For a state to function effectively it has to be properly funded. This is the starting point for Nematullah Bizhan's masterly analysis of Afghanistan's post-2001 transition, which demonstrates with great clarity how complications in this sphere can have vast ramifications for state building. This is truly a book to treasure.

William Maley, Professor of Diplomacy at
Australian National University

Impressive and well written. *Aid Paradoxes in Afghanistan* unpacks the challenges associated with the process of state building in situations of fragility. Building on his experience in international development, public policy, and reforms in post-2001 Afghanistan, Nematullah Bizhan persuasively explains paradoxes arising from well-intentioned foreign aid. Sometimes donor policies contribute to state building while in others aid undermines these gains. This book will be of great interest to scholars and practitioners of public policy, international development and political economy.

Ngaire Woods, Professor of Global Economic
Governance and Dean of Blavatnik School of
Government, University of Oxford

A fascinating, insightful and balanced exploration of the post-9/11 surge in aid to Afghanistan. Nematullah Bizhan undertakes extensive historical and comparative research, and also draws on his experience as a senior Afghan government official. Contrary to much state-building rhetoric, his study shows that in fact the ability of aid to strengthen domestic institutions is severely limited, and explains why this is.

Stephen Howes, Professor of Economics and
Director of Development Policy Centre at
Australian National University

This book is an exceptional and unique contribution to examine the role of foreign aid on state building process in Afghanistan. The goal, process, administration and effects of the substantial aid that flowed to Afghanistan since 9/11 are examined carefully and many useful and important lessons are drawn for effective use of foreign aid in the recipient countries.

M. Ishaq Nadiri, Jay Gould Professor of Economics at
New York University and Former Chief Economic
Advisor to the President of Afghanistan

T0270814

How can it be that, after the US appropriated more than US$100 billion in aid to Afghanistan, its government remains fragile and the country insecure?

To be sure, twenty years of Soviet invasion, civil war, and Taliban rule had left the state in shatters. But in this pioneering study, Nematullah Bizhan moves beyond this obvious truth to explore the sensitive question: did aid promote state building or hinder it? Focusing on reform plans, the resulting structure of aid, fiscal management in Kabul, and the relation between state and society, he shows how the best intentions can go awry. Rigorously analytic and meticulous in his research, Bizhan offers an unsettling perspective on US policy in Afghanistan and, no less, deep insights on foreign aid to weak states everywhere. This brilliant study should be a "must read" everyone involved with state building worldwide, whether as donor or recipient.

S. Frederick Starr, Chairman of Central Asia-Caucasus Institute at American Foreign Policy Council and author of Lost Enlightenment: Central Asia's Golden Age from the Arab Conquest to Tamerlane

This is an excellent work, a clearly written revelatory study on a highly complex subject-effects of aid on state building in situations of fragility that has long concerned those of us seeking answers to the question why billions of dollars of foreign aid to Afghanistan failed to build Afghan state institutions effectively. Nematullah Bizhan makes compelling arguments in support of his conclusions that the nature and modality of foreign aid, along with donor and Afghan government policies, were at the root of this failure and that foreign aid, in fact, reinforced building of a fragmented-aid based-rentier state. The book is a must-read for scholars and development practitioners specializing in state fragility and foreign aid.

Dr. Nipa Banerjee, Senior Fellow at University of Ottawa and Former Head of Canadian International Development Agency in Afghanistan

Aid Paradoxes in Afghanistan

The relationship between aid and state building is highly complex and the effects of aid on weak states depend on donors' interests, aid modalities and the recipient's pre-existing institutional and socio-political conditions. This book argues that, in the case of Afghanistan, the country inherited conditions that were not favourable for effective state building. Although some of the problems that emerged in the post-2001 state building process were predictable, the types of interventions that occurred—including an aid architecture which largely bypassed the state, the subordination of state building to the war on terror, and the short horizon policy choices of donors and the Afghan government—reduced the effectiveness of the aid and undermined effective state building.

By examining how foreign aid affected state building in Afghanistan since the US militarily intervened in Afghanistan in late 2001 until the end of President Hamid Karzai's first term in 2009, this book reveals the dynamic and complex relations between the Afghan government and foreign donors in their efforts to rebuild state institutions. The work explores three key areas: how donors supported government reforms to improve the taxation system, how government reorganized the state's fiscal management system, and how aid dependency and aid distribution outside the government budget affected interactions between state and society. Given that external revenue in the form of tribute, subsidies and aid has shaped the characteristics of the state in Afghanistan since the mid-eighteenth century, this book situates state building in a historical context.

This book will be invaluable for practitioners and anyone studying political economy, state building, international development and the politics of foreign aid.

Nematullah Bizhan is a Research Fellow at the Oxford University's Blavatnik School of Government. He is also a Senior Research Associate at the Oxford University's Global Economic Governance Program and a Fellow of Asia Pacific College of Diplomacy and Crawford School of Public Policy at the Australian National University. He has a PhD in Political Science and International Relations from the Australian National University and was previously a high-level participant in the post-2001 government of Afghanistan.

Routledge Studies in Middle East Development

Aid Paradoxes in Afghanistan

Building and Undermining the State

Nematullah Bizhan

LONDON AND NEW YORK

First published 2018 by Routledge

2 Park Square, Milton Park, Abingdon, Oxfordshire OX14 4RN
52 Vanderbilt Avenue, New York, NY 10017

Routledge is an imprint of the Taylor & Francis Group, an informa business

First issued in paperback 2019

British Library Cataloguing-in-Publication Data
A catalogue record for this book is available from the British Library

Library of Congress Cataloging-in-Publication Data
Names: Bizhan, Nematullah, author.
Title: Aid paradoxes in Afghanistan : building and undermining the state /
    Nematullah Bizhan.
Description: Milton Park, Abingdon, Oxon : Routledge, 2018. | Series:
    Routledge studies in Middle East development ; 1 | Includes bibliographical
    references.
Identifiers: LCCN 2017007968 | ISBN 9781138047617 (hardback) | ISBN
    9781315170701 (ebook)
Subjects: LCSH: Economic assistance, American—Afghanistan. | Nation-
    building—Afghanistan. | Afghanistan—Economic conditions—21st
    century. | Afghanistan—Politics and government—21st century.
Classification: LCC HC417 .B59 2018 | DDC 338.91/581—dc23
LC record available at https://lccn.loc.gov/2017007968

ISBN: 978-1-138-04761-7 (hbk)
ISBN: 978-0-367-88886-2 (pbk)

Typeset in Times New Roman
by Apex CoVantage, LLC

Contents

Figures

Tables

Note on transliteration, dates and currency

The US Library of Congress transliteration system is used for names, places and terms rendered in Dari (Persian) and Pashtu. However, for common names such as provinces and terms, officially used, the most common forms are employed.

As Afghanistan uses the *Solār Hijri* calendar, the dates are converted to Gregorian. Because a new *Solār Hijri* year starts on March 21, a complete year corresponds with two Gregorian years; the first year corresponds with the first nine months while the second corresponds with the last three months. Thus, where the dates are converted from *Solār Hijri* calendar to Gregorian, they show two years. However, for the analyses of the data available in the Gregorian calendar, the data of the first year is used as it corresponds to most of the months. The Ministry of Finance of Afghanistan also uses this method.

For 2001 and 2009 data, the unit of currency of Afghanistan, the Afghani, is converted to the US dollar. To do so, the average annual exchange rate of Da Afghanistan Bank is used. However, in Part I of the book the currency is mostly in Kabuli and Indian rupees as the analyses are in percentages.

Preface

I have been a part of Afghanistan's new generation. I was born when political changes led to a protracted conflict and uncertainty in the country. Our family were displaced three times. When I was about one year old, my family moved from our hometown in a village, about 40 miles away from Kabul in the south, to Kabul after conflict erupted in the countryside in 1978. Then we moved to Mazar-i-Sharif, the capital of Balkh province, in 1992 and back to Kabul in 1998 because of war among different *mujahidin* groups in Kabul and the Taliban aggression on Mazar city respectively. Each time we needed to start from scratch. Most Afghans lived under such harsh conditions for more than three decades.

While uncertainty was dominating hope, our family and many of whom I knew remained certain. We loved our country and kept our spirit high for solidarity. I have never lost my hope for or stopped the struggle in contributing to a better future for our people. But we lacked the mechanisms at the national level to build upon the energy and spirit of such people. The Afghan state neither provided services efficiently nor could it protect the citizens; not to mention its lack of will to allow political participation. Political leaders exacerbated this weakness. Above all, they failed us on multiple occasions.

But, unlike many of my fellows, I drew a different conclusion. I did not see heroism as a solution to our pressing challenges. For me what we needed the most was effective and accountable institutions that could keep predatory actors at bay, empower citizens and tap on local potentials for building peace and improving the living conditions of people. This does not mean that I underestimate a predatory or constructive role that external actors may play. This book is thus about institutions, not heroism. It examines state building in Afghanistan and how foreign aid as a major source of state revenue has affected it post-2001.

The writing of this book was a thoughtful journey. My work in Afghanistan at the very grassroots levels with people for raising awareness and addressing pressing local challenges, at the policy level with the post-2001 government in improving the effectiveness of budget and development cooperation, as well as supporting Afghanistan reconstruction, largely informed my analysis. During my research at the Universities of Princeton and Oxford, Australian National University and Williams College, I found that Afghanistan problems were not unique. Most fragile and conflict-affected societies have weak states, and the lives of their citizens are at risk. I thus hope that this book can make a contribution to understanding the challenges associated with state fragility and intervention as well as the building of a resilient state not only in Afghanistan but also other similar contexts.

I thank and acknowledge many people for their generous support, advice and comments in the last several years but can mention just a few by name. Ngaire Woods, Emily Jones, Thomas Hale, Richard Caplan, John Glidhell from the University of Oxford; Robert O. Keohane, John Ikenberry, Jennifer Widner, Atul Kohli from Princeton University and Francis Fukuyama from Stanford University. As this book is based on my PhD thesis at the Australian National University, I also thank my advisory panel, Amin Saikal, Peter Lourmor and Mark Evans, as well as William Maley, Stephen Howes, James Piscatori, Krill Nourzhanov, Mathew Gray, Valerie Braithwaite, Zahra Tahiri and Peter Quinn from the Australian National University as well as Clare Lockhart, Michal Carnahan and Barnett Rubin.

Ashraf Ghani and Ishaq Naderi, with whom I worked closely in the Finance Ministry and Office of the Chief Economic Advisor to the President in Afghanistan, generously shared their views and were open to respond to my questions on a number of occasions. Interviewees in Afghanistan and two anonymous reviewers of this book provided constructive critique. People, especially my former colleagues and friends, at the Ministries of Finance and Economy of Afghanistan, Chamber of Commerce, NGOs and political parties as well as the Australian Capital Territory Department of Treasury, Revenue Management Division provided necessary assistance during my fieldwork.

The University of Oxford, Princeton University, Australian National University and Williams College helped me to develop my ideas and interact with renewed scholars and practitioners, especially through Global Economic Governance Program, Niehaus Centre for Globalization and Governance, Development Policy Centre, Centre for Arab and Islamic Studies and Centre for Development Economics. The three awards which I received were instrumental: Oxford-Princeton Global Leaders Fellowship, the Australian Leadership Award and the Fulbright Scholarship.

Last but not least, it would have been impossible to complete this project without the support which I received from my family. My parents, brothers and sisters, nephews and nieces all provided support and encouragement. My daughters, Hadia and Diwa, and my son, Sina, particularly, made this project enjoyable by distracting me with their childhood concepts and dreams. Most of all, I cannot thank enough my caring wife, Safia Bizhan, whose love, support and understanding made possible the writing of this book. I dedicate this book to my late mother, an extraordinary woman of courage and vision, who provided me with endless support and love.

Glossary

Amir al-Muminin   commander of the faithful
arbakīs   local tribal militias
ausolī daftarī   administrative principles
bakhshishī   bonus
Bank-i Milly   National Bank
barāt   draft bill of exchange
bayt ul-māl   public property
bighār   unpaid compulsory work
bīst nafarī   a twenty-person system for conscription
chirāgh   lamp
Da Afghanistan Bank   refers to the Central Bank of Afghanistan
darbār   court
dasterkhvān pūli   table money, meaning business allowance
dastūr ul-amal   edicts
hakīm   the ruler of a province
girīb   a predetermined size of land
Jabha-i Mutahid-i Islāmī Barāī Najāt-i Afghanistan   the United Islamic Front for the Salvation of Afghanistan
jagirdārs   local rulers who were granted state land in exchange for military service
jam bast   a term for tax assessment based on a tribal community
jazyah   special poll tax levied on non-Muslim inhabitants
jihād   holy war, however, the word has wider implications
jirga   tribal assembly, also the national assembly
khālisa   crown lands
khānahdudah   chimney tax
Khalq   masses
kūt   used for a share of harvest for the purpose of in kind tax
Loya Jirga   traditional grand assembly
madrassa   an Arabic word meaning an education institution but is commonly used to refer to Islamic religious schools
malyat   taxes
malyat-i divāny   taxes levied by state

mantiqa   shared locality

mujahidin   From Arabic mujahidin, colloquial plural of mujahid, denoting a person who fights a jihad. It also refers to internal struggle.

mūlk   private property

mullā   religious clergy

mūstūfi   provincial finance director

mūstūfiat   provincial finance directorate

naqd'salār   cash-lord

niẓāmnāma   administrative code

Parcham   banner

Pashtunwāli   Pashtun tribal code of conduct

qawm   kin, village, tribe, or ethnic group

qāzi   Islamic Judge

sadr-i azam   prime minister

sargālah   cattle

sarrāfs   money changers

sāzmān ha-yi jāmah-yi madan-ī   civil society organizations

shah   king

sharia   Islamic Law

shurā   council, a term with Islamic root

shārvālī vulāyatay   provincial municipality

shārvālī vulūs'valī   district and rural municipality

shuraka-i dawlat   partners of the state

sī-kūt   one-third of a predetermined share, used for in kind tax on harvest

Sufi   practitioner of *Sufism*

tanzīms   organizations

tashkīl   personnel allotment or administrative structure

ulamā   Islamic religious scholars

vulāyat   province

valī   governor

vulūs'val   district officer

vulūs'valī   district

w'aqf   religious endowment

wolūsī jirga   lower house

zakāt   an obligatory Islamic tax, one of the five pillars of Islam

Abbreviations

AACA	Afghanistan Assistance Coordination Authority
ACCI	Afghanistan Chamber of Commerce and Industries
ACD	Afghanistan Customs Department
ADB	Asian Development Bank
ADF	Afghanistan Development Framework
AICC	Afghanistan International Chamber of Commerce
AISA	Afghanistan Investment and Support Agency
ANA	Afghan National Army
ANDS	Afghanistan National Development Strategy
ANP	Afghan National Police
ARTF	Afghanistan Reconstruction Trust Fund
ASI	Adam Smith International
ASP	Afghanistan Stabilization Programme
ASYCUDA	Automated System for Customs Data
BRT	Business Receipt Tax
CDCs	Community Development Councils
CENTO	Central Treaty Organisation
CEO	Chief Executive Officer
CGs	Consultative Groups
CGSC	Consultative Groups Standing Committee
CIA	Central Intelligence Agency
CSO	Central Statistics Organisation
CSOs	Civil Society Organisations
DDR	Disarmament, Demobilization and Reintegration
DFID	Department for International Development
DRC	Democratic Republic of Congo
EITI	Extractive Industries Transparency Initiative
FPU	Fiscal Policy Unit
GDP	Gross Domestic Product
GNI	Gross National Income
GPR	General Presidency of Revenue
I-ANDS	Interim Afghanistan National Development Strategy
IARCSC	Independent Administrative Reform and Civil Service Commission

ICD	Inland Customs Depot
IDLG	Independent Directorate of Local Government
IMF	International Monetary Fund
ISAF	International Security Assistance Force
IWA	Integrity Watch Afghanistan
JCMB	Joint Coordination and Monitoring Board
LOTFA	Law and Order Trust Fund for Afghanistan
LTO	Large Taxpayers Office
MoCI	Ministry of Commerce and Industries
MoMP	Ministry of Mines and Petroleum
MP	Member of the Parliament
MTO	Medium Taxpayers Office
NATO	North Atlantic Treaty Organization
NGOs	non-governmental organizations
NSP	National Solidarity Programme
ODA	Official Development Assistance
ODI	Oversees Development Institute
OECD	Organisation for Development Cooperation
PDPA	People's Democratic Party of Afghanistan
PRR	Priority Reforms and Restructuring
PRT	Provincial Reconstruction Teams
SAF	Securing Afghanistan's Future
SIGAR	Special Inspector General for Afghanistan Reconstruction
STO	Small Taxpayers Office
UAE	United Arab Emirates
UK	United Kingdom
UN	United Nations
UNAMA	UN Assistance Mission for Afghanistan
UNDP	United Nations Development Programme
UNICEF	United Nations Children Fund
US	United States
USAID	US Agency for International Development
USSR	Union of Soviet Socialist Republics
VAT	Value Added Tax
WB	World Bank

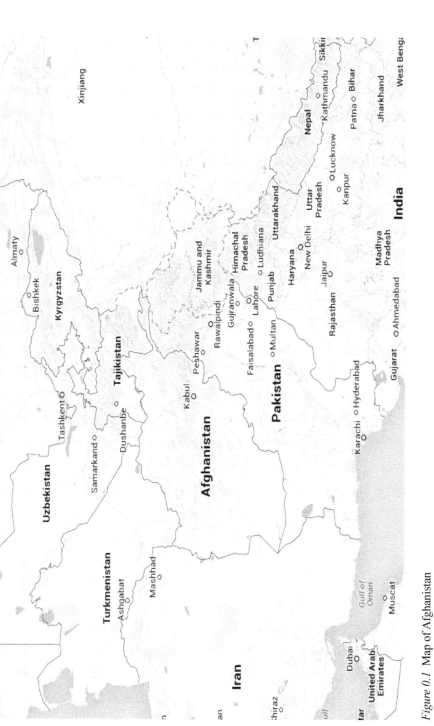

Figure 0.1 Map of Afghanistan

Source: Google Maps, November 24, 2013

Introduction

States are crucial not only for the security and prosperity of those who live under their jurisdiction but also for global security. Thirty six countries, home to more than a billion people, are fragile.[1] These states have weak institutions and capacity, and are vulnerable to conflict, or are failing or at the risk of failing to carry out the basic functions of the state. They are perceived to be the actual or potential ground for disease pandemics and mass migration or offer safe haven for terrorist groups, drugs and human trafficking. Often these so-called fragile states lack adequate revenue or fail to mobilize it to rebuild state institutions and provide services to their citizens. Thus, foreign aid plays a crucial role in the process of state building in situations of fragility, and understanding the effects of aid in fragile contexts has become increasingly urgent. Unprecedented attempts at state building and the substantial flow of aid in post-9/11 Afghanistan, with its dynamic history of state formation, makes an in-depth study of Afghanistan crucial for understanding the effects of aid on state building in fragile situations.

After a decade of neglect by the international community, in the wake of 9/11, Afghanistan has again attracted the attention of one of the most powerful states, the United States (US), and has become central to global security. Osama bin Laden, the Al-Qaeda leader, planned the 9/11 attacks on New York and Washington from his safe haven in Afghanistan under the Taliban regime (1996–2001). Following the removal of the Taliban regime by the US-led military intervention in late 2001, the country received substantial aid. From 2002 to 2014, after inflation adjustment, the US alone has appropriated $109 billion to reconstruct Afghanistan. This amount, though not being fully and efficiently spent in Afghanistan, exceeds an adjusted $103 billion that the US committed under the Marshall Plan between 1948 and 1952 for the recovery of Western Europe after World War II.[2] Despite some major achievements in expanding public services and building infrastructure in Afghanistan, the Afghan state remains weak and fiscally unsustainable, which invites critical examination of post-9/11 state building in Afghanistan.

Foreign aid played a crucial role after 2001 and reinforced the building of an aid-based rentier state, which had a long history in Afghanistan. Since the mid-eighteenth century, the Afghan government has largely relied on external revenue in the form of tribute, subsidies and foreign aid. Afghanistan had a weak tax system and a subsistence-based economy, with external income playing an important role in sustaining and reshaping the state-building process. Where external revenue fell short, political stability was undermined.

Two incidents remind us how state revenue can have an immediate impact in Afghanistan. The first is the attack of thirty angry farmers on King Amanullah Khan's (1919–1929) finance minister in rural Afghanistan because of the imposition of excessive and arbitrary taxes by the Ministry of Finance's officials (Chapter 2). The second incident occurred when, during a demonstration in 2004, a decommissioned officer threw his shoe towards the Finance Minister Ashraf Ghani's car when entering the building of the ministry in Kabul because of the failure of the government to pay the officers' benefits.[3] Joseph Schumpeter's argument, "The fiscal history of a people is above all an essential part of its general history,"[4] is highly relevant to the case of Afghanistan, where the fiscal history appears to be an essential part not only of its general history but also of the history of state building and failure.[5]

The interplay of social and political dynamics and geopolitical factors and the availability and type of revenue were all crucial for state building. Although the country has shown resilience in maintaining its independence from outside occupations, it has failed – except for a brief period under the reign of Amanullah Khan (1919–1929) – to pay for government expenditures from its domestic income. Hence, finding external sources of revenue to overcome this financial handicap has always been a top priority for Afghan rulers.

In the post-9/11 era, foreign donors primarily concentrated on the "war on terror" and chose to largely bypass the Afghan state to follow their national interests and to overcome the weakness of the Afghan state and corruption. More than half of the aid was allocated to security. In addition, donors largely abandoned hope of facilitating a large-scale reform of the state and instead chose an easy path to deliver aid outside the national systems. Out of US$56 billion in military and development aid that donors disbursed from 2002 and 2010, above three-fourths flew outside the Afghan government budget.[6] General Stanley McChrystal, commander of US and International Security Assistance Force (ISAF) in Afghanistan, for instance, wrote in an email (2009), "[w]e have to drop GIRA [Afghan government] and focus on people."[7] While aid fostered Afghanistan's economic growth and promoted primary and secondary education and the expansion of basic health services, the way that aid was administered produced paradoxical institutional and political outcomes based on mechanisms such as taxation, public spending and independent group formation.

This book argues that Afghanistan inherited conditions that were not favourable for effective state building. Although some of the problems that emerged in the post-2001 state-building process were predictable, the types of intervention that occurred – including the aid architecture, the subordination of state building to the war on terror, and donors and domestic policy choices – decreased the effectiveness of the use of aid and thus contributed to maintaining a weak state. This book shows that the relationship between aid and state building is highly complex and that the effects of aid on weak states depends on donors' interests, aid modality and the recipient's pre-existing institutional and socio-political conditions.

By examining how foreign aid affected state building in Afghanistan since the US militarily intervened in Afghanistan in late 2001 until the end of President Hamid Karzai's first term in 2009, this book reveals the dynamic and complex relations between the Afghan government and foreign donors in their efforts to rebuild state institutions. The work explores three key areas: how donors supported government reforms to improve the taxation system, how government reorganized the state's fiscal management system, and how aid dependency and aid distribution outside the government budget affected interactions between state and society. Given that external revenue in the form of tribute, subsidies and aid has shaped the characteristics of the state in Afghanistan since the mid-eighteenth century, this book situates state building in a historical context.

Revenues and state building

Since Max Weber (1864–1920) defined the modern state in the early twentieth century, scholars have argued that Weber underestimated the role of revenue and taxation in distinguishing the modern state from its predecessors. Weber focused on the organizational means employed by the state rather than the functions that it performed or the motivations that drove state-governing elites.[8] He defined the modern state as "a compulsory political organization with continuous operations . . ." that successfully claims a monopoly over the legitimate use of violence within a given territory.[9]

However, Joseph Schumpeter and Rudolf Goldscheid, Weber's contemporaries, challenged his view of the state and argued that taxation had a central role in social change.[10] They explored the historical shift in Europe from the "demesne state," which largely lived based on royal properties, to the "tax state," which supported itself by taxing its citizens. The important contribution of the "tax state" was that it employed many people, created a dynamic of state expansion, and became the driver of social change.[11] This notion inspired other scholars. Charles Tilly's historical work on the effects of war and the search for revenue on state formation in Western Europe is a notable example.[12]

Scholars have concentrated on studying the effects of taxation on state capacity and the development of representative institutions. As we will discuss in detail later, taxation assisted in building the capacity of the state and in improving state-society interactions by establishing representative institutions in Western Europe. However, little evidence exists, especially concerning government accountability, to support a similar role for taxation in the contemporary world because state building is complex and its outcomes depend on the interactions of revenue with pre-existing institutions and political and economic processes.

Scholars further developed the taxation and state-building framework to examine the effects of oil revenue on state formation in the late twentieth century. The development of a rentier state theory is an important example, arguing that states depending on rents tend to use low tax rates and higher spending, especially on patronage, to relieve the pressure for greater accountability.[13] State building in oil-rich countries thus produces different institutional and political outcomes than does state building in tax states.

In the contemporary world, despite economic growth, foreign aid still constitutes an important source of income for many low-income and strategically important countries. Net Official Development Assistance (ODA), excluding military expenditures and aid from non-traditional donors, totalled US$135 billion in 2014.[14] The question of how aid impacts state building thus arises. Two different schools of thought concerning the impacts of aid exist. The first perspective argues that aid can have rentier effects similar to those of revenue from oil or other fungible resources, while the second claims that the effects of aid differ from those of oil revenue because oil and aid have distinctive characteristics. Kevin M. Morrison argues that aid has an effect similar to the effect of revenue from state-owned oil enterprises in decreasing the likelihood of regime change.[15] Faisal Z. Ahmed concludes that aid and migrant remittances have similar effects in decreasing the likelihood of government turnover in authoritarian regimes.[16] Bruce Bueno de Mesquita and Alastair Smith argue that aid, similar to revenue from oil, decreases the likelihood of leader turnover and dampens the democratizing effects of mass political movements in nondemocratic countries.[17]

However, Paul Collier challenges the view that aid and oil revenue have similar impacts. Collier argues that aid conditionality and modality distinguish the impacts of aid from the impacts of oil revenue. As he argues, "aid comes with various donor-imposed mechanisms of scrutiny, which may spill over onto other expenditures, and so substitute for reduced pressure from citizens."[18] In addition, Sarah Blodgett Bermeo challenges both the negative political effects of aid and the similarity of aid to other resources. She argues that the negative relationship between foreign aid and democratic change is confined to the Cold War period.[19] Furthermore, Ceren Altincekic and David H. Bearce argue that aid is infungible, conditional and volatile over time and, thus, that it is unsuitable as a revenue source to pay for appeasement or oppression.[20]

Claims that aid has similar effects as oil revenue underestimate the complexities of aid impacts. First, the view that aid and oil revenue have similar effects underestimates differences in the characteristics of foreign aid and oil revenue and of their rentier implications through the mechanisms of taxation, government spending and group formation. Unlike oil revenue, aid is conditional, is not fully fungible (that is, the recipient government does not have full control over its use) and is not a reliable long-term source of state income.

In addition, although the view that "aid is not oil" highlights the differences between aid and revenue from oil, it does not adequately address the complex mechanisms of state building in aid-dependent states and of the democratization paradoxes that aid modality and donor preferences may induce. The flow of aid from Western donors appears to favour democratization of the recipient country, which is common in the post-Cold War period. However, the tendency of the recipient government to become increasingly accountable to foreign donors rather than to its citizens, especially if a large portion of aid bypasses the recipient budget, has negative implications for democratic decision making and domestic political process. First, although sometimes helpful, for example, for improving the public financial management system, the government's increasing accountability to donors undermines the basic principle of democracy – that the government is accountable to citizens. Second, donors' direct spending outside the recipient budget can subvert the budget as the major tool of policy. It creates institutions parallel to those of the recipient state that diverts political and financial resources from building state institutions; increases social and institutional fragmentation, especially in the presence of prior societal fragmentation and state weakness; and makes societal actors in turn accountable to donors as they rely on donors for funding.

This book contributes to rethinking externally aided state building and attempts to fill the gap in the literature on how an aid-induced parallel public sector affects state institutions as well as state-society interactions. This book argues that aid is less desirable than tax revenue for state building. However, when a country has a poor economy and is devastated by war or is failing to deliver services and protect citizens, domestic revenue may not sustain state building. Aid may thus be necessary until domestic institutions and economy thrive and short-term political stability is achieved. However, this stage of state development can have lasting effects. Aid can reinforce or hinder state building, depending on the alignment of donors' interests with recipients' needs, the recipient's type of state, the state's capacity, and whether interactions between aid and domestic institutions ensure continuity and support state capacity or undermine the state. Aid and state building have a highly complex relationship whose outcomes depend on historical legacies, aid modality, and policy choices of the recipient government and donors.

Research method

The book uses a qualitative methodology. Information on tax revenue, aid and budgets, as well as macroeconomic data, was collected from the Ministry of Finance and other Afghan government departments as well as from foreign donors in Afghanistan. These data were used to examine a simple correlation between different financial variables, such as aid and tax revenue, and to validate a situation of high aid dependency in Afghanistan.

Semi-structured interviews were undertaken in Afghanistan from March to August 2011, and interviewees were asked broad and less guided questions encouraging them to discuss issues that they considered important. These interviewees included government ministers and former ministers, presidential advisors, political party leaders, civil society activists, donor agency officials, foreign advisors who worked with government, provincial officials (including governors and *mūstufī*s or provincial financial directors), private sector representatives and academics at Kabul University. Notably, some of the interviewees were sometimes hesitant to share their views on sensitive political issues. This challenge was overcome by providing assurances that their identity would be anonymous.

Knowledge of Afghanistan, including familiarity with local languages (Dari/Persian and Pashtu) and earlier experiences of the author in Afghanistan, were crucial in building trust while conducting the interviews.

Additionally, informal discussions were held with income-tax payers, shopkeepers and members of local communities to gain a broader picture of the situation and to validate some of the questions that emerged during the fieldwork at that level. Published and unpublished works (in Dari/Persian and Pashtu) and original Afghan government and donor documents were consulted. Moreover, the author participated in two important national events in Kabul to observe the fiscal dynamics of state building and government-donor relations. These events were a seminar held by the Ministry of Finance (April 2011), attended by its financial, accounting and administration managers to assess achievements and challenges, and a conference organized by the "Transition Coordination Commission" (June 29–30, 2011) to assess the transfer of security responsibilities from the International Security Assistance Force (ISAF) to Afghan security forces in seven provinces as well as the economic implications of such a transition.

Moreover, my insights from my life experience including more than 13 years of field experience in Afghanistan at senior positions in the Ministries of Finance, Youth and Economy and the Office of *Chief Economic Advisor to the President of Afghanistan*, as well as with civil society at the grassroots level, have largely informed this study.

Two major challenges existed during data collection. The first challenge was a lack of reliable primary data on state revenue sources during the early years of state building in Afghanistan. To overcome this problem, the author consulted credible secondary resources such as published materials. Second, although financial data from the post-2001 period in Afghanistan were well documented, several shortcomings arose. The available data were subject to large margins of uncertainty and incompleteness, especially resulting from changes in the classification of information in relation to domestic revenue. In addition, different sources at various times offered diverse figures. Some figures the government produced did not match those from the World Bank, for example. To overcome this challenge in relation to government figures, this study used the World Bank data. Notably, the variation between the Afghan government and World Bank figures was sometimes significant.

Book outline

The book is divided into three parts: conceptual framework, the history of revenue and state formation in Afghanistan from 1747 to 2000, and post-9/11 state building in Afghanistan. It includes an introduction, six chapters and a conclusion. Chapter 1 establishes a conceptual framework to further assess the effects of aid on state building in the proceeding chapters. In so doing, the chapter considers whether aid rentier effects are similar to the rentier effects of oil revenue by comparing three mechanisms: taxation, spending and group formation. This part argues that aid, unlike oil revenue, is conditional and that the recipient does not have full discretion over it, which limits the recipient's ability to spend it on patronage. Thus, aid can have positive and negative effects on state building. The paradoxical effects of aid largely depend on donors' interests, aid modality and the recipient's pre-existing institutional and socio-political conditions. The relationship between aid and state building is thus highly complex, and the question of how aid affects state building cannot be answered unconditionally.

Chapter 2 provides the background for the study of post-9/11 state building in Afghanistan. It examines the relationship between Afghan state building and revenue during three distinctive periods. First, the chapter examines the Durrani Empire (1747–1824), in which the tribute arising from conquests was crucial for the state-building process. Second, this chapter examines the period following the collapse of the empire until the early twentieth century, when British subsidies partially replaced the tribute. Finally, the chapter examines the period from the mid-twentieth century through 2001, when foreign aid replaced subsidies and played a marked role in the state-building process. This chapter argues that the reliance of the Afghan state on different forms of external revenue has a long history.

Chapter 3 focuses on post-9/11 state building in Afghanistan. After the Taliban regime fell in late 2001, Afghan state building significantly depended on external military and financial support – more so than during any other period since 1747 – and the "war on terror" dominated the nature of foreign donors' engagement. Given Afghanistan's state weakness, this chapter examines how aid dependency and the ways that aid was spent reinforced the building of a transitional, yet fragmented, aid-based rentier state. In so doing, the chapter assesses how a new political order and the emergence of aid dependency shaped the characteristics of the state.

Building on the preceding chapters, Chapter 4 explores the effects of aid on taxation. The post-9/11 government inherited an empty treasury because of a devastated economy and limited capacity to collect provincial revenues from border customs that the local commanders and strongmen controlled. This chapter further examines the revenue reforms; its complexities and inherent contradictions; and the ways in which internal pressure, aid conditionality and political incentives shaped the development of the taxation system.

Another important aspect of post-2001 state building in Afghanistan included public spending and transparency. Although the Karzai government became fiscally more open after 2001 than its predecessors, the overall budget was divided between on-and off-budgets and suffered from poor transparency and secret cash transfers to strongmen and the President Office, ultimately spent on patronage. Accordingly, Chapter 5 examines the government budgetary process and budget transparency and explores whether the government and foreign donors adequately informed Afghan citizens of their fiscal activities.

Chapter 6 explores the effects of aid on the formation of independent groups. It examines the dynamics of budget support and off-budget aid, their implications for societal actors – especially civil society organizations (CSOs) – and state institutions, and the effects on state–society interactions. Finally, the book's conclusion discusses the major findings of this study and explores the implications for externally aided state building. It demonstrates not only that it is challenging to manage high aid dependency but also that the way aid is used has lasting consequences for state building. This book argues that the relationship between aid and state building is highly complex, and the question of how aid affects state building cannot be answered unconditionally.

Notes

 1 The Fund for Peace, "The Failed States Index," (2017). Also see World Bank, "Fragility, Conflict and Violence: Overview," www.worldbank.org/en/topic/fragilityconflictviolence/overview.
 2 U.S. Overseas Loans and Grants: Obligations and Loan Authorizations, July 1, 1945–September 30, 2014; Nematullah Bizhan, "The Limits of U.S. Aid in Afghanistan," *Foreign Policy* 2014; and SIGAR, "Quarterly Report to the United States Congress," (Arlington: July 30, 2014).
 3 Author's Personal Record, Kabul, 2004.
 4 Joseph A. Schumpeter, "The Crises of the Tax State," in *The Economics and Sociology of Capitalism*, ed. Richard Swedberg (Princeton: Princeton University Press, 1991), 100–1.
 5 Ibid.
 6 Islamic Republic of Afghanistan, "Development Cooperation Report," (Kabul: Ministry of Finance, 2010), 104; Nematullah Bizhan, "Continuity, Aid and Revival: State Building in South Korea, Taiwan, Iraq and Afghanistan," (Working Paper 2015/109, the Global Economic Governance Programme, University of Oxford, Oxford 2015).
 7 Sarah Chayes, *Thieves of State: Why Corruption Threatens Global Security* (New York: W. W. Norton & Company, 2015).
 8 Christopher Pierson, *The Modern State* (London: Routledge, 1996), 30; and Mick Moore, "Political Underdevelopment: What Causes Bad Governance," *Public Management Review* 3, no. 3 (2001): 399.
 9 Max Weber, ed., *Economy and Society: An Outline of Interpretive Sociology*. Vol. 2 (Berkeley: University of California Press, 1978), 54, 56.
10 Moore, "Political Underdevelopment: What Causes Bad Governance," 399.
11 Ibid., 400.
12 See Charles Tilly, ed., *The Formation of National States in Western Europe* (Princeton: Princeton University Press, 1975).
13 Michael L. Ross, "Does Oil Hinder Democracy?," *World Politics* 53, no. 03 (2001), 325–61.
14 OECD, Development Finance Statistics, Accessed on 15 January 2017. www.oecd.org/dac/stats/development-aid-stable-in-2014-but-flows-to-poorest-countries-still-falling.htm.
15 See Kevin M. Morrison, "Oil, Nontax Revenue, and the Redistributive Foundations of Regime Stability," *International Organization* 63, no. 01 (2009).
16 Faisal Z. Ahmed, "The Perils of Unearned Foreign Income: Aid, Remittances, and Government Survival," *American Political Science Review* 106, no. 01 (2012), 146–65.
17 Bruce Bueno de Mesquita and Alastair Smith, "Leader Survival, Revolutions, and the Nature of Government Finance," *American Journal of Political Science* 54, no. 4 (2010), 936–50.
18 Paul Collier, "Is Aid Oil? An Analysis of Whether Africa Can Absorb More Aid," *World Development* 34, no. 9 (2006): 482–1497.
19 Sarah Blodgett Bermeo, "Aid Is Not Oil: Donor Utility, Heterogeneous Aid, and the Aid-Democratization Relationship," *International Organization* 70, no. 1 (Winter 2016): 1–32.
20 Ceren Altincekic and David H. Bearce, "Why There Should Be No Political Foreign Aid Curse," *World Development* 64 (2014): 18–32.

Part I

Conceptual framework

Aid and state building

1 Aid and state building

Introduction

Scholars have different views on the impacts of aid. One group of scholars argues that aid has negative political effects similar to those of oil revenue and that aid reduces government accountability. The second group of scholars argues that aid is different from oil revenue and that its impacts are therefore distinguished from those of oil revenue. This chapter attempts to assess these two schools of thought on aid impacts and explores the causal mechanism that can explain the aid effects. The chapter concludes that the relationship between aid and state building is complex. Aid can thus have positive and negative effects that depend on the aid recipient's state capacity, aid modality, policy choices and pre-existing socio-political and economic conditions. This chapter provides the conceptual framework for analysis of the effects of different income sources on state building before 9/11 and of foreign aid after 9/11 in Afghanistan in the proceeding chapters.

Accordingly, this chapter reviews the effects of foreign aid on state building in the literature and builds on rentier state theory. The chapter explores whether aid rentier effects are similar to those of oil revenue by comparing the three mechanisms – taxation, spending and group formation – through which rentier effects work. This chapter argues that aid may have rentier effects but that such effects differ from the rentier effects of oil revenue and may have paradoxical implications for state building and democratic accountability based on prevailing conditions. These effects largely depend on donors' interests, aid modality and the recipient's pre-existing institutional and socio-political conditions.

Both aid and oil revenue are unearned. They enable states to derive revenue with little political and organizational efforts in relation to their citizens. Oil-rich countries use low tax rates and high spending to relieve pressure for greater public accountability, which works through the mechanisms of taxation, government spending and group formation. Oil-rich governments use fiscal measures such as lowering tax rates or not taxing the population at all; increasing government spending, especially on patronage; and dispensing of largess, preventing the formation of independent social groups, a necessary precondition for democracy.[1] These measures alleviate the pressure for greater accountability.

However, foreign aid, unlike oil revenue, is conditional and less reliable, and the recipient government does not have full control over its use. These characteristics of aid largely distinguish the effects of aid from the rentier effects of oil revenue. Unlike oil-rich states with a weak taxation function and low revenue collection,[2] the impact of aid on revenue collection is mixed.[3] Aid is often conditional on increases in revenue collection, and the recipient government may also have the incentive to strengthen the taxation system because the flow of aid is not permanent.

Because aid is conditional, the recipient does not have full discretion over it and is relatively constrained from spending it on patronage. How much discretion a recipient government has over the use of aid depends on foreign donors' intentions and the recipient capacity. Foreign donors typically use bypass tactics. They bypass the state by spending a large portion of aid outside the government budget process. Thus, unlike undemocratic oil-based rentier states with little government accountability, government accountability in aid-dependent states is largely to foreign donors, reducing the recipient government's accountability to its citizens. In addition, this type of aid can create a parallel public sector. Moreover, unlike oil revenue, aid is often used to promote the formation of groups independent of the recipient government – Civil Society Organisations (CSOs) or non-governmental organizations (NGOs). While such groups are independent of the recipient state, they are dependent on foreign donors for funding; hence, these groups tend to be accountable to donors rather than *vice versa*.

This chapter first explores why state revenue sources are relevant. Second, it discusses the pattern of state building when states are reliant on domestic tax revenue rather than oil revenue or aid. Third, we compare the rentier effects of aid and oil revenue on state building.

Why are state revenue sources relevant?

> The history of state revenue production is the history of the evolution of the state. . . . One major limitation on rule is revenue, the income of the government. The greater the revenue of the state, the more possible it is to extend rule. Revenue enhances the ability of rulers to elaborate the institutions of the state, to bring more people within the domain of those institutions, and to increase the number and variety of the collective goods provided through the state.[4]
>
> Margaret Levi

As the availability of revenue is crucial for a state to function, it is equally important how a state derives its income. Sources of state revenue have implications for the building of state institutions and governance. State building crucially depends on how revenue is collected, including the compromises that rulers make with their citizens to collect (and use) revenue, which institutional capacity the state develops to achieve this task and the extent to which the institutional arrangements reflect the interests of both the rulers and the ruled.[5] The state-building literature demonstrates that revenue sources may have different implications for the pattern of state building.[6] Tax and non-tax revenues (oil and foreign aid) thus produce particular political and institutional outcomes.[7]

Since Max Weber (1864–1920) defined the modern state in the early twentieth century, scholars have criticized him for underestimating the role of revenue and taxation in distinguishing the modern state from its predecessors.[8]

Scholars further developed the taxation and state-building framework to examine the effects of oil revenue on state formation in the late twentieth century. The development of a rentier state theory is a notable example, arguing that states depending on rents use low tax rates and higher spending to reduce the pressure for greater accountability.[9]

Tax and non-tax revenues are the two major sources of state revenue. The most common forms of non-tax revenue are foreign aid and oil revenue. Historically, taxation has been a major source of state income. Since the mid-twentieth century, some states have also derived a significant portion of their income from aid or oil revenue. States that derive a significant share of their income from tax, oil revenue (40 per cent or more of the budget) and foreign aid (10 per cent or greater share of GNI) are referred to here as tax states, rentier states and aid-dependent states respectively.[10]

Scholars have generally concentrated on the study of taxation effects on state capacity and of the development of representative institutions. As will be discussed in detail later, taxation helped build the capacity of the state and improved state–society interactions by establishing representative institutions in Western Europe; however, little evidence, especially concerning government accountability, exists to support a similar role for taxation in the contemporary world. This evidence is lacking because state building is complex and because the outcomes depend on the interactions of revenue with institutional, political and economic processes.

The ways in which different revenue sources affect political and institutional outcomes have captured an increasing amount of attention in the literature and policy arena. However, despite the existing consensus that different revenue sources produce distinctive outcomes, scholars differ in their views on the types of outcomes. For example, Kevin M. Morrison's study argues that taxation leads to instability, not representation.[11] Taxation, as Mick Moore and Debora Brautigam claim, will not guarantee improved governance in developing countries.[12] The outcome depends on how states negotiate (or fail to negotiate) with societies and how societies are organized, among other factors.

Oil revenue has different implications for state building. The literature demonstrates that oil revenue hinders democratic accountability.[13] Oil-rich countries use lower tax rates and higher government spending, especially on patronage, to relieve the pressure for greater accountability.[14] State building in oil-rich countries thus produces institutional and political outcomes that differ from the outcomes in tax states.

Two different views of the impacts of aid exist. In the first view, aid can have rentier effects similar to the effects of oil revenue, while the second view claims that the effects of aid differ from those of oil revenue because the processes and institutions surrounding oil revenue and aid themselves have distinctive characteristics.

Scholars such as Morrison, Bueno de Mesquita and Alastair Smith, and Faisal Z. Ahmed argue that aid extends regime stability and thus could undermine democratic transitions similar to the effects of oil revenue.[15] Morrison argues that the effect of aid is similar to that of oil revenue in decreasing the likelihood of regime change.[16] Ahmed concludes that aid and migrant remittances have similar effects, decreasing the likelihood of government turnover in authoritarian regimes.[17] Bueno de Mesquita and Smith argue that aid, similar to oil revenue, decreases the likelihood of leader turnover and weakens the democratizing effects of mass political movements in nondemocratic countries.[18]

However, in his paper "Is Aid Oil?" Paul Collier challenges the view that aid and oil revenue have similar impacts. Collier argues that aid conditionality and modality distinguish the impacts of aid from oil revenue. He argues that "aid comes with various donor-imposed mechanisms of scrutiny, which may spill over onto other expenditures, and so substitute for reduced pressure from citizens."[19] In her paper "Aid is Not Oil," Sarah Blodgett Bermeo considers a model incorporating changing donor preferences and foreign aid heterogeneity, in which donors provide fungible and infungible aid based on empirical tests for the period 1973–2010, challenges both the negative political effects of aid and the similarity of aid to other resources. She argues that the negative relationship between foreign aid and democratic change is confined to the Cold War period.[20] Furthermore, Ceren Altincekic and David H. Bearce argue that aid is infungible, conditional and volatile over time and, thus, that it is poorly suited as a revenue source to pay for appeasement or oppression.[21]

Claims that aid has similar effects as oil revenue underestimate the complexities of aid impacts. First, the view that aid and oil revenue have similar effects underestimates the differences in the characteristics of foreign aid and oil revenue and of their rentier implications through mechanisms such as taxation, government spending and group formation. Unlike oil revenue, aid is conditional; the recipient government does not have full control over its use. Additionally, aid is not a reliable long-term source of state income.

In addition, while the view that "aid is not oil" highlights the differences between aid and oil revenue, it does not adequately address the complex mechanisms of state building in aid-dependent states and the democratization paradoxes that aid modality and donor preferences may induce. The flow of aid from traditional (Western) donors tend to promote democratization of the recipient country, especially in the post-Cold War period. However, given the tendency of the recipient government to become increasingly accountable to foreign donors rather than to their citizens, and if a large portion of aid bypasses the recipient budget, the consequences may be negative for democratic decision making and state building. First, the government's increasing accountability to donors, even if it helps improve the recipient's public financial management system, undermines the basic principle of democracy – that is, government accountability to citizens. Second, donors' direct spending outside the recipient budget creates institutions parallel to those of the recipient state. It can result in diverting political and financial resources from state institutions, increase social and institutional fragmentation and encourage societal actors to become accountable to the donors providing their funding.

Before further exploring the effects of aid and oil revenue, we first define the following key terms: taxation, oil revenue, foreign aid and state capacity and state building. Taxation refers to a compulsory levy imposed by the state on citizens who receive nothing in return directly.[22] Governments place considerable organizational, bureaucratic and political demands on their state apparatus to tax citizens. However, when the state derives its revenue from rents, it exerts little organizational or political effort on the part of the state apparatus, particularly concerning such efforts that relate to citizens.[23] Oil revenue and foreign aid, also referred to as unearned income or non-tax revenue, are the two main types of non-tax revenue that are important in the contemporary world.

To define state capacity and state building, we first briefly assess the three main concepts of the state. The first, in the tradition of Hobbes, Rousseau and Locke, the state can be viewed as a social contract.[24] Accordingly, "the authority of the state rests upon an agreement among the members of a society to acknowledge the authority of a set of rules or a political regime."[25] This view emphasizes state and society relationships in a way that suggests not only the submission of all members of society to the state but also a responsibility of the state to deliver public goods in return.[26] The second concept, formulated by Max Weber, defines the state as "a human community" that monopolizes the legitimate use of force within a given territory, whether that legitimacy derives from charisma, tradition or law. This approach emphasizes a state's means instead of its ends.[27] The third approach focuses on juridical statehood rather than de facto attribution. Thus, according to the 1933 Montevideo Convention, the key characteristics of a state include "a defined territory," "a permanent population," "an effective government" and "the capacity to enter into formal relations with other states."[28]

Skocpol defines state capacity as the ability of a government to administer its territory effectively or "implement official goals, especially over the actual or potential opposition of powerful social groups or in the face of recalcitrant socioeconomic circumstances."[29] State capacity could be distinguished, according to Michael Mann, into infrastructure and the despotic power of the state. The former "derives from the range of actions that state elites can undertake without routine negotiation with civil society groups,"[30] whereas the latter refers "to the capacity of the state to actually penetrate civil society, and to implement logistically political decisions throughout the realm."[31]

The survival and functioning of a political system in the modern world depend on four basic state capacities. The first is the extractive capacity that enables the state to mobilize resources from society to pursue the "national interest." The second is the steering capacity, which guides national socio-economic development. The third, legitimization capacity, is the capacity to dominate by creating consensus. The fourth is coercive capacity, which involves dominating through the threat of force.[32]

State capacity is commonly measured in terms of tax extraction or extractive capacity. This approach measures capacity in two ways: "First, it takes capacity, however generated, in order to extract taxes; second, successful tax extraction provides resources that enable the government to operate in other domains."[33] Extractive capacity can be measured both by the percentage of taxes to gross domestic product (GDP) and by the nature of taxation. In the latter, it is important whether taxation is based on income or wealth or on indirect taxation (as income and wealth taxes are much more difficult to extract than indirect taxes).[34]

Tax extraction as an initial measure of state capacity has two main limitations. Potential and actual tax collections differ, and a given level of taxation does not necessarily translate into the efficient use of revenue.[35] Despite these limitations, extractive capacity, measured as the percentage of taxes to GDP, is one example of a general measure of state capacity.

States can also be distinguished based on how they are organized. The most common types of states are neo-patrimonial and Weberian. They are distinguished on the basis of how their public and private realms operate normatively and organizationally:

> [A] modern Weberian state . . . is supposed to be impersonal, formal, account-able and non-corrupt. The neo-patrimonial state is the precise opposite, with personalized and informal relationships between the boss or patron and his clients. The patron is accountable and hugely corrupt . . . and dispensing ben-efits to clients to stay in power.[36]

In Weberian states, recruitment is based on merit, unlike the system in neo-patrimonial states. Neo-patrimonial states suffer from uncertainty and the exis-tence of contradictory formal and informal rules.[37] State building in a neo-patrimonial state is much more challenging than that in a Weberian state.[38]

State building primarily refers to "interventionist strategies to restore and rebuild the institutions and apparatus of the state."[39] State institutions include bureaucracies, the legal system and the military. Two approaches exist for assess-ing the role of local (national) and external (international or foreign) actors in the state-building process. First, the "exogenous" school of thought views state building as an intervention by external actors to reform or consolidate a stable, sometimes democratic government over an internationally recognized territory. Thus, the US interventions in Afghanistan (2001) and Iraq (2003) are referred to as state building. The second views state building as an "endogenous" or national process driven by state–society relations. Accordingly, the role of external play-ers is limited, although they can foster or hinder state building. Supporters of this view argue that if state building is to be legitimate and sustainable, the efforts that shape it and lead it should be local, while external actors should play only a facilitating role in the state-building process.

Accountability is an important aspect of the state–society relationship. Fran-cis Fukuyama describes an accountable government as one in which "the rulers believe that they are responsible to the people they govern and put the people's interests above their own." Accountability can be achieved in different ways: it can arise from what Fukuyama calls moral education (as observed, for example, in China) or from a formal political system (as largely observed in the Western political system), largely referred to as procedural or formal accountability.[40]

Before we examine the effects of foreign aid and compare them to the effects of oil revenue, we assess the process of state building when the state derives its major source of revenue from taxation.

Tax states

Tax states tend to have a greater capacity and increased interaction with citizens. Historically, tax revenue has had a central role in the development of the state. As explained by Anoshyrvan, a Sassanian ruler (AD 531–579), "royal authority exists through the army, the army through money, money through taxes, taxes through cultivation, cultivation through justice."[41] The statement highlights the relation between state and citizens and indicates how taxes can be instrumental in the existence of a state and in the provision of effective governance. Taxes appear to have existed in some version since the emergence of advanced civilizations.[42] Governments of the ancient states of Persia, Greece, Egypt, Rome and China, for example, all levied taxes on property, the sale of goods, inheritances and customs duties to finance their expenditures.[43]

The ability of states to collect revenue has had a significant impact on state development. As Schumpeter notes, "[t]axes not only helped to create the state, they helped to form it."[44] Similarly, Michael Mann argues, between the eighteenth and mid-twentieth centuries, "Western states originated as war making monarchies."[45] Similarly, Tilly argues that war and perceived threats had a central role in the emergence of modern states in Western Europe by creating a demand for revenue.[46] Taxes and conscription were heavy because of the large, expensive armies and frequent wars. As tax extraction increased, popular resistance to taxes augmented. However, such resistance did not succeed in reducing the tax burden, as wars continued and became even larger and more expensive. The resistance in the eighteenth and nineteenth centuries eventually led to representative government, making bureaucracies responsible to legislatures. This development was based on "perceptions of mutual interest between controllers of state (monarchies) and larger taxpayers, especially merchants and others whose assets were mobile."[47]

The expansion of rulers' bargaining power in relation to powerful constituents during the thirteenth and fourteenth centuries in France and England resulted in the establishment of a national tax system. The development of military technology increased the costs of conflicts and improved the bargaining power of monarchs. War helped to justify taxation because it was defined as a collective good.[48] Although rulers did not make war to justify taxation, they used it to increase their power and demand for revenue. Accordingly, war laid the groundwork for the social contract theory of state, "in which rulers collected taxes to enable them to act on behalf of the common good."[49]

Two types of relationships between interstate war and revenue bargaining may exist. First, the perceived threat of war by a state leads to the search for higher state revenue. Second, this pursuit of revenue may encourage revenue bargaining between the state and taxpayers.[50] However, in some parts of the contemporary world, such as Africa, the absence of perceived external threats to the state has reduced the incentive to raise revenue.[51] For example, the *de facto* international guarantee of borders in Africa by the UN system after decolonization in the 1960s and the end of the Cold War since 1991 have made some African states "unmotivated to rule their frontiers and all their populations very actively, and therefore relatively unmotivated to tax widely."[52] The amount of aid that they have received might also have contributed to such a lack of motivation.[53]

However, Tilly's thesis of "war making state making" raises the question of whether war is necessary to create effective and accountable states. Although war has been a significant factor in the development of European states, war has not resulted in state creation in more recent times, especially given that war has been financed by other sources such as debt rather than increases in taxation. For example, case studies of eleven Latin American countries in four of the five geopolitical zones in Latin America (La Plata, Basin, Pacific Littoral, Northern Andes and Mexico) in the nineteenth century show that external threats did not prompt leaders to raise taxes; instead, they relied on debt.[54] Miguel A. Centeno argues that the "availability of external resources, state organizational capacity, and alliances with social actors are shown to help determine the political response to armed conflict."[55]

Similarly, Moore argues that in the developing world, war and external threats are no longer a major source of motivation for building states. He asserts that citizens primarily judge contemporary state elites based on their performance in terms of some combination of democratic or popular legitimacy and delivery of public benefits. Elites are therefore generally enthusiastic about reducing poverty, curbing inflation or maintaining high levels of employment, placing contemporary governments and regimes under clear threat of replacement through internal pressures if they fail.[56] In East Asia, such internal pressures motivated governments to construct effective developmental states in the late twentieth century.[57]

Taxation can also foster state capacity. Since the eighteenth century, for example, the need for revenue because of war and perceived threats created political incentives to establish a functioning bureaucracy in Europe, which in turn needed to collect revenue. This situation prompted rulers to strengthen their government's extractive capacity. The legislature in Britain used its "power of the purse" to hold the government accountable for the use of tax revenue by seeking regular reports. Government departments became more skilled and sophisticated in responding to demands from the legislature. Hence, accountability increased demands for capacity.[58]

Although researchers claim that the demand for "no taxation without representation" led to democratization,[59] taxation does not unilaterally lead to representation. The outcome of this process depends on how societies are organized and how the state interacts with society. For example, post-1979 Iran does not support the notion of "no taxation without representation"; taxation was declared a religious duty that would not entitle the taxpayer to have a voice in state affairs.[60]

Hence, taxation is not a guarantee for representation in the contemporary world.[61] In particular, Waterbury argues that in the Middle East,

> neither historically nor in the twentieth century is there much evidence that taxation has evoked demands that governments account for their use of tax monies. Predatory taxation has produced revolts, especially in the countryside, but there has been no translation of tax burden into pressures for democratization.[62]

The pattern of state formation in Western Europe was unique to a particular context and time. Hence, one should be cautious in expecting a similar state-building outcome in the contemporary world if a state wages external wars and relies on domestic taxation. However, the taxation and state-building framework provides a useful analytical tool to assess the relationship between non-tax revenue and state building.

Aid-dependent states

To determine whether aid has rentier effects, we need to unpack the characteristics of aid and the nature of its impacts in the state-building process. The view that aid and oil revenue may have similar impacts neglects the differences between the characteristics of foreign aid and oil revenue and their impacts. Despite some similarities between the political dynamics associated with oil revenue and aid, these dynamics also feature sharp distinctions. Both oil revenue and aid are unearned. As a result, both sources of revenue enable states to derive revenue with little political and organizational effort, especially effort involving citizens.[63] Hence, the autonomy of state power is increased relative to major power groupings of "civil society."[64]

However, aid and oil revenue have distinctive characteristics that have been underappreciated in the existing literature and that are important to understand. Unlike oil revenue, aid is conditional, and the recipient government does not have full discretion over its use – it is less fungible. Moreover, aid is not as reliable as oil revenue because of the smaller number of "sellers" and many potential "buyers." Circumstances in foreign donor and recipient countries may determine the reliability and flow of aid.

These differences result in greater contradictions associated with aid rentierism compared with oil rentierism, with profound implications for state building. Aid has specific implications for state building in terms of how heavily the government taxes its citizens, how the government spends its budget, and how it shapes the formation of independent groups.

The flow of aid has increased over time. The total flow of annual Official Development Assistance (ODA), excluding security expenditures, to recipient countries rose to US$134 billion (in constant 2013 USD) in 2014 from US$37 billion in 1960. While this amount represents only approximately 0.29 per cent of the gross national income (GNI) of the members of the Organisation for Economic Cooperation and Development (OECD), it constitutes a significant share of GNI in low-income (recipient) countries.[65]

Donors primarily use foreign aid as an instrument of foreign policy, which largely has geopolitical ramifications.[66] Aid is perceived as a post-World War II phenomenon, although the flow of financial assistance, such as subsidies and foreign aid, from patron states to client states existed well before the War. Since the nineteenth century, foreign aid has been used to ensure political control by donors in the colonial domain, to help the economic recovery of Western Europe under the Marshall Plan in the 1950s and subsequently to secure strategic alliances during the Cold War rivalry, to induce industrialization in the 1960s, to address poverty in the 1970s, to promote stabilization and structural adjustment in the 1980s and to enhance democracy and governance in the 1990s.[67]

Following the attacks on New York and Washington on September 11, 2001, aid has focused on the rebuilding of states in fragile situations.[68] Fragile states are those "failing or at risk of failing, with respect to authority, comprehensive basic service provision, or legitimacy."[69] The world's worse problems, such as terrorism and drug and human trafficking, often originate in these states.[70] Furthermore, "[b]y default, aid has become the chosen instrument for influencing the political and institutional development of [fragile] societies."[71] For instance, donors allocated one-third of their ODA to fragile states in 2012.[72]

In the late 1940s, three processes had significant impacts on the rise of foreign aid. The first processes related to the need to repair the widespread human, physical and economic devastation in post-World War II Europe. An atmosphere of "hope and renewal" among the Allies favoured the emergence of major initiatives in international cooperation, such as creating the United Nations and the Bretton Woods organizations, the International Monetary Fund (IMF) and World Bank (WB). Second, the beginning of a struggle for influence between two major economic powers, the US and the Soviet Union, led to early bilateral flows of aid with the political and strategic objective of assuring allegiance from aid recipients. Third, many colonized countries also gained their independence,[73] creating demand for the transfer of funds in the form of aid.

The Marshall Plan, designed for the economic recovery in Western Europe, was a major success in the history of aid for two reasons in particular.[74] First, the Plan provided generous, concerted aid. From 1948 to 1951, the US made available more than US$13 billion in aid – about US$100 billion in today's dollar terms, with 90 per cent in grants.[75] Second, Western Europe was well endowed with human resources and skills but was chronically short on capital, making the aid timely and appropriate.[76] In addition, the aid under the Plan was bilateral with a single donor, the US, and it never exceeded more than 3 per cent share of GDP of the recipient countries.[77]

Some characteristics of the aid from the Marshall Plan, however, have been missing in the contemporary relationship between donor and recipient countries. On the donors' side, the current recipients have to deal with dozens of bilateral and multilateral donors, multilateral organizations and hundreds of NGOs, involving hundreds of donor-funded and donor-managed projects.[78] In addition, aid consists of a higher percentage of the current recipient's GDP, especially in situations of aid dependency. More importantly, contemporary aid recipients are not only short on capital but also short on human resources and skills. Recent donor interventions have generally been less successful than expected.[79]

Given that the flow of aid has had a long history, to further assess the characteristics of aid and its impacts on the state-building process, we first discuss the rentier effects of oil revenue to establish a framework for assessing aid impacts and then distinguish the impacts of aid from the effects of oil revenue.

The effects of oil revenue

Following the two oil boom periods that began in the mid-1970s in the Middle East, scholars have developed rentier state theory to explain the effects of rents on governance and state–society relations.[80] Hossein Mahdavy is credited with introducing the fundamentals of rentierism. He used the term "rentier" for the first time to explore problems with Iran's economic development in 1970.[81] Hazem Beblawi later redefined the term, suggesting that rent in a rentier state is a predominant factor in the economy. While only a few are engaged in the generation of rent, the majority is involved in its distribution and utilization. Government is the principal recipient of this rent. Such a government role is argued to allow only a few to control the rent and to seize and hold political power.[82] As the relationship between rentier states and their people involves distribution of rents by the state instead of payment from the people to the government in the form of taxes, rentier regimes are financially independent of society. This situation may create the problem of "state autonomy" that enables elites to create and reshape institutions.

Thus, in the oil-rich Middle Eastern countries, the state and local institutions developed not to extract wealth but to spend it, thus allowing local rulers to circumvent the historical extractive process typical of productive economies. Oil revenue increases the autonomy of state power, which elites exercise over citizens. Rulers in rentier states do not need to "arrive at social contracts with their citizens against a backdrop of coercion; they can often buy out elites and social coalitions and convince them to trade power for wealth."[83]

However, states that are dependent on a small number of income providers are vulnerable to unexpected disturbances in those sources. When oil revenue decreases, for example, the state may adjust to alternative foreign sources, downsize the state apparatus or impose coercive taxation, especially when the existing taxation infrastructure is weak, without adequate time to negotiate with the population, or it may cut subsidies.[84] The decline in the state's income from oil revenue can in turn undermine political stability.

Arguments about the rentier state can be classified into two categories. First, oil wealth makes states less democratic. Second, oil wealth causes governments to be less effective in promoting economic growth. The causal mechanisms for the democratic effect of oil revenue include rentier effects, "repressive effects" and a "modernization effect."[85] The rentier effect focuses on the government's use of fiscal measures, the repression effect emphasizes the government's use of force, and the modernization effect involves social forces that can keep the public demobilized.[86] This process has implications for state building, and thus, state building in oil-rich countries produces different institutional and political outcomes from tax states. For our analysis here, we focus on the rentier effects of oil revenue.

Rentier effects, as noted earlier, work through three mechanisms: taxation, government spending and group formation. Oil-rich governments use fiscal measures such as lowering tax rates or not taxing the population at all, increasing government spending (especially on patronage to buy off adversaries), and preventing the formation of independent social groups, a necessary precondition for democracy, using its largess.[87] These mechanisms in rentier states relieve social pressure for greater accountability, and the effects can be severe when institutions are weak.

We first focus on taxation effects as measured by the share of government revenue collected from taxes on goods, services, income, profits and capital gains (excluding trade taxes). Building on the theory of taxation and state building, the causal mechanism suggests that when government has access to sufficient revenue from the sale of oil, it is less likely to heavily tax its population, if they are taxed at all. The public, in turn, would be less likely to demand accountability from the government.[88] The assured source of oil income can enable governments and politicians to make decisions independent of their citizen taxpayers. For example, governments can establish "mega-projects" without negotiating with citizens' representatives, if any exist, or without being held accountable. Governments may need to negotiate with certain societal actors who have the power to challenge their authority. Governments, however, tend to use some revenue to "buy off" citizens who can otherwise cause trouble and to maintain powerful armies and intelligence agencies to keep the others in line.[89] The degree of state autonomy might differ in varying contexts. However, a state is unlikely to have complete autonomy from its citizens.[90]

The government has little incentive to develop an effective civil bureaucracy because the financial existence of the state is not dependent on it. In the civil bureaucracy, jobs tend to be allocated primarily for patronage purposes rather than for merit. Instead of building an effective bureaucracy, the focus shifts towards building the military and intelligence apparatus of the state.[91]

In addition, when the state is weak, its failure to tax the bulk of its population can make it open to influence by armed insurgents, guerrillas or private armies that are dependent on narcotics and armed trades and other non-state movements of diverse types.[92] In addition to raising revenue, taxation keeps the state machinery active and ensures that the general population is connected to the political process. When the revenue-raising function of the state declines, it leaves open the threat from more committed and organized non-state actors.

The second component of the rentier effect is spending as measured by government consumption (on goods and services, including wages and salaries) as a share of GDP. Oil wealth may lead to increased government spending on patronage and programmes that demobilize the population, which can in turn reduce the demand for accountability. Saudi Arabia and Libya, for example, used their oil wealth to reduce pressure for democracy.[93] Additionally, the Mexican oil boom in the 1970s helped to sustain one-party rule.[94] While fiscal power is a tool for all authoritarian governments to reduce dissent, oil wealth provides the rentier states of the Middle East with exceptionally large and unconstrained budgets.

Fiscal transparency is poor in oil-rich countries. When public revenue comes from a small number of external sources, such as a mining enterprise and foreign oil companies, revenue and expenditures can easily remain hidden from public view.[95] George Kopits and Jon Craig define transparency as "openness towards the public at large about government structure and functions, fiscal policy intentions, public sector accounts, and projections." It also "involves ready access to reliable, comparable information on government activities."[96] The degree of fiscal transparency, however, may depend on the regime type. Many democracies, such as Brazil, New Zealand and Norway, make their oil revenue public; by contrast, undemocratic oil producers, such as Saudi Arabia, and some partially democratic ones, such as Iran and Venezuela, conceal oil revenues from public view.[97]

The second component of the spending effect of the rentier state includes the formation of independent groups. Although measuring the effects of group formation is difficult, Ross uses the government share of GDP to measure the effects of group formation. Oil-rich countries may use largess and design programmes to prevent the formation of independent groups. This argument is rooted in the study of state formation in Western Europe, in which the formation of an independent bourgeoisie helped to build representative institutions in England and France.[98] The cases of Algeria, Iran, Iraq and the Arab Gulf states show that oil wealth has impeded the formation of social capital and hindered transitions to democracy.[99] Despite some disagreements with the group formation argument that the government in, for example, Libya did not have a consistent policy against the development of an indigenous bourgeoisie,[100] evidence suggests that in the 1970s, the Middle East states developed programmes to depoliticize the population and destroy independent civil institutions while implementing others to advance state objectives.[101]

Oil wealth can hinder accountability and the building of an effective state. However, the presence and severity of such processes might differ under varying socio-economic conditions. The following section distinguishes between the rentier effects of aid and oil revenue.

Distinction between aid and oil-revenue rentier effects

Three characteristics of aid distinguish the rentier effects of aid from those of oil revenue: aid conditionality, the absence of the recipient's full discretion over the use of aid and the lack of aid reliability. Aid rentierism thus affects state building and can have specific implications for government accountability, the extent to which governments tax their citizens and the ways that governments allocate their budgets. In the following, we discuss each characteristic and the effects of aid in comparison to the three components of oil-revenue rentier effects – taxation, spending and group formation. Table 1.1 outlines the differences and similarities between aid and oil revenue.

First, aid taxation effects are mixed. Unlike in oil-rich states with a weak taxation function and low revenue collection,[102] the impact of aid on revenue collection

Table 1.1 Foreign aid and oil revenue

Characteristics	Oil Revenue	Foreign Aid
Reliability	Oil is more reliable.	Aid is less reliable.
Conditionality	No conditions attached.	Conditions attached.
Discretion and Control	State is the main recipient and has full discretion over the use of oil revenue.	State is not the sole recipient and does not have full discretion and control over the use of aid.

Source: Author's analysis

is mixed.[103] Aid is often conditional on increases in revenue collection, and the recipient government may also have the incentive to strengthen the taxation system because the flow of aid is not permanent. The recipient government needs to meet the revenue targets identified through negotiation with donors. This goal may result in distortions of formal procedures for tax collection and the misuse of power because the effective level of protection of taxpayer rights is weak.[104] The outcome varies in different contexts, however. Aid-dependent countries arguably inherit weak state institutions, but this does not always occur, as they are generally unable to generate sufficient revenue to sustain state building and provide public services.

Both aid and oil incomes create a situation in which the state becomes independent of domestic taxpayers, enabling the state to exist without much political and organizational effort in relation to citizens for tax collection. Aid donors frequently seek to influence the recipient government's domestic policies, which can potentially have a damaging impact on governance and can reconfigure state–society relations and conceivably undermine the emergence of a domestic social contract. Donors, for example, influence the taxation practices of recipient governments by providing technical assistance and funds with specific conditions. These include "conditional demands for specific policies on tax or other issues, sometimes [aid is] tied to signals about withdrawal of funding in cases of non-compliance."[105]

Moreover, foreign aid is less reliable than oil revenue because of the smaller number of "sellers" and many potential "buyers." Aid reliability is also predominantly linked with the recipient's and donor's geostrategic circumstances, which may change suddenly – a situation that is unlikely with oil. Thus, aid can shift from one country to another according to donor preference. Although oil prices may change, oil is unlikely to suddenly disappear from the wells.

A study by the OECD found that between 2000 and 2006, revenue collection in six highly aid-dependent countries (Afghanistan, Bolivia, the Democratic Republic of Congo, Nepal, Rwanda and Sierra Leone), except Bolivia, was less than 14 per cent, with Afghanistan having the lowest level of 5.3 per cent.[106] A negative relationship between tax revenue and aid is suggested by Todd Moss *et al.* using the four-year average of tax revenue (excluding trade taxes) as a share of GDP against the four-year average of aid as a share of GNI for fifty-five low-and middle-income countries between 1972 and 1992. Despite variation in the findings, such as situations of high aid and low tax and of low aid and high tax, no systems with high aid and high tax (when aid consists of more than 10 per cent of GNI and tax revenue is more than 18 per cent of GDP) were found.[107] However, the results of a number of country studies have been mixed.[108] For example, a negative relationship between aid and domestic revenue mobilization has been found in Pakistan (1998), Zambia (2004) and Cote d'Ivoire (2003). In contrast, a positive relationship between aid and revenue collection has been reported for Indonesia (1990), Ghana (2003), Uganda and Malawi (2004).[109]

Aid conditionality can undermine democratic state building by giving donors greater leverage to shape the recipient state's policy. Thus, unlike undemocratic oil-based rentier states where government accountability is weak, aid dependency can shift government accountability upward to foreign donors.[110] Collier argues that such conditionality substitutes for the weakness of recipient citizens to hold their government accountable.[111] This argument seems to be valid if the interests of donors and the recipient state's citizens are fully aligned and reinforce one another and if aid concentrates on specific technical reforms, such as modernizing the recipient budget. However, because aid largely follows donors' interests, the interests of foreign donors and the recipient country's citizens are less likely to be fully aligned. While government accountability to external actors may be better than the absence of accountability, it may undermine democratic decision making and deprive the recipient parliament (if any exists) of the right to hold the executive accountable.

Aid spending effects could be explained by aid modality, donors' intention and the context. However, compared with oil revenue, aid is more constrained from being spent on patronage. Unlike oil revenue, aid is generally conditional, and the recipient does not have full discretion over it. This does not imply that donors do not spend aid on patronage in recipient countries. In addition, donors often make their aid for the recipient country's budget conditional, for example, on the implementation of certain policies, or they earmark them for predetermined projects.[112] Donors directly allocate and manage the bulk of their aid through projects that bypass state and national mechanisms. Such aid is referred to as "off-budget" or "external budget" aid. NGOs, private companies and firms receive direct funding from donors for implementing projects. The state, therefore, does not have discretion and full control over the allocation and management of aid, "not even [on] general budget support or other less conditional types of aid."[113] Off-budget aid can also prevent the recipient parliament from overseeing off-budget aid spending. While "aid funds are never completely controlled by the recipient governments,"[114] the extent to which they are controlled still leaves room for buying political patronage,[115] although such opportunities are fewer than in the case of undemocratic oil-rich countries.

Aid can come in the form of government budget support, sector programme support, pool funding, projects through government systems, projects through parallel systems and NGOs. Government budget support and sector-based support flow through the recipient government systems, while projects through parallel systems and projects through NGOs do not use the recipient government systems. Projects through the government and pool funding can use both systems. How much total aid flows through the government budget depends on the recipients' state capacity and internal conditions as well as donor preferences.[116] Notably, donors adopt diverse approaches in a given context. However, although different approaches may have diverse effects in a given context, it is crucial to consider how major donors provide aid and support state building.

Hence, the amount of discretion that a recipient government might have over the use of aid depends on foreign donors' intention and the recipient state's capacity. Foreign donors generally use bypass tactics: they spend a large portion of aid outside the government budget, thus bypassing the state. Governments of OECD countries, for example, spent approximately one-thirds of their aid outside the recipient governments' budget in 2007.[117] This percentage does not include military spending, which typically flows outside the recipient government budget. In some countries, the total share of aid off-budget is extremely high. Donors spent more than 82 per cent of their aid outside the government budget in Afghanistan from 2002 and 2009 and almost all of their aid off-budget in Iraq from 2003 to 2014.[118]

Foreign donors' political economies, as Simone Dietrich argues, better explain the different aid policies. Countries that place a high premium on market efficiency, such as the US, the UK and Sweden, are more likely to outsource aid delivery in recipients with poor governance.[119] A single factor may not, however, be the key driver of aid policies. A combination of factors such as donors' political economies and the quality of recipient institutions may determine how much aid delivery should be outsourced outside the recipient state mechanisms.[120] Off-budget aid may have adverse implications for accountability and for state capacity, a topic that we discuss later.

In addition, the state and nature of fiscal transparency may differ in situations of aid dependency and oil rentierism. If we use state revenue and spending to measure fiscal transparency, then the government budget is a useful tool for doing so. Budget transparency is much more complex in aid-dependent contexts, which is an understudied topic in the literature. Until the open budget survey, assessing the state of budget transparency around the world, was conducted in 2006, data on budget transparency for a large number of countries did not exist.[121] This limitation constrained the study of budget transparency and aid dependency.

The open budget survey found in 2008 that highly aid-dependent countries suffer from a deficit of transparency. Thirty countries that received more than 5 per cent of their GNI in foreign aid ranked 24 on average by OBI, compared to a score of 62 for non-aid-dependent countries.[122] The 2010 open budget survey shows a modest improvement in the budget transparency of these countries. Individual cases may not support the view that aid dependency tends to have a converse relationship with budget transparency.[123] As legitimate stakeholders in the budget process of recipient countries,[124] donors urge governments to improve fiduciary control and make their budgetary information available to donors. This process neglects the need for improved budget transparency to the citizens of recipient countries. If a larger portion of aid is spent outside the recipient budget, this can fragment the budget into government budget (on-budget) and off-budget spending[125] and thus undermine transparency.

Aid also has distinctive implications for group formation. Foreign aid tends to promote the formation of groups that are independent of the recipient government, primarily non-profit NGOs, but in some contexts, these organizations can be referred to as CSOs. Aid effects work through two mechanisms: aid conditionality on democratization and the availability of aid funding for NGOs. However, sources of funding for NGOs or CSOs are diverse and include governments, private donations and private foundations, which may differ in varying contexts.[126]

NGOs are "those organizations that are officially established, run by employed staff (often urban professionals or expatriates), well-supported (by domestic or, as is more often the case, international funding), and that are often relatively large and well-resourced." However, NGOs are regarded as different from grassroots organizations, which are "usually understood to be smaller, often membership-based organizations, operating without a paid staff but often reliant upon donor or NGO support, which tend to be (but are not always) issue-based and therefore ephemeral."[127] The terms NGOs and CSOs overlap, and they are often used interchangeably; for example, these two terms are used interchangeably by the OECD.[128] Thus, interventions in support of NGOs largely show a pattern that is the opposite of the approach of oil-rich countries, which prevent the formation of independent groups.

Traditional donors finance CSOs to strengthen democracy. For example, Denmark financial support for civil society aims "to contribute to the development of a strong, independent and diversified civil society in the developing countries . . . to support democracy and poverty reduction."[129] Eric Werker and Faisal Z. Ahmed argue that because NGOs are an assumed part of civil society, "they also strengthen it through their activities, which in turn supports the democratic process."[130] The flow of aid to CSOs is an easy way to measure their development. The Development Assistance Committee (DAC) members, including European Union institutions, channelled 19.3 billion in ODA to and through CSOs in 2011, a significant increase from their US$14.5 billion commitment of 2008. The total ODA allocated to CSOs stabilized at approximately 14 per cent between 2009 and 2011.[131]

While donors' support for the development of NGOs/CSOs is important for promoting a civil society and democracy, this process has a number of limitations. First, in situations of aid dependency, although these groups are financially independent of the recipient state, they are in fact dependent on donors for funding to sustain their activities. Second, these groups often implement projects that donors envisage, frequently turning the role of CSOs into implementing agencies. Third, the dependence of these groups on donors impacts their relationship with the recipient state and can lead to divergence in the state–society fiscal relationship. These issues are further explored in the proceeding chapters.

The assumption is that a large flow of aid to NGOs might have negative effects on state capacity because it could encourage skilled government employees to shift to NGOs or could discourage skilled people from joining the government because the salary that they can receive while working with NGOs would be much better. However, the validity of this assumption greatly depends on the pre-existing conditions and the amount of time that NGOs have operated in a given country. In a weak state with a strong presence of NGOs, it seems more likely that NGOs can contribute to the capacity of the state if skilled NGO employees turn to the government for employment in the early years of state-building efforts; this process occurred in the early years of post-2001 Afghanistan (Chapter 3), but in the long term, the flow of a large portion of aid through NGOs could reverse such a trend. This area is understudied and requires further research.

Although the study of independent group formation in relation to state building in situations of aid dependency is understudied, the formation of independent groups generally appears to help strengthen civil society and, thus, state–society interactions. Arguably, NGOs can also contribute to the state-building process by training people who can join the government workforce. This situation occurred in Afghanistan after 2001, as many successful bureaucrats who joined the government had previously worked with NGOs.[132]

We noted that although both aid and oil revenue are unearned, their rentier effects through the mechanisms of taxation, spending and group formation differ. Although the effects of aid largely depend on the characteristics of foreign aid, the recipient context is equally important for the success of state building and of aid effectiveness. Aid seems to be more effective in building states that are modern with a Weberian bureaucracy. By contrast, aid seems to be less effective in building weak (fragile) and neo-patrimonial states. The outcome of the state-building process does not solely depend on the context. It is also crucial how donors react and which aid modality they use in response to state weakness. Therefore, the severity of aid effects differs based on the contexts and based on the types of aid received.

If the state is a relatively strong state with a Weberian bureaucracy, aid can further reinforce the state when spent through national systems, with efforts to ensure that the recipient leaders reinforce state effectiveness by implementing policies that require greater state capacity. However, even under more adverse initial conditions – as in neo-patrimonial states – the aid regime and state-building strategy are important. Under these conditions, aid undermines state building if it induces discontinuity in the existing state capacity and creates institutions parallel to those of the state. Post-World War II South Korea and Taiwan,[133] as well as Western European states, are notable examples of the former, whereas the latter include Iraq and Afghanistan, upon which we will further elaborate.[134]

Thus, aid can have positive and negative effects on state building. The paradoxical effects of aid largely depend on donors' interests, the aid modality and the recipient pre-existing institutional and socio-political conditions.

Conclusion

This chapter demonstrated that different sources of state revenue produce diverse political and institutional outcomes in the state-building process. Aid has paradoxical rentier effects through taxation, government spending and group formation, and these effects differ from the rentier effects of oil revenue.

Both oil revenue and aid are unearned. They enable states to derive revenue with little political and organizational effort, especially effort in relation to citizens. Oil-rich countries use low tax rates and higher spending to relieve the pressure for greater accountability. However, unlike oil revenue, foreign aid is conditional and less reliable, and the recipient government does not have full control over its use. Foreign donors' strategic relationship with the recipient government and the recipient state capacity may determine the degrees of aid conditionality, reliability and recipient control. Aid may also result in the recipient government being accountable to foreign donors rather than to citizens and may thus have paradoxical effects on state building.

When a large portion of aid is spent outside the recipient government budget, it creates a parallel public sector and undermines state building and democratic decision making. This use of aid diverts political and financial resources from state institutions and deprives the recipient state and parliament of the right to allocate and oversee the donor's off-budget spending.

The effects of aid on the formation of independent groups are paradoxical. Unlike oil revenue, aid tends to promote the formation of groups – especially CSOs – that are independent of the recipient government, although they are dependent on foreign donors for funding, which encourages upward accountability to donors.

Thus, aid can have positive and negative effects on state building. The paradoxical effects of aid largely depend on donors' interests, aid modality and the recipient's pre-existing institutional and socio-political conditions. The relationship between aid and state building is thus highly complex, and the question of how aid affects state building cannot be answered unconditionally.

Notes

1 Michael L. Ross, "Does Oil Hinder Democracy?," *World Politics* 53, no. 3 (2001) 325–61.

2 See for example Nazih Ayubi, "Arab Bureaucracies: Expanding Size, Changing Roles," in *The Arab State*, ed. Giacomo Luniani (London: Routledge, 1990), 144. There is no clear indication that what level of taxation is optimum. Jonathan Di John, "The Political Economy of Taxation and Tax Reform in Developing Countries," (Tokyo: World Institute for Economic Development Research, 2006), 4. However, still in some oil-producing countries, tax revenue as a percentage of GDP is low. For example, in 2009 the domestic taxation was 1 per cent share of Kuwait's annual GDP. World Bank, "World Data Bank: World Development Indicators," http://data.worldbank.org/indicator/GC.TAX.TOTL.GD.ZS/countries?display=default.

3 See Sanjeev Gupta, Robert Powell and Yongzheng Yang, *The Macroeconomic Challenges of Scaling up Aid to Africa: A Checklist for Practitioners* (Washington, DC: IMF, 2006); and Michael Carnahan, "Options for Revenue Generation in Post-Conflict Environments," in *Policy Paper Series on Public Finance in Post-conflict Environments* (New York: Center for International Cooperation and Political Economy Research Institute, New York University, 2007).

4 Margaret Levi, *Of Rule and Revenue* (Berkeley: University of California Press, 1988), 1, 2.

5 Dirk J. Vandewalle, *Libya since Independence: Oil and State-Building* (Ithaca: Cornell University Press, 1998), 17–18.

6 Mick Moore, "Revenues, State Formation, and the Quality of Governance in Developing Countries," *International Political Science Review* 25, no. 3 (2004), 297–319; Richard Snyder and Ravi Bhavnani, "Diamonds, Blood, and Taxes: A Revenue Centered Framework for Explaining Political Order," *Journal of Conflict Resolution* 49, no. 4 (2005), 563–97; Jeffrey F. Timmons, "The Fiscal Contract: States, Taxes, and Public Services," *World Politics* 57, no. 4 (2005), 530–67; and Deborah Brautigam, Odd-Helge Fjeldstad and Mick Moore, *Taxation and State-Building in Developing Countries: Capacity and Consent* (Cambridge: Cambridge University Press, 2008).

7 Levi, *Of Rule and Revenue*; Moore, "Revenues, State Formation, and the Quality of Governance in Developing Countries"; Di John, "The Political Economy of Taxation and Tax Reform in Developing Countries"; Brautigam, Fjeldstad, and Moore, *Taxation and State-Building in Developing Countries: Capacity and Consent*; Deborah Brautigam, "Building Leviathan: Revenue, State Capacity, and Governance," *IDS Bulletin* 33, no. 3 (2002); OECD, *Do No Harm: International Support for State Building* (Paris: OECD, 2009); Hazem Beblawi and Giacomo Luciani, *The Rentier State* (London: Croom Helm, 1987); Hossein Mahdavy, "The Patterns and Problems of Economic Development in Rentier States: The Case of Iran," in *Studies in the Economic History of the Middle East*, ed. M.A. Cook (London: Oxford University Press, 1970), 428–67.

8 Christopher Pierson, *The Modern State* (London: Routledge, 1996), 30; Mick Moore, "Political Underdevelopment: What Causes Bad Governance," *Public Management Review* 3, no. 3 (2001): 399; and Max Weber, ed. *Economy and Society: An Outline of Interpretive Sociology*. Vol. 2 (Berkeley: University of California Press, 1978), 54, 56.

9 See Ross, "Does Oil Hinder Democracy?"

10 Giacomo Luciani, "Allocation vs. Production States," in *The Rentier State*, ed. Hazem Beblawi and Giacomo Luciani (London: Croom Helm, 1987), 63–8; and Deborah Brautigam, *Aid Dependence and Governance* (Stockholm: Almqvist and Wiksell International, 2000).

11 Kevin M. Morrison, *Nontaxation and Representation* (Cambridge: Cambridge University Press, 2014).

12 Mick Moore, "Revenues, State Formation, and the Quality of Governance in Developing Countries"; and Deborah Brautigam, "Introduction: Taxation and State-Building in Developing Countries," in *Taxation and State-Building in Developing Countries: Capacity and Consent*, ed. Deborah Brautigam, Odd-Helge Fjeldstad, and Mick Moore, 1–33, (Cambridge: Cambridge University Press, 2008).

13 Ross, "Does Oil Hinder Democracy?"; Hazem Beblawi, "The Rentier State in the Arab World," in *The Rentier State*, ed. Hazem Beblawi and Giacomo Luciani, 49–62, (London: Croom Helm, 1987); and Giacomo Luciani, "Allocation vs. Production States."

14 Ross, "Does Oil Hinder Democracy?"

15 Morrison, *Nontaxation and Representation*; Barnett R. Rubin, *The Fragmentation of Afghanistan: State Formation and Collapse in the International System* (London: Yale University Press, 1995); and Moore, "Revenues, State Formation, and the Quality of Governance in Developing Countries."

16 Kevin M. Morrison, "Oil, Nontax Revenue, and the Redistributive Foundations of Regime Stability," *International Organization* 63, no. 1 (2009): 107–38; Faisal Z. Ahmed, "The Perils of Unearned Foreign Income: Aid, Remittances, and Government Survival," *American Political Science Review* 106, no. 1 (2012): 146–65; and Bruce Bueno de Mesquita and Alastair Smith, "Leader Survival, Revolutions, and the Nature of Government Finance," *American Journal of Political Science* 54, no. 4 (2010): 936–50.

17 Ahmed, "The Perils of Unearned Foreign Income".

18 de Mesquita and Smith, "Leader Survival, Revolutions, and the Nature of Government Finance".

19 Paul Collier, "Is Aid Oil? An Analysis of Whether Africa Can Absorb More Aid," *World Development* 34, no. 9 (2006), 482–1497.

20 Sarah Blodgett Bermeo, "Aid Is Not Oil: Donor Utility, Heterogeneous Aid, and the Aid-Democratization Relationship," *International Organization* 70, no. 1 (Winter 2016), 1–32.
21 Ceren Altincekic and David H. Bearce, "Why There Should Be No Political Foreign Aid Curse," *World Development* 64 (2014).
22 Simon James, ed., *Taxation: Critical Perspectives on the World Economy*. Vol. 3 (London: Routledge, 2002), 222.
23 Moore, "Revenues, State Formation, and the Quality of Governance in Developing Countries."
24 Sebastian von Einsiedel, "Policy Response to State Failure," in *Making States Work: State Failure and the Crisis of Governance*, ed. Simon Chesterman, Michal Ignatieff, and Ramesh Thakur (Tokyo: United Nations University Press, 2005), 15.
25 Ibid.
26 John Locke, *Two Treaties of Government*, ed. Peter Laslett (Cambridge: Cambridge University Press, 1988), 33; and see Jean-Jacques Rousseau, *The Social Contract*, transl. by Maurice Cranston (London: Penguin, 1968).
27 Max Weber, "The Profession and Vocation of Politics," in *Weber: Political Writings*, ed. Peter Lassman and Ronald Speirs (Cambridge: Cambridge University Press, 1994), 310–11.
28 The Montevideo Convention, in full Montevideo Convention on the Rights and Duties of States, was signed at Montevideo, Uruguay, on December 26, 1933. It established the standard definition of a state under international law and indicated that all states were equal sovereign units consisting of a permanent population, defined territorial boundaries, a government, and an ability to enter into agreements with other states. Among the convention's provisions were that signatories would not intervene in the domestic or foreign affairs of another state. See Encyclopaedia Britain s.v. "Montevideo Convention." www.britannica.com/EBchecked/topic/390844/Montevideo-Convention.
29 Theda Skocpol, ed., *Bringing the State Back In: Strategies of Analysis in Current Research*, (Cambridge: Cambridge University Press, 1985).
30 Michael Mann, "The Sources of Social Power: The Rise of Classes and Nation-States, 1760–1914, Vol. II," (Cambridge: Cambridge University Press, 1993), 59.
31 Michael Mann, States, War and Capitalism: Studies in Political Sociology (Oxford: Basil Blackwell, 1988), 5.
32 Andrew George Walder, The Waning of the Communist State: Economic Origins of Political Decline in China and Hungary (Berkeley: University of California Press, 1995), 89.
33 Francis Fukuyama, "What Is Governance?," *Governance* 26, no. 3 (2013): 353.
34 Ibid.
35 Ibid.
36 Mushtaq Husain Khan and Hazel Gray, "State Weakness in Developing Countries and Strategies of Institutional Reform: Operational Implications for Anti-Corruption Policy and a Case Study of Tanzania," Paper commissioned by the Department for International Development (DFID). School of Oriental and African Studies (SOAS) University of London, 2006), available at http://eprints.lse.ac.uk/50337/1/Gray_State_weakness_developing_2006.pdf. in *LSE Research Online* (London School of Econmomics and Political Science, May 2003), 28.
37 Ibid., 3; Tam O'Neil, "Neopatrimonialism and Public Sector Performance and Reform," (September 2007).
38 Nematullah Bizhan, "Continuity, Aid and Revival: State Building in South Korea, Taiwan, Iraq and Afghanistan," (Working Paper 2015/109, the Global Economic Governance Programme, Oxford: University of Oxford, 2015).
39 Zoe Scott, "Literature Review on State-Building," (Working Paper, University of Birmingham, Birmingham, 2007), 3.
40 Francis Fukuyama, The Origins of Political Order: From Prehuman Times to the French Revolution (New York: Farrar, Straus and Giroux, 2011), 321.

41 Ibn Khaldun, *The Muqaddimah: An Introduction to History, Translated by Franz Rosenthal* (Princeton: Princeton University Press, 1967), 40.
42 David F. Burg, A World History of Tax Rebellions: An Encyclopedia of Tax Rebels, Revolts, and Riots from Antiquity to the Present (New York: Routledge, 2004), x.
43 Ibid.
44 See Joseph A. Schumpeter, "The Crises of the Tax State," in *The Economics and Sociology of Capitalism*, ed. Richard Swedberg (Princeton: Princeton University Press, 1991), 108.
45 Michael Mann, "The Crises of the Latin American Nation-State," in *Conference on The Political Crises and Internal Conflict in Colombia* (Bogota: University of the Andes, April 10–13, 2003), 3.
46 See for details Charles Tilly, "War Making and State Making as Organized Crime," in *Bringing the State Back In*, ed. Peter B. Evans, Dietrich Rueschemeyer and Theda Skocpol (Cambridge: Cambridge University Press, 1985), 161–91.
47 Moore, "Political Underdevelopment: What Causes Bad Governance," 401.
48 Levi, Of Rule and Revenue, 120.
49 Ibid.
50 Mick Moore, "Between Coercion and Contract," in *Taxation and State-Building in Developing Countries: Capacity and Consent*, ed. Deborah Brautigam, Odd-Helge Fjeldstad, and Mick Moore (Cambridge: Cambridge University Press, 2008), 53.
51 Ibid., 53.
52 Jeffrey Herbst, States and Power in Africa: Comparative Lessons in Authority and Control (Princeton: Princeton University Press, 2000); and Robert H. Jackson, Quasi-States: Sovereignty, International Relations, and the Third World (Cambridge: Cambridge University Press, 1990); as quoted in Moore, "Between Coercion and Contract," 53.
53 See Dambisa Moyo, Dead Aid: Why Aid Is Not Working and How There Is a Better Way for Africa (New York: Farrar, Straus and Giroux, 2009).
54 See Miguel A. Centeno, "Blood and Debt: War and Taxation in Nineteenth-Century Latin America," *American Journal of Sociology* 102, no. 6 (1997), 1565–1605. The case studies included all the countries in four of the five geopolitical zones of Latin America. These were Argentina, Uruguay (La Plata Basin), Chile, Peru, Bolivia (Pacific Littoral), Ecuador, Colombia, Venezuela (Northern Andes) and Mexico.
55 Ibid., 1565.
56 Moore, "Between Coercion and Contract," 53.
57 See Bryan K. Ritchie, Richard F. Doner, and Dan Slater, "Systemic Vulnerability and the Origins of Developmental States: Northeast and Southeast Asia in Comparative Perspective," *International Organization* 59, no. 2 (April 2005), 327–61. Developmental state is a state that plays a central role in economic development. It has a bureaucracy that is given sufficient scope to take initiatives and operate effectively. See Huck-ju Kwon, "Transforming the Developmental Welfare State in East Asia," *Development and Change* 36, no. 3 (2005): 481.
58 Brautigam, "Introduction: Taxation and State-Building in Developing Countries," 7–
59 Mann, "The Crises of the Latin American Nation-State," 3.
60 See Afsaneh Najmabadi, "Depoliticisation of a Rentier State," in *The Rentier State*, ed. Hazem Beblawi and Giacomo Luciani (London: Croom Helm, 1987), 211–27.
61 Morrison, *Nontaxation and Representation*; Moore, "Revenues, State Formation, and the Quality of Governance in Developing Countries"; and John Waterbury, "Democracy without Democrats? The Potential for Political Liberalization in the Middle East," in *Democracy without Democrats: The Renewal of Politics in the Muslim World*, ed. Ghassan Salame (London: I.B. Tauris 1994), 23–47.
62 John Waterbury, "Democracy Without Democrats?" 29.
63 See Moore, "Revenues, State Formation, and the Quality of Governance in Developing Countries."

64 For detailed discussions about the power of the state, see Mann, Michael. "The Auton-omous Power of the State: Its Origins, Mechanisms and Results." *European Journal of Sociology* 25, no. 2 (1984): 185–213.
65 OECD, "States of Fragility 2015: Meeting Post-2015 Ambitions," (Paris: OECD Pub-lishing, 2015), 57–8.
66 Helen V. Milner and Dustin Tingley, eds., "Introduction," *Geopolitics of Foreign Aid* (Cheltenham: Edward Elgar, 2013).
67 See Moyo, Dead Aid, 10–28.
68 See Francis Y. Owusu, Post-9/11 U.S. Foreign Aid, the Millennium Challenge Account and Africa: How Many Birds Can One Stone Kill? (Ames: Iowa State Uni-versity, 2004).
69 Frances Stewart and Graham Brown, "Fragile States," (Centre for Research on Inequal-ity, Human Security and Ethnicity, Oxford, 2010), 9.
70 Ashraf Ghani and Clare Lockhart, *Fixing Failed States: A Framework for Rebuilding a Fractured World* (New York: Oxford University Press, 2008).
71 Miles Kahler, "Aid and State Building," (Working Paper, University of California, San Diego, 2007), 3.
72 OECD, "States of Fragility 2015: Meeting Post-2015 Ambitions," 57; "Total Flows by Donors," (April 9, 2016).
73 Stephen Browne, *Foreign Aid in Practice* (London: Pinter Reference, 1990), 1.
74 For detailed discussion on Marshall Plan Aid see Eliot Sorel and Pier Carlo Pdoan, eds., *The Marshall Plan: Lessons Learned for the 21st Century* (Paris: OECD, 2008).
75 Ibid., 55.
76 Browne, Foreign Aid in Practice, 12.
77 See Barry Eichengreen et al., "The Marshall Plan: Economic Effects and Implications for Eastern Europe and the Former Ussr," *Economic Policy* 7, no. 14 (1992): 15; and Moyo, *Dead Aid: Why Aid Is Not Working and How There Is a Better Way for Africa*, 10–28.
78 Knack, Stephen, and Aminur Rahman, "Donor Fragmentation and Bureaucratic Qual-ity in Aid Recipients," Policy Research Working Paper 3186, World Bank, 2004, 1, available at doi:10.1596/1813-9450-3186. doi:doi:10.1596/1813-9450-3186.
79 See Kahler, "Aid and State Building," 2.
80 Matthew Gray, "A Theory of 'Late Rentierism' in the Arab States of the Gulf," Cen-ter for International And Regional Studies (Qatar: Georgetown University School of Foreign Service in Qatar, 2011), 1.
81 Mahdavy, "The Patterns and Problems of Economic Development in Rentier States: The Case of Iran."
82 Beblawi, "The Rentier State in the Arab World," 51–2.
83 Vandewalle, Libya since Independence: Oil and State-Building, 8.
84 For example, the government of Saudi Arabia cut massive oil subsidies as low oil prices suppressed revenue and resulted in a budget deficit of US$98 billion. Ahmed AL Omran and Summer Said, "Saudi Arabia Cuts Spending, Raises Domestic Fuel Prices," *The Wall Street Journal*, December 28, 2015. www.wsj.com/articles/saudi-arabia-announces-2016-budget-1451312691.
85 Ross, "Does Oil Hinder Democracy?"
86 Ibid., 337.
87 Ibid.
88 Luciani, "Allocation vs. Production States."
89 Moore, "Revenues, State Formation, and the Quality of Governance in Developing Countries," 306; and Ross, "Does Oil Hinder Democracy?"
90 See Gray, "A Theory of 'Late Rentierism' in the Arab States of the Gulf," 10.
91 See Moore, "Revenues, State Formation, and the Quality of Governance in Develop-ing Countries," 307–8; and Ross, "Does Oil Hinder Democracy?" Overinvesting on military apparatus is also referred to as the repressive effect of oil revenue. Ibid., 335.

92 Moore, "Revenues, State Formation, and the Quality of Governance in Developing Countries," 307.
93 John P. Entelis, ed., *Oil Wealth and the Prospects for Democratization in the Arabian Peninsula: The Case of Saudi Arabia*, Arab Oil: Impact on the Arab Countries and Global Implications (New York: Praeger, 1976); and Vandewalle, *Libya since Independence: Oil and State-Building*.
94 Carlos Bazdresch and Santiago Levy, "Populism and Economic Policy in Mexico, 1970–1982," in *The Macroeconomics of Populism in Latin America*, ed. Rudiger Dornbush and Sebastian Edwards (Chicago: University of Chicago Press, 1991), 223–62.
95 Moore, "Revenues, State Formation, and the Quality of Governance in Developing Countries," 307.
96 George Kopits and Jon D. Craig, *Transparency in Government Operations*, Occasional Paper (Washington: IMF, 1998). Transparency is believed to be a "preventative remedy" for corruption. Stephen Kotkin and Andras Sajo, *Political Corruption in Transition: A Skeptic's Handbook* (Budapest: Central European University Press, 2002), 2.
97 See Michael Ross, *The Oil Curse: How Petroleum Wealth Shapes the Development of Nations* (Princeton: Princeton University Press, 2012), 59.
98 Bazdresch and Levy, "Populism and Economic Policy in Mexico, 1970–1982."
99 Ross, "Does Oil Hinder Democracy?," 334.
100 Ruth First, "Libya: Class and State in an Oil Economy," in *Oil and Class Struggle*, ed. Petter Nore and Terisa Turner (London: Zed Press, 1980), 137.
101 Kiren Aziz Chaudhry, "Economic Liberalization and the Lineages of the Rentier State," *Comparative Politics* 27, no. 1 (1994): 9.
102 See, for example, Ayubi, "Arab Bureaucracies: Expanding Size, Changing Roles," 144. There is no clear indication of what level of taxation is optimum. John, "The Political Economy of Taxation and Tax Reform in Developing Countries," 4. However, in some oil producing countries, tax revenue as a percentage of GDP is very low. For example, in 2009 the domestic taxation was 1 per cent share of Kuwait's annual GDP. World Bank, "World Data Bank: World Development Indicators."
103 See Gupta, Powell and Yang, *The Macroeconomic Challenges of Scaling up Aid to Africa: A Checklist for Practitioners*; and Carnahan, "Options for Revenue Generation in Post-Conflict Environments."
104 See Florens Luoga, "Taxpayers' Right in the Context of Democratic Governance: Tanzania," *IDS Bulletin* 33, no. 3 (July 2002), 1–14.
105 Ole Therkildsen, "Keeping the State Accountable: Is Aid No Better Than Oil?," *IDS Bulletin* 33, no. 3 (2002): 3.
106 Net ODA (official development assistance) disbursements (the sum of grants, capital subscriptions and net loans – loans extended minus repayments of loan principal and offsetting entries for debt relief) in 2005 were almost 40 per cent of gross national income (GNI) in Afghanistan, around 50 per cent in the DRC (Democratic Republic of Congo) and 25 per cent or more in Rwanda and Sierra Leone. OECD, *Do No Harm: International Support for State Building*, 101–2.
107 Todd Moss, Gunilla Pettersson, and Nicolas Van de Walle, "An Aid-Institutions Paradox? A Review Essay on Aid Dependency and State Building in Sub-Saharan Africa," (Center for Global Development, Washington, January 2006), 11.
108 Ibid.
109 See ibid., 13, 28.
110 Knack and Rahman, "Donor Fragmentation and Bureaucratic Quality in Aid Recipients."
111 Collier, "Is Aid Oil? An Analysis of Whether Africa Can Absorb More Aid."
112 Nematullah Bizhan, "Continuity, Aid and Revival: State Building in South Korea, Taiwan, Iraq and Afghanistan," (Working Paper 2015/109, the Global Economic Governance Programme, Oxford: University of Oxford, 2015).

113 Therkildsen, "Keeping the State Accountable: Is Aid No Better Than Oil?," 2.
114 Ibid.
115 Stephen Knack, "Aid Dependence and the Quality of Governance: Cross-Country Empirical Tests," *Southern Economic Journal* 68, no. 2 (2001): 313. Furthermore, the aid flow is locked into the budget system of the donor countries, while the priorities of these countries may change over time in order to assure their interests. Hence, it is difficult for the recipients to secure multi-year assistance from donors.
116 Sara Bandstein, "What Determines the Choice of Aid Modalities? A Framework for Assessing Incentive Structures," (Karlstad: SADEV, 2007), 11.
117 Simone Dietrich, "Donor Political Economies and the Pursuit of Aid Effectiveness," *International Organization* 70, no. 1, (2014): 2.
118 Islamic Republic of Afghanistan, "Development Cooperation Report," (Kabul: Ministry of Finance, 2010); and Bizhan, "Continuity, Aid and Revival: State Building in South Korea, Taiwan, Iraq and Afghanistan."
119 Dietrich, "Donor Political Economies and the Pursuit of Aid Effectiveness."
120 See Bizhan, "Continuity, Aid and Revival."
121 Paolo De Renzio and Harika Masud, "Measuring and Promoting Budget Transparency: The Open Budget Index as a Research and Advocacy Tool," *Governance* 24, no. 3 (2011), 607–11.
122 IBP, "Open Budgets Transform Lives: The Open Budget Survey of 2008," (2008), 18.
123 IBP, "Open Budget Survey 2012," (Washington, DC, 2012); and World Bank, "World Development Indicators," (2014).
124 Vivek Ramkumar and Paolo de Renzio, "Improving Budget Transparency and Accountability in Aid Dependent Countries: How Can Donors Help?," in *Budget Brief*, (IBP [International Budget Partnership], 2009).
125 Nematullah Bizhan, "Budget Transparency in Afghanistan: A Pathway to Building Public Trust in the State," (Washington: International Budget Partnership, 2013).
126 Roger C. Riddell, *Does Foreign Aid Really Work?* (Oxford: Oxford University Press, 2007), 259–64.
127 Eric Werker and Faisal Z. Ahmed, "What Do Nongovernmental Organizations Do?," *The Journal of Economic Perspectives* 22, no. 2 (2008): 6.
128 See OECD, "Aid for CSOs," (2013).
129 Ministry of Foreign Affairs of Denmark, "Partners: Civil Society Organisations," http://um.dk/en/danida-en/partners/civil-society-organisations/.
130 Werker and Ahmed, "What Do Nongovernmental Organizations Do?," 7.
131 OECD, "Aid for CSOs," 5.
132 Also see Seema Ghani and Nematullah Bizhan, "Contracting out Core Government Functions and Services in Afghanistan," in *Contracting out Government Functions and Services: Emerging Lessons from Post-Conflict and Fragile Situations*, ed. OECD, 97–133 (Paris: OECD, 2009).
133 See Atul Kohli, State-Directed Development: Political Power and Industrialization in the Global Periphery (Cambridge, UK; New York: Cambridge University Press, 2004).
134 Bizhan, "Continuity, Aid and Revival."

Part II

The history of revenue and state formation in Afghanistan, 1747–2000

2 Reliance on external revenue

Afghanistan from 1747 to 2000

Introduction

Since the establishment of the Durrani Empire in 1747, Afghanistan has suffered from a weak taxation system and has frequently and significantly relied on external revenue in the form of tributes, subsidies and foreign aid to finance state-building efforts. The country lacked a viable economy, its state institutions remained weak and conflicts negatively impacted development and institution building. Given the geopolitical importance of Afghanistan, external revenue has been made available under geostrategic considerations. Sources of state revenue have thus profoundly impacted state building.

Although Afghanistan has historically shown resilience in maintaining its independence, it has failed to pay for government expenditure from domestic revenue, except for a brief period under the reign of Amanullah Khan (1919–1929). Access to an external source of revenue has therefore been a top priority for Afghan rulers to overcome their financial limitations. External revenue has played a major role in sustaining and reshaping the state-building process and producing particular political outcomes as a result of the interplay with the pre-external revenue dynamics and state revenue sources. Moreover, the loss of external revenue has undermined the state's stability at various times.

Although the dependence of various Afghan regimes on external revenue has varied over time, Afghanistan became an aid-based rentier state after the mid-twentieth century, especially as the share of domestic revenue from direct taxation declined considerably. External revenue has increased the government's autonomy from society and allowed it to finance the army and implement projects without facing increasing pressure to tax the rural population.

Prior to 2001, except for the aid to *mujahidin* groups, who fought the People's Democratic Party of Afghanistan (PDPA) regime and the Soviet Union troops in Afghanistan, the government was the main recipient of aid. Aid has played an important role in sustaining state institutions and empowering rulers.

This chapter examines revenue sources and state building in Afghanistan from 1747 to the US-led intervention of 2001. This examination covers three distinctive periods: the Durrani Empire (1747–1824), where the tribute arising from its conquests was crucial for the state-building process; the period following the collapse of the Empire until the early twentieth century, when British subsidies partially replaced the tribute; and the period from the mid-twentieth century to late 2001, when foreign aid replaced subsidies and played a marked role in the state-building process.

The society: an inheritance of history

Landlocked Afghanistan is a regional crossroad. It has been an important part of the enlightenment age of the greater central Asia.[1] It is often portrayed as a "highway of conquest" for migratory peoples and expanding empires, a "round-about" for various trade paths linking Europe with the Far East and the Indian subcontinent, and a crossroads of civilizations and religions. The country was previously called Arianna (1000 BC) and Khurasan (after the seventh century) which comprised a much larger territory than today's Afghanistan.[2] Its geography has been important in determining the course of Afghanistan's history for millennia as the entry point for invaders from Iran or Central Asia into India as well as the launching path for the country's own offensive campaigns on a number of occasions. Cyrus the Great, Alexander the Great, Mahmmud of Ghazni, Changyz Khan, Timurlane and Babur are some examples. Under these circumstances Afghanistan was either ruled by outsiders as part of different empires or became the centre of its own Empires.[3] The sharp racial, ethnic and linguistic differences throughout the country also point to its unique historical and geopolitical position.[4] Afghanistan's current territory emerged as a recognizable political unit in the mid-eighteenth century in a much larger territory than what it is today.

The mosaic nature of Afghan society highlights a number of "divisive" factors, which underscore the difficult legacy of Afghanistan. As Vartan Gregorian puts it, this difficult legacy is significantly disclosed in its ethnic mosaic and socio-economic structure. "Linguistic, racial, cultural and religious diversities, coupled with the country's predominantly semi-feudal, tribal, and nomadic social organization, presented great obstacles to the development of a modern state [in Afghanistan]."[5] The major ethnic groups that are living in Afghanistan range from Pashtuns to Tajiks, Hazaras, Uzbeks, Turkmen, and Aimaqs. About 99 per cent of the population are Muslim (of which 85–90 per cent is Sunni and 10–15 per cent is Shia).[6]

However, no reliable census is available to indicate the total population and different ethnic groups. Population statistics are loosely validated more by repetition than by any reliable data.[7] The government estimated the total population at about 16 million and 25 million in the 1970s and 2008 respectively.[8] The people mostly converse in one of the two languages, Dari (Persian) and Pashtu, which are recognized as the official languages of the state by the 2004 Constitution of Afghanistan. However, other languages spoken around the country, such as Uzbeki, Turkmani, Baluchi, Pashai and Nuristani, are considered the third official language in areas where they are spoken by a majority.[9] Around one-and-a-half-million Afghans are estimated to be living either a fully nomadic or semi-nomadic existence.[10] They are called Kuchi and are mostly Pashtun, who move as a group from summer to winter pasturages and back again.

Although only 12 per cent of the land is arable,[11] the vast majority of the population relies directly on agriculture for their livelihoods. Thus, Afghanistan's economy is dominated by agricultural and pastoral activities. As a consequence of the problem of water scarcity, the already limited area of arable land is not entirely cultivated each year. Armed conflict and drought since 1979 worsened this situation. While about 3.6 million hectares of land was irrigated in the 1970s, this number declined to 1.6 million hectares in the 2000s. The way the land is used affects how local communities organize themselves.[12] Since almost 80 per cent of the population live in small villages and are engaged in subsistence agriculture and farming, this way of living has provided these villages with significant autonomy.[13]

Relying on tribute for state building: the importance of external revenue to the Durrani Empire (1747–1824)

From the rise of the Durrani Empire in 1747 until 1809, revenue, mostly in the form of tribute from its conquests in what is now in India and Pakistan, remained the major source of income for the Empire, comprising about three-fourths of its revenue. However, the availability of tribute depended on the military strength of the Empire and its ability to assure the transfer of the tribute.[14] The Empire did not have "an elaborate, institutionalised administrative and security apparatus which could provide for what could resemble a governmental system in the modern sense of the term."[15] While the Empire imposed taxes on its constituencies, its taxation system was weak and complex, granting tax exemptions to favour certain groups while heavily taxing others. The fiscal base of the Empire compounded with institutional weakness had perverse implications for the development of state institutions. This confirms the notion that the fiscal base of the state has major implications for state building, something we noted in Chapter 1.

After Nadir Shah Afshar, King of Persia (today's Iran) was assassinated in 1747, Ahmad Khan Abdali (later Ahmad Shah Durrani, 1747–1773), a commander in Nadir's army, returned to Kandahar, and a tribal *jirga* (grand assembly) declared him s*hah* (king). He successfully assembled the Pashtun chieftains and subsequently formed a grand ethno-tribal confederation, founding the Durrani Empire in the vast region extended from the rivers Oxus to Indus.[16] Ahmad Shah's reign coincided with successful revenue mobilization from external sources largely in the form of tribute. This relieved him of the problem of taxing those on whom he relied for military strength on the one hand, while helping him to fund his initial alliance and military efforts on the other.[17] Ahmad Shah's army confiscated a caravan transporting Nader's taxes to Persia after his assassination. The value of the caravan was about 260 million rupees (of which 20 million rupees were in cash and the rest included precious jewellery); almost nine times the annual income of Ahmad Shah's treasury in the last years of his reign.[18]

The "economic foundation of the Durrani Empire was the feudal state's ownership of land, . . . the state collected rent-tax from the territories under its suzerainty."[19] The conquest of new territories therefore supplied the state with significant amounts of revenue, which was fundamental in cementing the Afghan tribes together on the one hand, and relieving them of the heavy burden of the tax payment on the other.[20] As revenue from outside its territories was vital to the Empire, Ahmad Shah therefore relied on an expansionist policy of enlarging and maintaining its territorial control.[21]

The Durrani Empire depended excessively on the personalized politics and the charismatic leadership of Ahmad Shah. It took the form of a "nomad and conquest empire" where the ruler temporarily and partially succeeded in transforming it into a patrimonial state.[22] For the tribes who allied with Ahmad Shah, the aim of the state apparatus was to "administer their conquests" but not themselves to be governed.[23] Ahmad Shah in the east annexed Kashmir, Sindh and part of the Punjab, while in the west he consolidated Herat and Mashhad into his empire.[24] He also extended his rule to Kabul and the north of today's Afghanistan as far as the Oxus.[25] These developments were rapid due to the dissolution of the Safavid Empire in Persia and that of the Mughuls in India. In addition, Russia under the reign of Catherine II (1762–1796) did not carry out a planned campaign towards Iran and Central Asia which could have had an impact on the expansion of the Durrani Empire.[26]

In the absence of a detailed account of the Durrani Empire's sources of revenue and expenditures, the study of the Empire taxation and tax system by Yuri Gankovski can serve as a reliable source.[27] The Empire, according to this study, collected over three-fourths of its revenue from its conquests of India, especially Punjab and Kashmir.[28] The Empire did not directly rule most of these territories. However, the flow of revenue was mainly dependent on the continued military domination of the Empire over them.[29] The wealth that flowed to Afghanistan in this period did not have an economic base in the country, nor was it invested to enhance economic activities. Instead, the resources were used largely for buying land or given to Indian *sarrāfs* (money changers) to be taken care of in Kabul and Kandahar. The Indian *sarrāfs* mostly invested these funds outside Afghanistan.[30]

The Durrani Empire's ineffective tax system

The Empire used the existing Safavid administrative apparatus. However, the Durrani monarchs' power was balanced by a strong class of Pashtun Khans (tribal chieftains),[31] who played an important role in the rise and fall of the Empire.[32] Four types of relationship existed between the central government and the provinces. First, the former rulers of the provinces were allowed to remain in power in return for yearly tribute and pledges of allegiance. Second, Afghan military commanders acted as the overlords of the local power holders. Third, the local *khans* undertook to supply the government with military contingents but otherwise remained autonomous. Fourth, governors were directly appointed by the crown to exercise power over provinces.[33] In the first three cases, the local rulers preserved their power, but in the fourth, if the governor was a member of the royal family or a prominent Pashtun Khan, he would resist dismissal by the s*hah*, bringing the central government into conflict with the provinces. The governors' control over provincial revenue and the military would increase the likelihood of turning such resistance into acts of riot and armed conflict.[34] As such, the balance of the forces between the *shah* and the *khans* was such that neither side could effectively subordinate the other. In 1775, because of a contentious relation with Pashtun *khans* and tribal leaders, Timur Shah (1773–1793) shifted the capital from Kandahar to Kabul to reduce their influence.[35]

The Durrani Empire also collected taxes from its constituencies. However, its tax system was weak and unfair, favouring certain groups while penalizing others. Land taxes made up the major portion of the state revenue. Taxes were predominantly paid in kind, which consisted of direct and indirect taxes – called *malyat-i divāny* (taxes levied by state). Taxes in cash were paid directly to the treasury, while in-kind taxes were delivered to state storehouses.[36] The main categories of land ownership that existed in the latter half of the eighteenth century generally consisted of crown lands (*khālisa*), private property (*mūlk*), and religious endowment (*w'aqf*). The state lands, which were in the *shah*'s possession such as *khālisa* and the land of *divān* (state) increased during the first years of the Empire's existence because of its successful conquests.[37] According to Ashraf Ghani, in the eighteenth and nineteenth centuries most of the lands were in the possession of private landowners.[38] Taxes on private lands were paid by landlords with rates which varied in different provinces.

In addition, other taxes existed in the latter half of the eighteenth century. Taxes were levied on water, which was sometimes collected in cash from the owner of the canal. However, if a canal belonged to the state, the tax was collected on the plot of irrigated land. The tax rate on water was determined by the productivity of the land. Chimney (*khānahdudah*) tax was also imposed (e.g. it accounted to two rupees per house in Kandahar). Cattle (*sargālah*) tax was paid in cash or kind per head of cattle. Mill tax was usually levied in kind (half of milled harvest of grain a year). Extraordinary requisition was paid in kind for upkeep of the army. In addition, taxes for maintenance of the *qāzi* (Islamic judge) and the village elder were levied. The population had to report for unpaid compulsory work (*bighār*), for construction and repair of palaces and fortresses, bridges and roads, and cleaning and digging of canals. The inhabitants were also obliged to provide carting facilities and the means of transportation for the *shah*'s messengers and officials. There was also a special poll tax (*jazyah*) levied on non-Muslim inhabitants.[39]

In town, taxes were collected from craftsmen with the rates determined on the basis of the value of goods they produced.[40] While mines belonged to the state, they were farmed out. For example, the mining of salt was contracted out to merchants and craftsmen who had to pay a tax amounting to one-fifth of their income annually.[41] Road taxes and customs, at the rate of 2.5 per cent of the value of the goods, made up a significant portion of the state revenue. However, the civilian rulers of provinces (*hakīms*) sometimes arbitrarily raised these taxes to 5 per cent or more. The customs duties were heavy for merchants because they were collected at multiple points and more than once. There were also small taxes and duties imposed on the population. For example, people who were entering Kabul had to pay a *chirāghi* (lamp) fee for lighting the customs houses.[42]

Although in some cases tax farmers were Durrani *khans*, usually they were Indian merchants and usurers.[43] The merchants provided loans to the Afghan *khans* and the government at high interest rates. For the loans, provincial taxes were used as a security.[44] The tax farmers had arbitrary power in collecting taxes, especially if they were close to the *shah*'s court and were major landlords. They acquired a substantial amount of wealth by extracting extra taxes from the population.[45] The tax farmers and officials would extract as much as possible from the population by using government armed forces. The officially determined tax rates were seldom put into practice and the provincial authorities and department of finance arbitrarily introduced extra taxes. This would often lead to harsh exploitation of some peasants, merchants and craftsmen. For example, the Tajiks and Aymaks were pleased if the tax collectors extracted only twice as much as was due under the law,[46] especially as they were too militarily and politically weak to resist. This situation largely resulted from the weakness of central government and absence of fixed salaries for government employees, especially the tax officials.[47]

The Durrani taxation system exempted a certain category of population while heavily taxing others. Neamatollah Nojumi *et al.* observe, "Government authorities and military leaders have long provided preferential access to land as a reward to certain population groups and supporters, and have levied heavy land taxes against groups who were in political or social disfavour."[48] Many Pashtun tribes were exempt from taxes in exchange for military services. The *jagirdārs* (local rulers who were granted state land in exchange for military service) were immune from taxes. Many of the *w'aqf* lands were tax-free. Ahmad Shah abolished or lowered many taxes like land tax, taxes on cattle, orchards and vineyards and chimney duty on the Pashtun tribes, in particular the Durrani tribe, to which the *shah* himself belonged.[49] For example, the tax on arid lands was lowered considerably for the Durrani tribes, while it was increased for the non-Pashtun peasants, who had to pay one-tenth of their gross harvest to the *shah*'s treasury. The Pashtun tribes were also not treated equally by the taxation system, which privileged the Durrani tribe.[50]

The provinces under the Durrani Empire's suzerainty were sending a percentage of their revenue to the Durrani Shah's treasury, while the rest was used to cover their expenditures. This percentage varied between different provinces on the basis of their annual revenue and expenditure. The total annual income of the *shah*'s treasury reached 30 million rupees by the end of his rule (1773). However, during Timur Shah's reign (1773–1793) the figure decreased drastically and in the 1780s the total annual income did not exceed 10 million rupees.[51]

The major revenue came from the eastern provinces of the Empire (Kashmir, Multan, Derah Ismail Khan, Deh Ghazi Khan, Shikārpur, Muzaffarābād, Attok, Indian Hazara and Sukkur), including the tribute from Sind, Bahawalpur and Layah. It comprised about three-fourths of the Empire's central treasury annual revenue, while the rest came from the western provinces of the Empire (Kabul, Peshawar, Jalalabad, Ghūrband, Bangashat, Ghazni, Kalāt-i Ghilzai, Chārikār and Panjshir, Kandahar, Farah, Herat, Bamyan and Hazarajāt).[52] The tribute from Indian conquests was an important source of income, although it was neither paid in full nor paid regularly.[53] External revenue and tribute was coming directly to the treasury of the *shah* and the *shah* had full discretion where and how to spend it. They largely sustained the institutions and the polity of patronage, which existed before the creation of the Empire and access to the external revenue transformed some of the institutions based on the imperative that the Empire should maintain its military domination over the territories it ruled to secure the flow of external revenue.[54]

The major items of the Durrani Shah's treasury expenditure (1793–1809) consisted of military expenditure (31.6 per cent), palace services (25.3 per cent) and the *shah*'s personal expenses (26 per cent). A very small portion of expenditure around 4 per cent went to construction, and another 4 per cent was allocated for subsidies for Balkh and Aqcha provinces. These two provinces were not sending revenue to the *shah*'s treasury, but instead they were receiving subsidies as they were tasked with the defence of the northern area of Afghanistan against the attacks from Amir of Bukhara.[55] The state revenue shrank further under Zaman Shah (1793–1801) and it was reduced to 6.7 million rupees. The annual maximum revenue under Shah Shuja (1803–1809) was estimated at 10 million rupees.[56]

However, within two generations after Ahmad Shah's death, the Durrani Empire lost its Indian territories due to internal decay and expansion of regional powers such as the Sikhs and British, leading to a substantial loss in state revenue and increase in tribal rivalry.[57] The Empire therefore no longer had the alternative of territorial conquest and resource extraction from abroad. The decay of the central government also resulted in the loss of state lands to *khans*. Only in Kandahar, for example, could the influential Durrani *khans* seize approximately half of all tax-levied lands.[58] The Empire therefore failed to establish a reliable source of revenue in its home territory to sustain its institutions, such as the army.

Subsidies and state building: the loss of tribute and search for alternative revenue (1824–1879)

The loss of tribute from the Indian conquests forced the new ruler of Afghanistan, Dost Muhammad Khan (1826–1839 and 1843–1863), to look for new sources of revenue within the limit of his kingdom. While Dost Muhammad Khan inherited the structure of an Empire, his government had very little revenue. Hence, he imposed taxes on the Pashtun *khans* and tribes who were exempted earlier or lightly taxed.[59] This policy was applied more "out of desperation than a choice."[60] Dost Muhammad Khan, however, was not able to introduce major changes in the tax system which he inherited from the Durrani Empire.[61] At the beginning of his reign, the government revenue was about a half-million rupees collected from Kabul and the territories in the north. Although this increased to two-and-a-half-million rupees by the 1830s,[62] this was less than 10 per cent of the annual revenue of Ahmad Shah's reign. Therefore, the inhabitants of Afghanistan had to pay for the state's expenditure.[63] Despite Dost Muhammad Khan's success in consolidating his power, he was not able to back it with a centralized administration to tap local resources efficiently and only a small fraction of local surplus reached the central administration by way of revenue payment.[64]

Although the administration was already downsized, the need for revenue led to its re-expansion. Dost Muhammad Khan therefore imposed heavy taxes and relied on harsh methods of collection.[65] The rural population often resisted arbitrary government tax collection that was supported with mounted troops. The imposition of heavy taxation also discouraged the development of greater economic activities in the urban centres. Since the state income was inadequate to finance governance expenditures, Dost Muhammad Khan began looking for British subsidies. In his second reign, he signed a friendship and alliance treaty with the East India Company in 1855 and two years later followed with another treaty. Accordingly, Britain provided him with an annual subsidy of 1.2 million Indian rupees and weapons.[66] This fund was conditional on the defence of Herat from Russian-backed attacks from Persia. The British justified the subsidy as part of their anti-Russian strategy in Afghanistan, Persia and Central Asia.[67] Considering the size of domestic revenue, the amount of the subsidy was significant in helping Dost Muhammad Khan consolidate his power. The British annual subsidies made up about 18 per cent of the total annual state income in 1863.

Institution building

The British subsidies to Dost Muhammad Khan were given to support him "against internal dissent and external threats that were invariably deemed to be inspired by Russia,"[68] and as a condition he was required to strengthen his army. The fiscal weakness of the state further increased the vulnerability of Dost Muhammad Khan to British influence. For example, although domestic revenue was very low, almost half of it was spent on the upkeep of the military and almost another half was spent on the allowances to the numerous members of the royal family. The soldiers did not have regular salaries and thus they often resorted to plunder for their upkeep, which became a source of insecurity and fear for people. In addition, the royal family members occupied the government senior positions, using them for making money, and the government lacked a solid official recording system.[69] The government officials were mostly working from their homes and were reporting to Dost Muhammad Khan while keeping the papers in their pockets.[70]

The major state-building initiative in this period took place in the military field. Between 1830 and 1836, Dost Muhammad Khan employed three foreign advisors to modernize the army – a former Qajar officer, a British officer and an American doctor. The assistance from these advisors helped him to introduce British-type uniforms and European pattern-type drills into the army. During the second reign of Dost Mohammad Khan, the Cavalry officially consisted of 15,300 men and the entire infantry amounted to 9,250 men.[71]

In 1839, in order to increase its influence in Afghanistan in response to the expansionist policy of Russia,[72] the British invaded Afghanistan and displaced Dost Mohammad Khan from Kabul and his brothers from Kandahar and Herat. This terminated the reforms which Dost Mohammad Khan had initiated. The British installed Shah Shuja, an exiled Durrani prince and a former ruler of Afghanistan (1803–1809) as the new ruler. Subsequently, the British focused on restructuring the state and its financial system. However, these interventions had paradoxical impacts. For example, while the British abolished state grants, for example, to notables and *khans*, they distributed cash to those who cooperated with them.

The flow of British cash increased the power and influence of those who engaged in trade, providing needed commodities and services. It also "undermined the social and political standing of those whose influence was based on feudal obligations to the state, or who owned unproductive landed estates."[73] The British total cost over the three years of war was estimated around eight million British pounds,[74] including the cost of occupation and distribution of cash. Although the British troops did not face resistance at the beginning, the people of Afghanistan soon rose against them, declaring *jihād* (holy war). The British failed to repress the popular uprising and withdrew, creating Britain's "greatest military humiliation of the nineteenth century" in 1841. They lost their entire army of 16,000 troops in Afghanistan.[75]

During his second reign (1843–1863), Dost Muhammad concentrated on consolidating his power over all Afghanistan. In 1963, the annual state revenue rose to 7 million rupees.[76] Dost Muhammad Khan farmed out the provincial tax collection to his sons alone. They in turn sublet the tax farming of the districts to individuals of their choice. The government system in this period was based on the ties between a father and his sons where the father's rule remained unchallenged by the sons. This system of governance collapsed after Dost Muhammad Khan's death. When his son Sher Ali Khan (1863–1866 and 1868–1879) tried to impose his authority over the whole country, it resulted in a civil war between him and his brothers from 1863 to 1868.[77]

Whilst receiving subsidies from the British, Sher Ali Khan too sought reforming the government taxation system. Between 1863 and 1869, he received a total of 1.2 million rupees in British subsidies.[78] However, the British neglected Sher Ali Khan's petition to increase the transfer of the subsidies to strengthen his army, deeming it strategically insignificant for their interest.[79] Later they became suspicious of Sher Ali Khan's relations with Russia.[80] Unlike his father, Sher Ali Khan did not allow his sons to take over the administration of the provinces and relied on those whom he trusted.[81] He abolished the three months advanced tax payment on actual agriculture production that was imposed in the first three months of the New Year and the *barāt* (draft bill of exchange) for the army and government employees that the peasants and craftsmen were to reimburse against their tax dues.[82] Although not a great deal of information about the overall system of taxation is available, the reports on a number of districts suggest that the revenue on land was assessed on the basis of *sī-kūt* (one-third of production) and *jam bast* (assessment based on a tribal community). The government would take one-third of the produce in the former case while a fixed amount was assessed in the latter. A lighter rate was imposed on the private land than on the *khālisa*.[83]

Additionally, Sher Ali Khan established a council of twelve members, directly appointed by him, to advise him on state affairs. This later became the state cabinet. He created the office of *sadr-i azam* (prime minister) and assigned ministers for war, foreign affairs, interior, finance and treasury as well as a general secretary.

In order to improve government linkages with the periphery, he also established a department of post and communication in Kabul and provinces with a branch in Peshawar. Sayyid Jamāl ad-Dīn al-Afghāni (lived 1837–1897), a prominent Islamic reformist who advised Sher Ali Khan, inspired most of these reforms.[84]

The army salary became fixed (seven rupees per month) and was paid directly from the government's treasury. The army's permanent bases were kept outside the cities, something not commonly practised before. The total number of the standing army was 50,000 men who were placed in Kabul, Ningarhar, Paktia, Kandahar, Herat, Maimana and Balkh on the border areas of the country.[85] To collect taxes and implement the reforms, the administration had to grow. To pay for the new employees of the government, Sher Ali Khan increased existing taxes and introduced new ones. Yet the government was unable to have direct control over the entire country. It controlled only those cities where troops were placed. The tribes, mainly those of the frontier regions, remained autonomous. *Pashtunwāli* (Pashtun tribal code of conduct) and *sharia* (Islamic Law) were the basic platforms for solving their problems.

Although the reforms were important for institution building, "the ties between [Sher Ali Khan] and subjects were still personal in character rather than institutional."[86] In 1878, the second British invasion of Afghanistan due to Sher Ali's growing relationship with Russia terminated these reforms[87] and facilitated the rise of a modern buffer state. The British invasion, as noted by the Viceroy of India in a communication to the secretary of state of India at that time, had "left the civil government and the military resource of the Afghans in a state of dilapidation which [would] require a long time to repair."[88]

Consolidation of a modern buffer state (1880–1919): the significance of subsidies and external military support

The two Anglo-Afghan wars (1839–1842, 1878–1880) imposed a major cost on the country, with agriculture and trade declining significantly. Although the British military campaigns ended after the second invasion of Afghanistan, the Britain retained control over the foreign relations of Afghanistan (1879–1919). This isolated the country from the rest of the world and became a major obstacle for its development.[89] The defeat of the British military after their invasions of Afghanistan led to a shift in their foreign policy towards Afghanistan.[90] The British therefore found it desirable to support an Afghan ruler who would be dependent on them for resources, be prepared to subdue the peoples of Afghanistan, and be strong enough to defeat rivals.[91] They thus recognized Abdur Rahman Khan's (1889–1901) accession to the throne as the Amir of Afghanistan.[92] He compromised with the British, agreed to Britain having control over the foreign policy of Afghanistan and later signed the territorial agreement establishing the Durand Line (1893). This line fixed the spheres of influence between British and Afghan interests. Afghanistan subsequently became a buffer state between the British Empire that ruled much of South Asia, and the Russian Empire, which ruled most of Central Asia.

After the British assured Abdur Rahman Khan of its regular subsidies and protection against external aggression, Abdur Rahman Khan focused on centralizing
government and bureaucratizing affairs. The British granted him a yearly subsidy of 1.2 million Indian rupees in 1882, which was raised to 1.85 million by
1897. During his reign, he received a total of 28.5 million rupees in cash from the
British. Abdur Rahman Khan remained the sole recipient of the British subsidies
and military assistance which helped to build his government's coercive capacity
and consolidate his power. However, it did not contribute to making him accountable to his people or any other authority. Abdur Rahman Khan opposed political
participation and abolished the cabinet system which was established under Sher
Ali Khan and replaced it with a system centred on himself.[93] As will be discussed
in the next section, he remained autonomous in formulating his tax and distribution policy. The availability of a supply of weapons and cash partly freed him
from having to rule in alliance with local power holders such as the tribal chieftains and religious establishment. Yet the resources were not generous enough to
make the state fully independent of the society. Abdur Rahman Khan largely used
the subsidies to strengthen his army.[94]

Although Abdur Rahman Khan was aware of his financial constraints, Afghanistan's natural resources and the potential benefit that he could gain from European
technical assistance, he relied on British subsidies, domestic taxes and income
derived from a few government-run factories in Kabul.[95] As the British subsidies
were not enough, Abdur Rahman Khan heavily taxed the population. He did so by
using the army and harsh coercive measures. In this period, the country remained
subsistence-based and "in terms of transport, communications, industry, or education, little distinguished the Afghanistan of 1800 from that of 1900, beyond a few
government-run factories in Kabul."[96]

To mobilize support for his centralizing policies, Abdur Rahman Khan used
Islam "as an ideology of state building in a country inhabited by diverse ethno-
linguistic groups. . . ."[97] He mobilized some *ulamā* (Islamic religious scholars)
to interpret Islam to justify his policies. He used Islam to stress the duty of the
unconditional obedience of his subjects.[98] Abdur Rahman Khan deprived *ulamā*
of their earlier economic privileges and instead offered them a regular allowance
from the state treasury. This made them dependent on the state, obliging them to
propagate Abdur Rahman Khan's doctrine.[99] He declared taxation as a religious
duty and replied to a dignitary that "exemption from paying taxes was equivalent
to disobedience to God's commands, and that since the country was threatened by
the infidels it was the duty of every Muslim to contribute to the strengthening of
the Islamic state."[100] Thus, "subjects not paying their taxes and officials guilty of
corruption are, indeed, betraying the religion."[101] This type of approach to taxation, defining it as a mandatory religious duty and payment, therefore would not
entitle the taxpayer to a say in state affairs.[102]

Accordingly, taxpayers had to pay their due without failure; if not, tax was
realized from their nearest relatives or tribe.[103] Abdur Rahman Khan argued that
the revenue belonged to *bayt al-māl* (public property) and it was collected for the
protection of the borders and the honour of the religion and the nation. He ordered

that everyone, even religious groups which had held free-rent lands should pay tax.[104] Despite the appeal to religious obligation, some taxpayers resisted the tax policy in the form of non-payment of taxes and appeals, leading to confrontations between them and the government. However, the resistance to tax policy did not help to reduce the tax rates. The imposition of taxes was so heavy that a number of people emigrated to neighbouring countries. The system was inflexible and sometime poor taxpayers had to sell their lands, property and even their children to pay their due taxes.[105]

To pay for government wages and maintain the large army, Abdur Rahman Khan modified the taxation system. As security considerably improved in this period,[106] the government was able to extract significant amounts of tax from landowners, which formed the bulk of the state domestic revenue. He raised the rates of land taxes, introduced new ones and imposed tax on rent-free lands. In order to improve tax collection, he developed a new system of collection, whereby the taxpayers had to pay their taxes by a predetermined date. The arrears were then collected by mounted troops. Tax farming was practised as before.[107] He used taxation to penalize his political opponents. For example, he imposed higher tax rates on Ghilzai Pashtun tribes than on the Durrani ones because the former supported his rival cousin, Ayub Khan (1857–1914),[108] the ex-governor of Herat and the victor of the Maiwand battle (1880) against the British.[109]

Hakīms were in charge of revenue collection in provinces, which were issuing receipts to taxpayers after they paid their taxes.[110] The proportion of tax in kind and cash was not fixed; Abdur Rahman Khan himself ordered that taxes could be collected in cash or kind based on the availability of grain or the need for coin. The new systems of tax collection, like *kūt* (a share of harvest) and *girīb* (a predetermined size of land), increased the role of government officials in tax collection and expanded the administration.[111] However, this process allowed government officials to exact unofficial fees and bribes from taxpayers.[112] State revenue increased to 50 million rupees in 1891 from 14 million in 1889.[113] The major items of spending were on the army (about one-third of the annual revenue) and the court.[114] Although Abdur Rahman Khan occasionally provided the British government with the statement of revenue and expenditure of Afghanistan,[115] there is no record available that he accounted to his people through mechanisms existing in his time.

The annual subsidy of the British consisted of about 3.5 per cent of the state annual revenue, using the average of domestic revenue in 1889 and 1891 and the average of the subsidies. The British also granted a significant amount of weaponry to Abdur Rahman Khan, who, in addition purchased further supplies of weapons from the market in Europe, using domestic revenue and income from government factories. Ghubār observes that he took a month's salary from government employees each year to purchase weapons in order to strengthen the defence of Afghanistan.[116] This challenges Barnett Rubin's view that under Abdur Rahman Khan Afghanistan became a rentier state by financing about 40 per cent of its expenditure from subsidies and in the form of weapons from the British.[117]

However, a generous estimation of the weapons granted to Abdur Rahman Khan from 1880 to 1895 in terms of value, on average, could have amounted to 20 per cent of annual state revenue and by including the subsidies this amount could have become 25 per cent.[118]

Civil and military administration

Abdur Rahman Khan established a centralized unitary state,[119] which was administratively unified and governed directly by a centralized authority based on a superior military rule, with internationally recognized boundaries. He established fairly well-defined and universally applied administrative and judiciary rules and regulations which helped to transform an indirect rule which had been instituted under the Durrani Empire on the basis of feudal ties.[120] He bureaucratized all "spheres of administration, involving the clear demarcation of spheres of responsibility based on . . . hierarchy and record keeping," and the administration was mainly conducted through written mediums. The different edicts (*dastūr ul-amal*) that he issued were essential in formalizing these changes.[121] To maintain security and achieve stability, Abdur Rahman Khan did not rely on *hakīm*, or civilian *qazī* (judge). Instead, he depended on a trained standing army of around 96,400 men,[122] whose authority was superior to that of *hakīm*.[123] In addition, since 1887 Abdur Rahman Khan relied on a conscription system called *bīst nafarī* (twenty-person system) whereby twenty families were required to identify and provide a soldier for a year at their own expense (except for food).[124] The government army mostly engaged in subduing rebellions and combating the Amir rivals, and according to Abdur Rahman Khan, the army participated in four civil wars and one hundred major and minor revolts under his reign.[125]

Abdur Rahman Khan divided the country into six provinces (*vulāyats*)[126] to enhance central government authority. In each province, a network of small administrative units was established. They were "strong enough to control their constituencies, but not with sufficient power to pose any threat to Kabul's pre-eminence."[127] In addition, each province was divided into smaller units. For example, Kabul province was divided into districts, mostly independent of each other, such as Jalalabad, Kunar, Laghman and Ghazni (Khost was part of Ghazni). These districts sent their revenue directly to Kabul. Such division of traditionally independent provinces into smaller administrative units gave Abdur Rahman Khan direct control. There was no systematic cooperation among these districts, except in cases of military cooperation in putting down rebellions. However, if larger forces were required, Kabul would supply them, while Abdur Rahman Khan himself closely controlled such processes. The administrative units were headed by *hakīms*.[128] There was a *qāzi* in each administrative unit under the jurisdiction of the *hakīm*.[129] In the Pashtun tribal areas the administration came into conflict with tribal authorities because the main platform to the tribes for bestowing justice was *pashtunwāli* through *jirga* (tribal assembly).[130]

State–society relations

Abdur Rahman Khan's state-building project significantly reshaped state–society relations. He acted as a despotic reformer, and he showed little or no concern for human lives. During his reign "violence committed in the name of state was without parallel in Afghan history."[131]

> He destroyed and subordinated the regional elite in the north, west, and south who had previously challenged the national government's primacy in the nineteenth century to such an extent that one could be forgiven for thinking that they had been wiped from the map. The tribal structure of the Pashtun areas in the east remained intact, but [Abdur Rahman Khan] had so brutally repressed their rebellions that the Pashtuns withdrew from national politics entirely.[132]

This process also reduced the influence of Islamic clerics and *Sufi* pirs (spiritual guides) who had an independent political role during the end of the second Anglo-Afghan war.[133]

Those who directly confronted the government, especially the Hazaras, were suppressed brutally by the army and suffered the most.[134] Abdur Rahman Khan governed the country through fear by heavily relying on coercive measures. For instance, when Mirza Amir Abu al-Hassan, a senior government official, learned that his father was under arrest by order of Abdur Rahman Khan, he committed suicide because he was afraid that he would also be punished.[135]

Abdur Rahman Khan used a redistribution policy to reshape the structure of the elite polity. However, this policy remained biased by favouring Abdur Rahman Khan's clan – Muhammadzai – whom he made "partners of the state" (*shuraka-i dawlat*).[136] He ordered a regular annual stipend of 400 rupees for each male and 300 rupees for each female of his clan, which on average was almost three and a half times higher than the annual salary of an infantry officer in the army.[137] They were also able to receive land on easy terms.[138] His clan dominated power for about eighty years following his death in 1901.[139] His state building also produced a new class of national elites who were dependent on state patronage. These elites had a much narrower social, political and regional base than those of the nineteenth century. Although they were mostly dominated by Muhammadzais,[140] the elite also included members of other groups such as urbanized Tajiks and other ethnic groups based in Kabul. This widened the gap between a rising elite in Kabul and the inhabitants of the countryside and provincial cities. Although the national elites were smaller in number, their influence was greater because they dominated state institutions. They advocated for state reforms while the provincial elites were suspicious of change.

Abdur Rahman Khan's heavy reliance on the military and intelligence improved the security for the trade and businesses. But in the long run it undermined national consciousness and courage among the people.[141] In order to repress the rebels on many occasions he mobilized one ethnic group and used them against another.[142] This further complicated the relationship among these groups, and between them and the state.

Amanullah Khan's reforms: the loss of subsidies, budget surplus and fiscal decline (1919–1929)

After the death of Abdur Rahman Khan, his son Habibullah Khan (1901–1919) largely followed his state-building policies. Annual government revenue under his reign increased to 80 million rupees,[143] while still being in receipt of the regular British subsidies. However, following the assassination of Habibullah Khan in 1919, Afghanistan experienced a dramatic change under the reign of his son, Amanullah Khan (1919–1929). In this period three interrelated events happened which shaped the politics of state building and state–society relations. First, Afghanistan gained control of its foreign policy from the British, referred to as independence. Second, Amanullah Khan lost the British subsidy. Third, the new regime initiated comprehensive socio-economic and political reforms to modernize Afghanistan. Although these events increased the Amanullah Khan regime's dependency on its citizens for their tax revenue and political legitimacy, the reforms brought it into conflict with the most conservative segments of the society such as *ulamā* and tribal leaders. As a result of their revolts, the state was deprived of the bulk of land and livestock revenue.

A number of Afghan reformists and nationalists, members of or inspired by Afghanistan's Constitutional movement, mostly young, dominated Amanullah Khan's regime and backed the reforms in order to transform the socio-economic structure of Afghanistan. Gaining Afghanistan's independence in 1919 increased Amanullah Khan's prestige and legitimacy among the people. Afghanistan became the only Muslim member of the League of Nations.[144] Although Afghanistan received some military and technical aid from the Soviet Union, Turkey, Germany, France and Italy, it did not replace the British regular subsidy and establish a reliable external source of revenue for the state.[145] The government improved and centralized the administration by unifying the legal system and introducing a new tax law. The tax system was regularized and tax farming was abolished. The taxpayers had to pay their taxes in cash to the government. The rates of direct tax on land and livestock increased, which together accounted for around three-fifths of the government's domestic revenue.[146] The government simplified the customs duties; however, collection was a problem and brought the government into conflict with landowning *khans* and with the border tribes who largely benefited from smuggling on the border.[147]

Additionally, the government abolished *jazyah* on non-Muslims to promote equal rights and responsibilities for all citizens, which was promised in Article 16 of the first Constitution of Afghanistan (1921).[148] The Constitution established the *Loya Jirga* (grand assembly) as the highest representative organ of the state and Amanullah Khan convened it three times.[149] The first budget was introduced in 1922 and the Afghani became the new unit of currency in 1923. *Bank-i Milly* (National Bank) was established in 1928.[150] The establishment of an *ausolī daftarī* (administrative principles) school in Kabul helped to build up the government financial management capacity by appointing its graduates to key financial positions. Moreover, Amanullah Khan founded a well-structured cabinet/ministers' council headed by himself.[151]

Under the social reform agenda, Amanullah officially abolished slavery and expanded the education system. This included formal education for women and reformation of the *madrasses* (Islamic religious schools). Universal conscription was imposed. The government tried to curtail polygamy, child marriage and *bad* (exchange of women for settling disputes). Additionally, a written code of law defined family matters,[152] allowing the government to intervene in the private sphere of family life, something which was not practised before.

The economic reforms led to increased revenue collection. At the beginning of Amanullah Khan's reign, revenue increased to 180 million rupees. The major portion of the revenue came from land taxes (44 per cent of total revenue), cattle tax (14 per cent of total revenue) and customs duties (22 per cent of total revenue). The major expenditures of the government were 22 per cent on the army, 11 per cent on the King's *darbār* (court), and around 8 per cent on education. The government even produced a budget surplus. Therefore approximately 37 per cent of the annual revenue was allocated for contingency expenditures and savings.[153]

The main problems of the reforms arose from the attempts to extend central government power into provinces where they affected people's lives directly. These came in three ways: "taxation, conscription and perceived interference in family life."[154] However, it was the cost of these reforms which made the people feel the most pressure because they were financed through taxation. A "combined weight of taxation and administrative abuses encouraged brigandage in the countryside and contributed to social disturbances."[155] A remarkable example was in 1927, when some thirty peasants attacked the finance minister.[156] The government heavily taxed both the peasants and the urban population. Duties on exports and imports increased hitting the merchant class. For example, customs duties ranged from 10–14 per cent on useful or necessary items to 100 per cent on luxury items, but in practice it ranged from 20 per cent to 200 per cent.[157] Even internal trade was subject to a 5 per cent tax. Furthermore, a poll tax was imposed on the inhabitants of Kabul city. The low salary of government officials and the new method of tax collection in cash made it difficult for Amanullah Khan to realize his anti-corruption measures,[158] particularly as it was easy for tax collectors to pocket the cash in comparison to in-kind payments.

The reforms, however, led to changes that seriously disturbed the relationship among the governing elites and with the other social actors such as religious establishments and the different ethnic groups, as it reconfigured the structure of polity and the state role in Afghanistan.[159] This seriously undermined the relative stability which existed for the previous four decades, and consequently Amanullah Khan faced revolts from the countryside.[160] In 1924, the Khost revolts cost the government about two years of its income. The Khost rebellion was because of Amanullah Khan's *niẓāmnāma* (administrative code), which he passed in 1923. Among other things, in particular this policy attempted to liberalize the position of women and to allow the government to regulate various family problems. Some *mullāhs* (clergies) deemed the administrative code to be contrary to instructions of Islamic law and the spirit of the Quran. The rebellion continued for more than nine months.[161] Because of the social pressure, the government was not only deprived of the resources to fund the reforms, but had to modify some parts of the reforms too.

The instability from the reforms was exacerbated by the British interference and occasionally blockage of Afghanistan trade route to the outside world through India. British granted subsidies to some tribal chieftains and clergies and encouraged them to undermine Amanullah Khan's legitimacy. When, for example, Amanullah Khan was in desperate need of weapons during the uprisings, the British did not allow any weapons to be transited in a timely manner to Afghanistan.[162]

In 1928, violent anti-government demonstrations and rebellion by conservative leaders spread across the country. This situation deprived the government of 30 per cent of land tax.[163] The rebel leaders gave Amanullah Khan an ultimatum, among other things, to abolish the family law, reduce taxes and restore the *ulamā* to their previous positions of distinction.[164] Although Amanullah Khan was prepared to comply with these demands to secure the throne, the general decay in the central government and the constant revolts led to the fall of his regime. Subsequently, Habibullah Kalakani, an ethnic Tajik and a former army non-commissioned officer from Kalakān district of Kūhdāman (north of Kabul), took power after his militia forces overthrew Amanullah Khan in 1929.[165]

Although Amanullah Khan failed to implement his reforms and lost the throne, most of the reforms initiated under his reign were gradually implemented by the *Musahiban* family and inspired subsequent leaders, except Habibullah Kalakani whose anti-reform stand was the basis for his legitimacy among the most traditional and conservative segments of the society. Nonetheless, the reforms paved the way for limited modernization of administration and expansion of secular public education.

However, Habibullah Kalakani held the throne of Kabul for only a short period (January 17 to October 13, 1929) and his reign was associated with political instability and severe economic dislocation. His rule did not extend beyond the major urban centres. He soon promised to eliminate all of his predecessor's reforms, which he deemed anti-Islamic. Habibullah Kalakani cancelled compulsory military service, shut all modern schools and liquidated taxes imposed by Amanullah Khan. He used 750,000 British pounds that he captured in the royal palace to consolidate his power temporarily through patronage.[166] But his regime soon faced financial crisis due to a decline in agriculture and trade caused by unrest and he was forced to break his promises. He not only retained the previous taxes levied under Amanullah Khan,[167] but levied new ones as well. Habibullah Kalakani forced merchants and citizens of Kabul to contribute to his treasury.[168] This cost him the support of peasant masses and merchants and added to their increased discontent arising from a lack of security and high inflation. Subsequently, he lost the support of some of the Pashtun tribal allies.[169] The lack of revenue for his government, either domestic or external, accelerated the fall of his regime.

Foreign aid and state building: reshaping the state-building process (1929–1978)

In 1929, Nadir Khan, the former war minister of Amanullah Khan, who lived in exile, overthrew Habibullah Kalakani and captured Kabul. He was aided by the British and supported by trans-border Pashtun tribes. The leaders of a 12,000 strong tribal army crowned him *shah* (king) in a *jirga*.[170] To institute his programme and consolidate the rule of his dynasty, Nadir Khan relied on his brothers and on the cooperation of the religious establishment and the Afghan tribes. "His government was virtually a family circle."[171] Between 1929 and 1978, Nadir Shah and his four brothers, referred as the Musahiban family, as well as their descendants remained in power.[172] Although they shared to some extent the goal of modernization with Amanullah Khan, they shifted their domestic policy from Amanullah Khan's radical modernization to a policy of gradual modernization and development. They concluded from Amanullah Khan's experience that the balance of forces in the country prevented a "state-imposed global transformation."[173] Although they compromised with traditional actors, the tribes and religious establishment, they forged their links with the international state system and the market. The latter steadily facilitated a "state-dominated export enclave centred in Kabul."[174] The state became less and less dependent on the peasant-tribal society which largely remained fragmented, and the state–society relationship was mediated through local notables.[175]

Nadir Shah divided Afghanistan into nine areas, consisting of five major provinces around the major urban centres, Kabul, Kandahar, Herat, Mazar-i Sharif, Qataghan and Badakhshan; and four minor provinces that included Farah and Maimana and the eastern and southern provinces. These provinces and sub-provinces were divided into three classes of prefecture (first, second and third) based on their size and importance. *Valīs* (governors) headed provinces.[176] After World War II the British withdrew from the region leaving Afghanistan with a new international order and Pakistan as a new country, after its partition from India in 1947, on its border. The Afghan government thereafter opposed Pakistan because of Afghanistan's claim of sovereignty over Pashtun tribal areas separated by the Durand Line from Afghanistan. However, Afghanistan also became dependent on Pakistan for its link to the international market.[177]

The Musahiban family reduced the state's economic pressure on the countryside in return for a greater political obedience from the rural population.[178] The new Constitution, which was adopted in 1931, provided an opportunity for representation of tribal *khans* and gave a concession allowing the *ulamā* to review laws prior to approval. Consequently, "no government in such an arrangement since then has succeeded in persuading the legislature to raise land and livestock taxes."[179] This type of arrangement decreased the share of agriculture and livestock tax revenue which was historically the main source of state income. Although the tax was collected in cash, it continually diminished and the share of domestic revenue from agriculture and livestock fell significantly from 62.5 per cent in 1926, to 18.1 per cent in 1953, and then to 7 per cent by 1957 and in the 1970s to less than 2 per cent.[180] These changes demonstrate the state's limited ability to penetrate the society. However, for its revenue the state instead largely relied on trade tariffs, government monopoly enterprises and (especially in the last two decades of Musahiban reign) foreign aid in the form of grants and loans.[181] During this period, the proportion of indirect taxes, particularly taxes on foreign trade, was higher in Afghanistan than in other countries at similar stages of development. This put the country at some economic disadvantage in the area of domestic production.[182] Afghanistan's tax efforts (the ratio of potential revenue versus that collected) seemed to be the last, after Nepal, in a comparison of 55 developing countries.[183]

Such low tax performance resulted because of the fear of the government from a popular reaction against government tax in the countryside and Afghanistan's economic structure – which was largely agricultural based with the industrial sector contributing little to the economy. Moreover, tax collection was hampered by weak administration as well as corruption. Last but not least, the government's reluctance to strengthen its taxation system was exacerbated by the availability of economic assistance from the east and west after the 1950s.[184]

The rise of a weak rentier state

During the early 1950s and 1960s, the Cold War strengthened Afghanistan's bargaining position for receiving economic aid from the US and the Soviet Union,[185] both of which sought to influence the country through economic assistance. This type of relationship, however, disrupted state–society relations in the subsequent decades by making Afghanistan highly dependent on the Soviet Union, especially when the US refused to increase its economic assistance and provide military support because of the US alliance with Pakistan, and the refusal of Afghanistan to join the US-sponsored military pacts of Baghdad (1955) and its successor, the Central Treaty Organisation (CENTO, 1964). The Afghan government declined to join these military pacts as it

> deemed it to be in the general interest of Afghanistan to preserve {six} with its traditional policy of neutrality in world politics; and thus avoid any complication in its relations with the Soviet Union in the absence of all-ground goodwill on the part of the [US].[186]

The US reluctance to respond to Prime Minister Daud Khan's request for support (1953–1963), prompted him to accept a longstanding offer from the Soviet Union of significant military equipment and aid.[187] Foreign aid funded state building increased the autonomy of the government and undermined "old patterns" of social control in Afghanistan.[188] It relieved Daud of whatever incentive he might have had to make his government accountable to his people.[189] At the same time, it allowed him to implement his state-building policy to:

> centralize control of the means of violence in a strong, well-equipped and trained modern army; to strengthen commercial agriculture and exports by investing in economic infrastructure such as dams and roads; to make state enterprises rather than private joint stock companies the main sources of capital accumulation; to expand modern education to train personnel necessary for the new institutions; and to create a national transportation and

communication network. To help run development projects, the schools, and the military, foreign advisors entered the country by the thousands, especially the Soviets.[190]

This period therefore became an exceptional era for socio-economic progress in Afghanistan's history. The government also developed "close ties with, and ideological vulnerability to, the Soviet Union."[191] Yet the government had difficulty in paying for 20 per cent of projects earmarked for domestic financing and for operating costs after projects were in place.[192] A major portion of aid was invested in infrastructure, such as transport and communication, which counted for 54.2 per cent of all government allocations during the government's first Five-Year Plan (1956–1961).[193] The new asphalted highways and air links connected the main cities of the country and provided better access to neighbouring countries such as Pakistan, Iran and the Soviet Union.[194] A credit of US$100 million in economic aid that was granted to the government of Afghanistan by the Soviet Union in 1955, and the US$350 million of US aid that followed it,[195] led to an increase in the number of civil servants from 10,000 in 1955 to 60,000 in 1963.[196] Foreign aid and revenue from gas exports increasingly became important for state building. Between 1958 and 1968 and again in the 1970s the state financed over 40 per cent of its budget from foreign aid and the sales of natural gas to the Soviet Union (see Figure 2.1). Consequently, Afghanistan became a rentier state.[197] The government concentrated on managing aid as well as building patronage networks with aid and services.[198]

Since the activities and size of the state expanded, it needed new forms of legitimacy among the intellectuals and traditional actors.[199] This was envisaged in the new Constitution adopted in 1964 which introduced aspects of representative government. The government therefore permitted limited freedom for intellectuals during the two parliaments (1949–1952 and 1964–1973), also referred to as decade of democracy. However, the government did not grant intellectuals access to real power.[200] King Zahir Shah did not sign the bill to legalize parties so that they could effectively exercise power.[201]

The state was not accountable to the people for its policies in a meaningful sense. The ruling elites were fragmented severely at a time when "expectations of state performance were rising"[202] and a dysfunctional bureaucracy was inherited. M. Hasan Kakar noted that "Afghan civil servants are probably among the lowest paid in the world,"[203] making it difficult for them to have a decent life in the absence of other sources of income. Kakar observes, "Corruption and embezzlement [were] accepted facts of Afghan bureaucratic life and [were] objected to only when excesses [were] committed."[204]

Decline in foreign aid

Unlike the oil-rich states, which can control their sales volume, Afghanistan had no control over foreign aid, which declined after 1963.[205] This caused increasing levels of unemployment and underemployment among high school and university

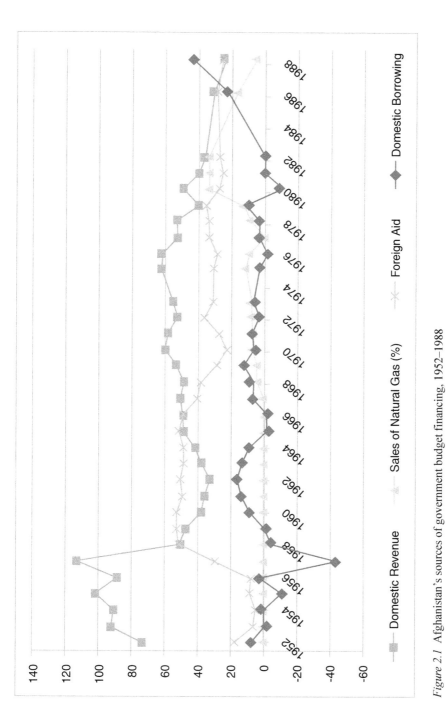

Figure 2.1 Afghanistan's sources of government budget financing, 1952–1988

Source: Barnett Rubin, *The Search For Peace in Afghanistan: From Buffer State to Failed State* (Karachi: Oxford University Press, 1995) 148–9.

graduates. In addition, the elites became polarized along ideological lines, ranging from traditional conservatives to Islamists and Marxists, shaping the power struggle of the coming decades.[206] The famine of 1971 and 1972 was a notable event which left around 50,000 deaths. The poorest regions, such as the highlands of Hazarajat were most affected. Following a government appeal, the US provided 200,000 tons of wheat, though much of it was wasted through "pilfering, profiteering and a corrupt and inefficient administration." In the process thousands of peasants lost their lands to money-lenders.[207]

In 1973, while Zahir Shah was in Italy, Daud Khan (Zahir Shah's step cousin and brother-in-law) seized power through a military coup and proclaimed Afghanistan a republic, with himself as the first president.[208] The decline in foreign aid had already alerted the government to seek alternative revenue from domestic and external sources. In 1976, the government introduced a progressive land tax policy under its Graduated Land Tax Law. However, it was not implemented in full due to the fall of the regime in 1978.[209]

Daud Khan had become acutely aware of the perverse impact of Afghanistan's overreliance on the Soviet Union for economic aid and technical assistance. By 1978, the total of Soviet Union aid to Afghanistan stood at US$1.265 billion which was in the form of soft loans with a low interest rate (2–3 per cent) and long-term repayment (usually up to 12 years). The Soviet aid was three times higher than the US aid to Afghanistan (US$471 million) in the same period. While Afghanistan was the third main recipient of Soviet Union aid among the developing countries, it ranked thirteenth in US assistance to developing countries.[210] In order to reduce the Soviet Union influence and maintain the flow of external revenue, Daud Khan looked to other sources for aid.

The US agreed but on condition that Afghanistan would join in a regional grouping dominated by Iran. This resulted in a billion US dollar promise of Iranian investment in Afghanistan,[211] although it did not materialize due to regime change in both Afghanistan and Iran (1979). However, this shift in Daud Khan's foreign policy and his suppression of opposition parties, such as the People's Democratic Party of Afghanistan (PDPA) toward the end of his reign in particular, led to a military coup by the PDPA in 1978. The coup resulted in the death of Daud Khan and his immediate family members. The incoming PDPA regime held power until 1992.

The state and the *mujahidin tanzīms* (organizations) and sources of revenue: conflict in state–society relations (1978–2000)

As the PDPA regime faced increasing resistance from the opposition-armed groups in the cities and countryside, Soviet troops entered Afghanistan in 1979 to prevent its fall. This changed the earlier policy of the Soviet Union and the US towards Afghanistan. They replaced the process of economic competition for influence over Afghanistan to competition through military domination by supporting their local allies. This situation led to a "rentier conflict" which was entirely funded externally. The Soviet Union supported the PDPA regime, while the US, Saudi Arabia, China, Iran and Pakistan funded and provided military equipment to its armed opposition, the *mujahidin* (known as Islamist fighters), who were mainly based in Pakistan. Between 1986 and 1990, about US$5 billion worth of weapons were supplied to the *mujahidin tanzīms*, while the Soviet Union sent weapons worth about US$5.7 billion to the PDPA regime in the same period.[212]

The way assistance was channelled had an impact on the polity of the PDPA regime and the *tanzīms*. As the Soviet aid was channelled from a single source to a single organization (the party-state), it brought with it an artificial unity to that which was in effect a fragmented PDPA between *Khalq* (masses) and *Parcham* (banner) factions. At the same time, aid to *mujahidin tanzīms*, of which 15 were recognized by Pakistan and Iran,[213] came from various sources to different organizations, exacerbating their existing disunity and creating new conflicts.[214] While the government in Kabul largely would use its systems to account for the aid, though not perfectly, transactions to the *mujahidin tanzīms* remained secret and were managed through Pakistan's Inter-Services Intelligence (ISI).[215] The situation, to borrow from Rubin, made the "tension between state and society into a part of the struggle between the East and West."[216] Thus, the attempt to depose the PDPA regime diluted the weak state itself.[217] This conflict transformed the role of traditional actors (tribal and village leaders, *mullās* and *Sufi* figures) and replaced them with (*mujahidin*) commanders, who emerged as new types of strongmen, having links with sources beyond the traditional establishments such as Islamic groups, foreign countries and international organizations. Aid and military assistance increased their autonomy from local populations,[218] making a political settlement far more difficult. Because of the conflict, the Afghan society was devastated and the state continued to disintegrate. Out of a population of fifteen to seventeen million people, about one million lost their lives, over five million people became refugees in Pakistan and Iran and two to three million were internally displaced.[219]

Since the reign of Abdur Rahman Khan, it was the first time that violence had emerged as a decisive factor in state–society relations. Due to increasing resistance in the countryside after 1987, the PDPA regime abandoned its plans for social transformation of the rural area. Instead of using military force to disarm *qawm-* (kin, village, tribe or ethnic group) based formation, it relied on patronage financed by the Soviet Union.[220]

The PDPA regime increasingly became dependent on the Soviet aid and the sales of natural gas which on average financed about half of the government total expenditure between 1978 and 1988 (see Figure 2.1). Between 1978 and 1992, the PDPA regime received about US$10 billion in Soviet soft loans.[221] The dependence of the state on rents in this period indicates similarity with the 1958–1963 period, when on average 52 per cent of the government total expenditure was funded by aid. However, in 1988, the state was able to fund only 24 per cent of the government expenditure from domestic revenue, while 32 per cent came from sales of natural gas (6 per cent) and foreign aid (26 per cent) and 44 per cent from domestic borrowings. The domestic revenue further deteriorated in this period because of armed conflict and social unrest.[222]

In 1989, the Soviet Union troops withdrew from Afghanistan mainly due to resistance against them and international pressure. Subsequently, agriculture and trade revived. Yet much of the agriculture production took the form of heroin growing, heroin processing and smuggling. The enterprise was organized by a combination of internal and external actors, including Afghan armed militia groups under the *mujahidin tanzīms*, Pakistani military officers, and Pakistani drug syndicates.[223] The opium revenue further complicated the relationship of the actors who were dependent on it and the local communities. However, following the disintegration of the Soviet Union in 1991, the PDPA regime lost the Soviet aid and collapsed in 1992.

The *mujahidin* government financial crises and Pakistani aid to the Taliban

After the fall of the PDPA regime, the US abandoned Afghanistan, and the US and Soviet Union rivalry was replaced by competition between Afghanistan's neighbours Pakistan and Iran, as well as Saudi Arabia which supported Pakistan's policy towards Afghanistan. They sought to broaden their military and political influence in Afghanistan. Although the *mujahidin* groups formed a coalition government in 1992 without the US and Soviet Union aid,[224] it had almost no reliable source of revenue. The major source of revenue for the new government was from provincial customs which were under the control of strongmen in the provinces who spent the revenue locally without accounting to central government.[225]

The regional *mujahidin* commanders retained their autonomy from the central government of President Rabbani. The government maintained its connection with them through cash transfer as means of patronage.[226] In the absence of a unifying political vision,[227] the *mujahidin* leaders fought each other and a civil war erupted among them in 1992. Thus, the government failed to provide basic services to protect its citizens, turning Afghanistan into a seriously disrupted state. Absence of substantial external revenue neither resulted in such reforms that could bolster the economic base of the state nor improved the bargaining of the government with the society. This situation instead further weakened the decay of the state institutions and undermined what internal administrative accountability was practised earlier.[228]

The failure of the *mujahidin* groups to stabilize Afghanistan, and Pakistan's ambition to assert its influence over Afghanistan, contributed to the rise of the Taliban, a cross border movement largely led by Afghan Pashtuns trained in Pakistani *madrassas* (refers to Islamic religious schools). The Taliban first took control of Kandahar in 1994 and then captured Kabul in 1996, expelling the *mujahidin* government. By the end of the 1990s, they controlled most of the country.[229] In the south, the Taliban promised to improve security and property rights which were poor but as they were well established, they implemented their radical and oppressive policies and consolidated their theocratic rule under the banner of Islam.[230]

The Taliban resorted to some of the Abdur Rahman Khan's state-building approach and they attempted to interfere in every walk of the people's lives and impose the same system across the country. In addition, the Taliban remained over-whelmingly dependent on Pakistan instead of British-India for logistic and finan-cial support; they governed the country through fear and the military remained their core strength. While they perceived to be independent, they conducted their foreign policy through Pakistan, as was the case under the reign of Abdur Rahman Khan. They established a theocratic regime and called it the Islamic Emirate of Afghanistan, headed by Mullah Muhammad Omar, who fought against the Soviet troops, referred by the Taliban as *Amir al-Muminin* (commander of the faithful). Their extreme interpretation of Islam inspired a "new extremist form of funda-mentalism across Pakistan and Central Asia, which refused to compromise with traditional Islamic values, social structures or existing state systems."[231]

The Taliban officially banned women from employment and education, espe-cially depriving 25 per cent of the government women employees of the right to work. They banned pictures, television and recreational activities (such as kite running), and ordered all males to grow long beards. They committed a series of war crimes by killing civilians and targeting minority groups such as the Hazaras while fighting to capture different cities. These crimes further isolated Afghani-stan from the rest of the world and Afghanistan became a rogue state. Only Paki-stan, Saudi Arabia and United Arab Emirates (UAE) recognized it,[232] although UAE and the Saudi Arabia withdrew their recognition in 1998.

Although the Taliban enhanced revenue collection, the economy was devas-tated and thus government income did not much improve.[233] The average revenue during the Taliban regime was not clear. They imposed a 10 per cent Islamic tax (*zakāt*) on public and private income and *mūstufiats* (provincial financial directorates) were charged to enforce this tax. Furthermore, taxes were levied on imported goods, agriculture production and landholdings. The Taliban forced people to repay their customs duties which they already had paid in the north of Afghanistan, such as at Balkh from the era under regional commander Abdul Rashid Dustum. They deemed the financial arrangements under commanders like Dustum unlawful.[234] The budget under the Taliban rule was kept in various con-tingency funds and was allocated to a very small number of ministries without clear mandate. For example, 80 per cent of the 2000 budget seemed to be in con-tingency, while the state budget was more of a general policy statement.[235]

Pakistan played a central role in the rise and survival of the Taliban regime[236] as its financial and military support was vital in changing the Taliban militias into a dominant military actor in Afghanistan. Pakistan's involvement was very intrusive to the extent that the Afghan leaders in post-2001 called it a "hidden occupation."[237] After Saudi Arabia and the United Arab Emirates stopped sup-porting the Taliban, the Taliban remained dependent on Pakistan, which saw them as their strategic asset to counter the Indian influence in Afghanistan. However, Pakistan's support of the Taliban was limited in financial terms and could not sub-stitute for the revenue derived from richer countries on which the earlier Afghan regimes were dependent. The Taliban turned to the United Nations (UN) for assis-tance, but their request was not met (except for some humanitarian assistance). This was mainly because of their violation of human rights and women's rights.[238]

Although by the end of 1990s the Taliban took most parts of the country, a momentous but small force, called *Jabha-i Mutahid-i Islāmī Barāī Najāt-i Afghanistan* (the United Islamic Front for the Salvation of Afghanistan), under the military leadership of Ahmad Shah Masoud (who was assassinated on September 9, 2001), resisted them. Following the horrific attacks by Al-Qaeda on September 11, 2001 on New York and Washington, the US in alliance with the Islamic Front commanders in the north and commanders in other parts of Afghanistan, deposed the Taliban regime, which had hosted Al-Qaeda's leader, Osama Bin Laden.[239]

Conclusion

This chapter demonstrated that Afghanistan historically suffered from a poor economy unable to pay for state expenditures, weak institutions, conflicts and invasion by powerful states. The reliance of the state on tributes, subsidies and foreign aid in this complex environment has been crucial in sustaining and reshaping institutions and state–society relations. Since 1747, except for a brief period in the 1920s, external revenue has constituted a substantial portion of state income and has been an important source of income for state building in Afghanistan. The degree of state dependence on external revenue has varied over time, and its absence has undermined the stability of states.

As shown in Figure 2.2 below, the tribute from the Indian conquests under the Durrani Empire, the British subsidies following the collapse of the Empire until the early twentieth century, and foreign aid from the mid-twentieth century to 2001 constituted a significant portion of state income. However, in all these cases, external revenue was not reliable and was available only under certain geostrategic conditions.

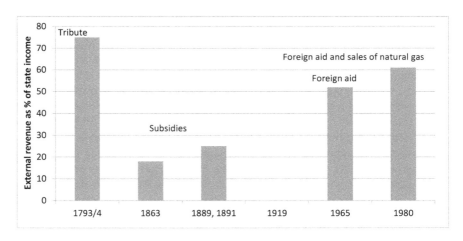

Figure 2.2 Percentage of Afghan state income from external revenue as a share of total annual state revenue (selected years)[240]

External revenue increased the domestic autonomy of the government, but it was not sufficient to make it fully independent of society. A large portion of external revenue was spent on building the army, helping rulers to suppress their rivals, improving stability and, more importantly, diffusing the external threats posed by rivals of the patron/donor states. External revenue did not contribute much in the building of more inclusive institutions that could foster accountability.

The availability of external revenue was associated with increases in domestic revenue. In this process, external revenue funded the army, which in turn helped to improve security and the state capacity for coercive tax enforcement. Improved security fostered trade and increased government revenue. The termination of external revenue to a great extent led to reshaping state-building priorities and a harsh taxation arrangement.

The loss of the tribute after the collapse of the Durrani Empire challenged Dost Muhammad Khan to reform the army and taxation system. His tax policy, however, remained extractive, and he taxed the rural and urban population heavily without negotiating with them or allowing their participation in government. Meanwhile, the government remained virtually in the hands of his immediate family members. His government not only failed to change the patronage system inherited from the Durrani Empire but also created its own patronage system. The British invasion in 1838, however, disrupted Dost Muhammad Khan's state-building efforts and exposed Afghanistan to new international dynamics that subsequently played a key role in Afghan state building.

In the late nineteenth century, subsidies and military assistance from Britain became important for Abdur Rahman Khan's state-building project. Abdur Rahman Khan's superior army, which was assisted by the British subsidy and weapons, facilitated the extraction of unprecedented taxes to fund the state-building project. However, he did not address the taxpayers' demands to reduce tax rates or negotiate with them on tax policies. His lack of action in this regard widened the gulf in state–society relations. This type of arrangement did not foster an effective taxation system to encourage taxpayers' compliance, which could have strengthened state–society relations and accountability by promoting a fiscal social contract between the state and society.

This fiscal dynamic changed under Amanullah Khan's reign largely as a result of his ambitions to modernize Afghanistan and the loss of British subsidies (see Figure 2.2), as well as the pressure that he asserted to fund his comprehensive reform programmes. Hence, the state became increasingly dependent on people for tax revenue and thus brought direct contact with them, especially through the use of *loya jirga*. Because of the weakness of the state in negotiating with the people and the existence of a weak tax administration, the state failed to either negotiate with or coerce the people. Subsequently, Amanullah Khan was overthrown. After a brief period of instability, the Musahiban reign fostered state autonomy by accessing international markets and foreign aid. As such, from the mid-twentieth century, Afghanistan became a rentier state as a result of its dependence on foreign aid and sales of natural gas.

The failure of Daud Khan's government to maintain a balanced relationship between the US and the Soviet Union, as well as its increasing reliance on Soviet economic and military assistance, exposed Afghanistan to the Cold War between the US and the Soviet Union. Following the Soviet invasion of Afghanistan in 1979, foreign aid therefore funded and sustained the conflict instead of building the economy and financing state-building efforts. This process contributed to the emergence of commanders as a new form of strongmen who replaced the previous ones, making a political settlement far more difficult and making state and society relations more contentious, which in turn reinforced the rise of the Taliban.

While Abdul Rahman Khan, the Musahiban family and the PDPA regime were the sole recipients of the subsidies and foreign aid, thus playing an important role in sustaining the institutions and the superiority of rulers, such a method for the delivery of external assistance did not render rulers accountable to the people. However, the delivery of Western aid to *mujahidin tanzīms*, through fragmented channels reinforced and institutionalized the differences among them. The chapter also found that the absence of external revenue and dependence on taxation, although important, does not necessarily guarantee the government's accountability to its people.

Historically, external revenue has played a major role in sustaining and reshaping the state-building process and producing particular outcomes as a result of the interplay with pre-external revenue dynamics and the international context, determining the availability and type of the revenue. The loss of external revenue has undermined the stability of the state at various times.

Notes

1 S. Frederick Starr, Lost Enlightenment: Central Asia's Golden Age from the Arab Conquest to Tamerlane (Princeton: Princeton University Press, 2013).
2 M. Ghulām M. Ghubār, *Afghanistan Dar Masyr-i Tārykh (Afghanistan in the Course of History)* (Peshawar: Dārulsalām Kitābkhānah, 1388 *Solār Hijri* Calendar [2009]), 9.
3 Thomas Barfield, *Afghanistan: A Cultural and Political History* (Princeton: Princeton University Press, 2010), 1; and Vartan Gregorian, *The Emergence of Modern Afghanistan* (Stanford: Stanford University Press, 1969), 10.
4 Gregorian, The Emergence of Modern Afghanistan, 10.
5 Ibid., 25.
6 The World Factbook, "Afghanistan: People and Society," CIA, www.cia.gov/library/publications/the-world-factbook/geos/af.html.
7 Barfield, Afghanistan: A Cultural and Political History, 23–4.
8 Barfield indicates that the total population was estimated around sixteen million during 1970s and 1990s. Ghubār, using the 1962 census of the Afghan government, estimates the total population of Afghanistan at around fifteen million (15,271,687). See ibid., 23; and Ghubār, *Afghanistan Dar Masyr-i Tārykh (Afghanistan in the Course of History)*, 11. Even to date there is no precise population census available in Afghanistan. The Afghan government and donors use different estimations. Islamic Republic of Afganistan and European Commission, "Summary of The National Risk and Vulnerability Assesment 2007/8: Profile of Afghanistan" (n.d.).
9 Ministry of Justice of Afghanistan, "Qānoni Asāsī Afghanistan," http://moj.gov.af/fa/page/1684.

10 Islamic Republic of Afghanistan, *Afghanistan Statistical Yearbook (2007/8)* (Central Statistics Organization [CSO], Kabul, 2008), 8.
11 Ibid., 137.
12 See Liz Alden Wily, *Land Rights in Crises: Restoring Tenure Security in Afghanistan* (Kabul: AREU, 2003), 2–4; and William Maley, *The Afghanistan Wars* (Basingstoke: Palgrave MacMillan, 2009), 10. The GDP share of the agriculture sector in Afghanistan has fallen from 65 per cent in 1978 to 27 per cent (excluding the opium) in 2007. Nematullah Bizhan, "Beyond Armed Stabilization in Afghanistan: Poverty and Unemployment," in *Petersberg Papers on Afghanistan and the Region*, ed. Wolfgang Danspeckgruber (Princeton: Princeton University Press, 2009), 126.
13 See Barfield, *Afghanistan: A Cultural and Political History*, 32–5; and Louis Dupree, *Afghanistan* (Karachi: Oxford University Press, 1973), 164.
14 Barfield, Afghanistan: A Cultural and Political History, 311.
15 Amin Saikal, Modern Afghanistan: A History of Struggle and Survival (London: I.B. Tauris, 2004), 22.
16 Ibid., 17.
17 Barnett R. Rubin, The Fragmentation of Afghanistan: State Formation and Collapse in the International System, 2nd ed. (New Haven: Yale University Press, 2002), 45.
18 Mir M. Seddiq Farhang, *Afghanistan Dar Panj Qarn-i Akhyr*. Vol. 1 (Sadir Qum: Ismāaylian, 1371 *Solār Hijri* Calendar [1992]), 105.
19 Yuri Gankovski, "The Durrani Empire: Taxes and Tax System, State Incomes and Expenditures," in *Afghanistan Past and Present*, ed. Social Sciences Editorial Board (Moscow: USSR Academy of Sciences, 1981), 77.
20 Ghubār, Afghanistan Dar Masyr-i Tārykh (Afghanistan in the Course of History), 368.
21 See Saikal, Modern Afghanistan: A History of Struggle and Survival, 21.
22 Barnet R. Rubin, "Lineages of the State in Afghanistan," *Asian Survey* 28, no. 11 (1988): 1191.
23 Ibid.
24 Percy Molesworth Sykes, *History of Persia*, 2nd ed. (London: Routledge, 2004), 370.
25 The present frontiers of Afghanistan were established at the beginning of the twentieth century. The frontier with the Indian subcontinent was denounced in 1893 by the Durand line, which has become the main source of conflict between Afghanistan and Pakistan. The frontier with Russia was settled in 1896 (with minor adjustments in the 1920s, the 1930s and 1948), and the final correction along the frontier with Iran (originally defined between 1903 and 1905) was made in 1935. Gregorian, *The Emergence of Modern Afghanistan*, 10.
26 Farhang, Afghanistan Dar Panj Qarn-i Akhyr, 1, 107–9.
27 See Gankovski, "The Durrani Empire: Taxes and Tax System, State Incomes and Expenditures."
28 Ibid., 90.
29 Barfield, Afghanistan: A Cultural and Political History, 100.
30 Farhang, Afghanistan Dar Panj Qarn-i Akhyr, 1, 143.
31 Ashraf Ghani, "Afghanistan xi Administration," in *Encyclopedia Iranica*, Online Edition, 1982, available at www.iranicaonline.org/articles/afghanistan-xi-admin 2:10. For details on Durrani Empire structure also see Gregorian, *The Emergence of Modern Afghanistan*, 46–51.
32 Ghani, "Afghanistan xi Administration," 2:10.
33 Ibid., 3:10.
34 Ibid.
35 See ibid., 2:10.
36 Gankovski, "The Durrani Empire: Taxes and Tax System, State Incomes and Expenditures," 76.

37 See ibid.
38 Ashraf Ghani, "Production and Domination: Afghanistan, 1747–1901," (PhD Dissertation, Columbia University, New York, 1982), 133; and Gankovski, "The Durrani Empire: Taxes and Tax System, State Incomes and Expenditures," 96.
39 Gankovski, "The Durrani Empire: Taxes and Tax System, State Incomes and Expenditures," 79–80.
40 Ibid., 80.
41 Ibid., 81.
42 Ibid.
43 Ibid., 84.
44 Ibid.
45 Ghubār, Afghanistan Dar Masyr-i Tārykh (Afghanistan in the Course of History), 391.
46 Gankovski, "The Durrani Empire: Taxes and Tax System, State Incomes and Expenditures," 83.
47 Ibid., 84.
48 Neamatollah Nojumi, Dyan Mazurana, and Elizabeth Stites, *After the Taliban: Life and Security in Rural Afghanistan* (Lanham: Rowman and Littlefield, 2009), 135.
49 See Gankovski, "The Durrani Empire: Taxes and Tax System, State Incomes and Expenditures," 91.
50 Ibid.
51 Ibid., 86.
52 Ibid., 88–9.
53 Ibid., 85.
54 See ibid.
55 Ibid., 93–4.
56 Ibid., 86.
57 Rubin, *The Fragmentation of Afghanistan: State Formation and Collapse in the International System*, 46. In the early nineteenth century under Qajar, Iran reclaimed some territories in the west of Afghanistan, while Murad Big, an Uzbek Chief, occupied the territory claimed by Bukhara in Afghan Turkistan.
58 Gankovski, "The Durrani Empire: Taxes and Tax System, State Incomes and Expenditures," 95.
59 Christine Noelle, State and Tribe in Nineteenth-Century Afghanistan: The Reign of Amir Dost Muhammad Khan (1826–1863) (London: Routledge Curzon, 1997), 226; and Barfield, Afghanistan: A Cultural and Political History, 113.
60 Barfield, Afghanistan: A Cultural and Political History, 113.
61 Noelle, State and Tribe in Nineteenth-Century Afghanistan, 226.
62 Barfield, Afghanistan: A Cultural and Political History, 112.
63 See Ghani, "Afghanistan xi Administration," 3:10. Also for details on the position of the Pashtun tribes see Noelle, *State and Tribe in Nineteenth-Century Afghanistan: The Reign of Amir Dost Muhammad Khan (1826–1863)*, 123–227.
64 Noelle, State and Tribe in Nineteenth-Century Afghanistan, 228.
65 Barfield, Afghanistan: A Cultural and Political History, 113.
66 Ahmad Shayeq Qassem, *Afghanistan's Political Stability: A Dream Unrealised* (Farnham: Ashgate, 2009), 29.
67 Shah Hanifi, Connecting Histories in Afghanistan: Market Relations and State Formation on a Colonial Frontier (Stanford: Stanford University Press, 2011), 99.
68 Ibid.
69 Ghani, "Afghanistan xi Administration," 3:10.
70 Noelle, State and Tribe in Nineteenth-Century Afghanistan: The Reign of Amir Dost Muhammad Khan (1826–1863), 228–76.
71 Ibid., 259–60.
72 Ghubār, Afghanistan Dar Masyr-i Tārykh (Afghanistan in the Course of History), 549.
73 Barfield, Afghanistan: A Cultural and Political History, 120.
74 Ibid.

75 William Dalrymple, Return of A King: The Battle for Afghanistan (London: Blooms-
    bury, 2013); and Patrick Macrory, Retreat from Kabul: The Catastrophic British Defeat
    in Afghanistan, 1842 (Guilford, CT: Lyons, 2002).
76 Barfield, Afghanistan: A Cultural and Political History.
77 Ghani, "Afghanistan xi Administration," 4:10.
78 Hanifi, Connecting Histories in Afghanistan, 99.
79 Ibid., 99–100.
80 Qassem, Afghanistan's Political Stability, 30–1.
81 Ghani, "Afghanistan xi. Administration," 4:10
82 Ghubār, *Afghanistan Dar Masyr-i Tārykh (Afghanistan in the Course of History)*,
    618–19. For details on Sher Ali Khan's reforms see ibid., 617–21.
83 M. Hasan Kakar, A Political and Diplomatic History of Afghanistan, 1863–1901
    (Leiden: Brill, 2006), 19.
84 Ghubār, Afghanistan Dar Masyr-i Tārykh (Afghanistan in the Course of History),
    617–21.
85 See ibid., 618–20.
86 Kakar, A Political and Diplomatic History of Afghanistan, 1863–1901, 22.
87 Ghani, "Afghanistan xi. Administration," 4:10.
88 Ibid.
89 See Ghubār, *Afghanistan Dar Masyr-i Tārykh (Afghanistan in the Course of His-
    tory)*, 669. Jafar Rasuly argues that Afghanistan's foreign policy has been a major
    cause of its underdevelopment. This has been very much shaped by the existence
    of strong powers in the region, surrounding Afghanistan. See Jafar Rasuly, "Tāsir-i
    Siāsati Khārijy Bar Tawseah Nayāftagy-i Afghanistan (The Impact of Foreign Policy
    on Afghanistan's Underdevelopment)," (Kabul: Maiwand, 1384 *Solār Hijra* Calendar
    [2005]).
90 Amin H. Tarzi, "A Tax Reform of the Afghan Amir, 'Abd Al-Rahman Khan'," *Jour-
    nal of Asian History* 27, no. 1 (1993): 36.
91 Barnett R. Rubin, The Fragmentation of Afghanistan: State Formation and Collapse in
    the International System (London: Yale University Press, 1995), 48.
92 Abdur Rahman Khan provided the British with "the necessary opportunity for a face-
    saving withdrawal." He was son of Mohammad Afzal Khan and grandson of Dost
    Muhammad. In 1868, after his defeat by Sher Ali Khan (half-brother and arch-rival
    of his deceased father), Abdur Rahman Khan lived in exile in Samarkand and Tash-
    kent for twelve years. He was then impressed by centralizing policies of the Czarist
    Empire. In February 1880, the Russians, believing him to be pro-Russian, assisted his
    return to Afghanistan. He mobilized the support of Afghanistan's northern *khans* and
    Begs (Uzbek and Turkmen leaders) and rallied to Kabul. In the absence of any other
    strong leader, the British found it desirable to support his accession to the throne.
    See Saikal, *Modern Afghanistan: A History of Struggle and Survival*, 35; and Ashraf
    Ghani, "Islam and State-Building in a Tribal Society, Afghanistan: 1880–1901," *Mod-
    ern Asian Studies* 12, no. 2 (1978): 272.
93 Ghubār, Afghanistan Dar Masyr-i Tārykh (Afghanistan in the Course of History), 670.
94 See ibid., 677–84.
95 Gregorian, The Emergence of Modern Afghanistan, 134.
96 Barfield, Afghanistan: A Cultural and Political History, 165.
97 Ghani, "Islam and State-Building in a Tribal Society, Afghanistan: 1880–1901," 283.
98 See ibid. For example, Abdur Rahman Khan was propagating through religious pub-
    lications that "if a king becomes tyrannical towards his subjects, they are not to rise
    against him but show patience in bearing his excesses." Where "[t]he oppression and
    injustice of the rulers is "a result of our sins and not of faults on the parts of kings."
    Government of Afghanistan, *Resala Mawaza* (Kabul: Government Press, 1311 Solār
    Hijri Calendar [1932]), 63; and Abu Bakr, *Taqwim Din*, 2nd ed. (Kabul: Government
    Press, 1306 A.H.), 116; quoted in Ghani, "Islam and State-Building in a Tribal Soci-
    ety, Afghanistan: 1880–1901," 281.

99   Ghani, "Islam and State-Building in a Tribal Society, Afghanistan: 1880–1901," 272.
100 Ibid., 274.
101 Republic of Afghanistan, *Resala Mawaza*, 92–5, quoted in "Islam and State-Building in a Tribal Society, Afghanistan: 1880–1901," 278.
102 For discussion on a similar approach to taxation in Iran's context after 1979, see Afsaneh Najmabadi, "Depoliticisation of a Rentier State," in *The Rentier State*, ed. Hazem Beblawi and Giacomo Luciani, 211–27, (London: Croom Helm, 1987).
103 See M. Hasan Kakar, Government and Society in Afghanistan: The Reign of Amir'Abd al-Rahman Khan (Austin: University of Texas Press, 1979), 78–85.
104 Ibid., 75.
105 The people who were not able to pay their tax dues and escaped the country were estimated to be around hundreds of families. They were mostly constituents of beyond the Hindu Kosh (Baghlan, Ghuri, Qataghan and Badakhshan). See ibid., 87–8.
106 Ghubār, Afghanistan Dar Masyr-i Tārykh (Afghanistan in the Course of History), 675.
107 Kakar, Government and Society in Afghanistan, 73.
108 Barfield, Afghanistan: A Cultural and Political History, 148.
109 Kakar, A Political and Diplomatic History of Afghanistan, 1863–1901, 50.
110 Kakar, Government and Society in Afghanistan, 78.
111 See ibid., 77–8.
112 In the distant areas from Kabul the situation was even worse. The government officials often exacted much more tax than the official dues.
113 Kakar, Government and Society in Afghanistan, 90.
114 Ghubār, Afghanistan Dar Masyr-i Tārykh (Afghanistan in the Course of History), 675.
115 Kakar, Government and Society in Afghanistan, 90.
116 Ghubār, Afghanistan Dar Masyr-i Tārykh (Afghanistan in the Course of History), 672.
117 See Rubin, The Fragmentation of Afghanistan: State Formation and Collapse in the International System, 49.
118 Between 1886 and 1889, the price of a rifle was about 25–40 rupees at Mascut. This price excluded the price of a rifle in a local market on the border of Afghanistan. Because the British Empire granted the weapon to the Amir of Afghanistan, it is safe to calculate the mentioned price, not the one in the local market. By estimating the price of each rifle at 40 rupees, the total price of 33,302 rifles, which the British Empire granted to Abdur Rahman Khan between 1880 and 1895, could have been, on average, ninety thousand rupees per year. For information about the price of rifles see Tim Moreman, "Arms Trade on the N.W. Frontier 1890–1914," http://archive.is/UBNuk#selection-107.0-109.4; and Rubin, *The Fragmentation of Afghanistan: State Formation and Collapse in the International System*, 49.
119 Barfield, Afghanistan: A Cultural and Political History, 160.
120 M. Nazif Shahrani, "State Building and Social Fragmentation in Afghanistan: A Historical Perspective." In *The State, Religion and Ethnic Politics: Afghanistan, Iran, and Pakistan*, edited by Ali Banuazizi and Myron Weiner, (Syracuse: Syracuse University Press, 1986), 39.
121 Ghani, "Afghanistan: Administration," 5:10.
122 Ghubār claims that the estimated number of troops under Abdur Rahman Khan's reign was around 96,400, while Ghani notes that this number was around 79,000. However, Abdur Rahman Khan in his autobiography highlighted the need for a million armed men to defend the country from foreign invasions. Therefore, Ghubār's figure seems to be a closer estimation. See Ghubār, *Afghanistan Dar Masyr-i Tārykh (Afghanistan in the Course of History)*, 671; Ghani, "Afghanistan xi Administration," 5:10; and Abdur Rahman Khan, *Tāj ul-Tawārikh (Amir Abdur Rahman Khan's Autobiography)*, 2 vols. (Kabul: Maiwand, 1387 *Solār Hijri* Calendar [2008]), 446.
123 Kakar, Government and Society in Afghanistan: The Reign of Amir'Abd al-Rahman Khan, 39.

124 Ghubār, Afghanistan Dar Masyr-i Tārykh (Afghanistan in the Course of History), 672.
125 Tarzi, "A Tax Reform of the Afghan Amir, 'Abd Al-Rahman Khan'," 40; and Khan, *Tāj ul-Tawārikh (Amir Abdur Rahman Khan's Autobiography)*.
126 Ghani, "Afghanistan xi Administration," 5:10.
127 Gregorian, The Emergence of Modern Afghanistan, 37.
128 Tarzi argues that all the governing heads of administrative units under Abdur Rahman Khan were called *hakīm*. The word *hakīm* has its root in Arabic verb *hakamā* (in command). See Tarzi, "A Tax Reform of the Afghan Amir, 'Abd Al-Rahman Khan'," 38.
129 Kakar, Government and Society in Afghanistan: The Reign of Amir'Abd al-Rahman Khan, 51.
130 Tarzi notes that Abdur Rahman Khan by the end of his reign succeeded in replacing the judicial authority of the tribe with the justice of *Quran* and *qāzi's* court, at least in Khost. Tarzi, "A Tax Reform of the Afghan Amir, 'Abd Al-Rahman Khan'."
131 Kakar, Government and Society in Afghanistan: The Reign of Amir'Abd al-Rahman Khan, 232. Also see Ghubār, *Afghanistan Dar Masyr-i Tārykh (Afghanistan in the Course of History)*, 675.
132 Barfield, Afghanistan: A Cultural and Political History, 165–66.
133 Ibid.
134 See Kakar, Government and Society in Afghanistan: The Reign of Amir'Abd al-Rahman Khan.
135 Ghubār, *Afghanistan Dar Masyr-i Tārykh (Afghanistan in the Course of History)*, 682. *Mirza* was used as a title for a civil office or military rank, usually under monarchies and emirates.
136 Barfield, Afghanistan: A Cultural and Political History, 167.
137 Ghubār, Afghanistan Dar Masyr-i Tārykh (Afghanistan in the Course of History), 671.
138 Barfield, Afghanistan: A Cultural and Political History, 167.
139 Ibid.; and Rubin, The Fragmentation of Afghanistan: State Formation and Collapse in the International System, 90–2.
140 Muhammadzai is a subtribe from Barakzai branch of Durrani tribe. From 1826 to 1978 most of the Afghan rulers were Mohammadzais. See for example Francis Y. Owusu, "Post-9/11 U.S. Foreign Aid, the Millennium Challenge Account and Africa: How Many Birds Can One Stone Kill?," (Ames: Iowa State University, 2004), 53–5.
141 Ghubār, Afghanistan Dar Masyr-i Tārykh (Afghanistan in the Course of History), 675–82.
142 For details see ibid., 690–700.
143 Said S. Hashimi, The First Book on Constitutional Movement In Afghanistan, During the First Quarter of the Twentieth Century, 2nd ed. Vol. 1 (Kabul: Afghanistan Cultural Association, 2008), 145; and Ghubār, Afghanistan Dar Masyr-i Tārykh (Afghanistan in the Course of History), 742.
144 Rubin, The Fragmentation of Afghanistan: State Formation and Collapse in the International System, 54.
145 Ibid.
146 Ghubār, Afghanistan Dar Masyr-i Tārykh (Afghanistan in the Course of History), 850.
147 Rubin, The Fragmentation of Afghanistan: State Formation and Collapse in the International System, 55.
148 Ghubār, Afghanistan Dar Masyr-i Tārykh (Afghanistan in the Course of History), 853–4.
149 Rubin, The Fragmentation of Afghanistan: State Formation and Collapse in the International System, 55–6.
150 For further discussions on Amanullah Khan's reforms see Ghubār, Afghanistan Dar Masyr-i Tārykh (Afghanistan in the Course of History), 847–61; Saikal, Modern Afghanistan: A History of Struggle and Survival, 73–90; and Gregorian, The Emergence of Modern Afghanistan, 239–74.

151 Saikal, Modern Afghanistan: A History of Struggle and Survival, 73.
152 Barfield, Afghanistan: A Cultural and Political History, 182–3.
153 Ghubār, *Afghanistan Dar Masyr-i Tārykh (Afghanistan in the Course of History)*, 850. The exchange rate in this period was at 100 Kabuli rupees to 60 Indian rupees. Ibid., 850.
154 Barfield, Afghanistan: A Cultural and Political History, 183.
155 See Gregorian, The Emergence of Modern Afghanistan, 271. Also see Ghubār, Afghanistan Dar Masyr-i Tārykh (Afghanistan in the Course of History), 848.
156 Gregorian, The Emergence of Modern Afghanistan, 271.
157 Ibid.
158 Barfield, Afghanistan: A Cultural and Political History, 183–4.
159 See Saikal, Modern Afghanistan: A History of Struggle and Survival, 58; Gregorian, The Emergence of Modern Afghanistan, 8; and Angelo Rasanayagam, Afghanistan: A Modern History (London: I.B. Tauris, 2005), 17.
160 See Saikal, Modern Afghanistan: A History of Struggle and Survival, 58.
161 See Gregorian, The Emergence of Modern Afghanistan, 254–5.
162 For more discussion see Ghubār, Afghanistan Dar Masyr-i Tārykh (Afghanistan in the Course of History), 847–61.
163 Gregorian, The Emergence of Modern Afghanistan, 270.
164 Saikal, Modern Afghanistan: A History of Struggle and Survival, 87–8.
165 Ibid., 88.
166 Ibid., 96.
167 Ghubār, Afghanistan Dar Masyr-i Tārykh (Afghanistan in the Course of History), 901–2.
168 Gregorian, The Emergence of Modern Afghanistan, 281.
169 Saikal, Modern Afghanistan: A History of Struggle and Survival, 96.
170 Ibid., 97; and Dupree, *Afghanistan*, 458–9.
171 See Gregorian, The Emergence of Modern Afghanistan, 294.
172 Ghani, "Afghanistan xi Administration," 6:10. During the reign of Amanullah Khan four families played a dominant role in shaping the politics. They were his royal family, the Musahiban family whose head was Nadir Khan, the Charkhi family led by Ghulam Nabi Khan Charkhi and the Tarzi family headed by Mahmud Tarzi. Abdur Rahman Khan exiled the Musahiban and Tarzi families. However, Habibullah Khan allowed them to return to Afghanistan and gave them the positions of honour and influence. Leon B. Poullada, *Reform and Rebellion in Afghanistan, 1919–1929; King Amanullah's Failure to Modernize a Tribal Society* (Ithaca: Cornell University Press, 1973), 35–6.
173 Rubin, "Lineages of the State in Afghanistan," 1200.
174 Ibid.
175 Ibid.
176 Gregorian, The Emergence of Modern Afghanistan, 298.
177 Rubin, "Lineages of the State in Afghanistan," 1203.
178 Barfield, Afghanistan: A Cultural and Political History, 198.
179 Maxwell J. Fry, The Afghan Economy: Money, Finance, and the Critical Constraints to Economic Development (Leiden: Brill, 1974), 174.
180 Rubin, "Lineages of the State in Afghanistan," 1201; and Fry, The Afghan Economy, 170–3.
181 Barfield, Afghanistan: A Cultural and Political History, 198.
182 Fry, *The Afghan Economy: Money, Finance, and the Critical Constraints to Economic Development*, 169–70. Taxes on exports were high. For instance in 1944, taxes at the rate of 51.8 per cent were imposed on cotton exports, 50.9 per cent on wool exports and 43.4 per cent on Karakul. See ibid., 226.
183 In the initial comparative study of forty-nine countries, where taxable capacity was calculated, Afghanistan was not included. Fry later added Afghanistan in the assessment. See ibid., 183.

184 Islamic Republic of Afghanistan, "Policy Directions and Strategies for Sustainable Sources of Revenue for Afghanistan: Official Tax Policy Framework and Revenue System Strategy," (Kabul: Ministry of Finance, 2007), 3–4. Also for details on foreign aid in the 1960s and 1970s; see Dupree, *Afghanistan.*
185 Rubin, The Fragmentation of Afghanistan: State Formation and Collapse in the International System, 73.
186 Saikal, Modern Afghanistan: A History of Struggle and Survival, 119.
187 See Rubin, "Lineages of the State in Afghanistan," 1203; and Saikal, *Modern Afghanistan: A History of Struggle and Survival*, 134.
188 Rubin, The Fragmentation of Afghanistan: State Formation and Collapse in the International System, 75.
189 Ibid.
190 Rubin, "Lineages of the State in Afghanistan," 1204.
191 Saikal, Modern Afghanistan: A History of Struggle and Survival, 119.
192 Rubin, "Lineages of the State in Afghanistan," 1204.
193 Saikal, Modern Afghanistan: A History of Struggle and Survival, 130.
194 See Rubin, "Lineages of the State in Afghanistan," 1204.
195 Ghani, "Afghanistan xi Administration," 7:10.
196 Ibid.
197 See Rubin, *The Fragmentation of Afghanistan: State Formation and Collapse in the International System*, 48, 65, 66; and Giacomo Luciani, "Allocation vs. Production States," in *The Rentier State*, ed. Hazem Beblawi and Giacomo Luciani (London: Croom Helm, 1987), 80.
198 Amin Saikal, "Afghanistan's Weak State and Strong Society," in *Making States Work: State Failure and the Crisis of Governance*, ed. Simon Chesterman, Michael Ignatieff and Ramesh Chandra Thakur (Tokyo: United Nations University Press, 2005), 198.
199 Rubin, "Lineages of the State in Afghanistan," 1205.
200 Ibid.
201 Ibid.; and Ghani, "Afghanistan xi Administration," 7:10.
202 Maley, The Afghanistan Wars, 12.
203 Hasan Kakar, "The Fall of the Afghan Monarchy in 1973," *International Journal of Middle East Studies* 9, no. 2 (1978): 200.
204 Ibid.
205 Fry, The Afghan Economy, 70.
206 Rasanayagam, Afghanistan: A Modern History, 59.
207 Ibid., 60.
208 Rubin, "Lineages of the State in Afghanistan," 1206.
209 Republic of Afghanistan, "Graduated Land Tax Law," The World Law Guide, n.d.
210 M. Siddieq Noorzoy, "Long-Term Economic Relations between Afghanistan and the Soviet Union: An Interpretive Study," *International Journal of Middle East Studies* 17, no. 2 (1985): 160.
211 Rubin, "Lineages of the State in Afghanistan," 1207.
212 Rubin, The Fragmentation of Afghanistan: State Formation and Collapse in the International System, 179.
213 Antonio Giustozzi, Koran, Kalashnikov and Laptop: *The Neo-Taliban Insurgency in Afghanistan* (London: Hurst, 2007), 81.
214 Rubin, The Fragmentation of Afghanistan: State Formation and Collapse in the International System, 181.
215 Ibid.
216 Ibid., 279.
217 Ibid.
218 For details see ibid., 179–83.
219 Ibid., 1; Also see Nematullah Bizhan, "The Effects of Afghanistan's Political Evolution on Migration and Displacement," *Migration Policy and Practice* vi, no. 3 (June–September 2016), 4–9.

220 Ibid., 171–72.
221 The record at the Ministry of Finance of Afghanistan shows that Afghanistan in total received US$11 in soft loans from the Soviet Union, most of it was given to Afghanistan under the PDPA regime.
222 Islamic Republic of Afghanistan, "Policy Directions and Strategies for Sustainable Sources of Revenue for Afghanistan: Official Tax Policy Framework and Revenue System Strategy," 4. Also see "Review of Afghanistan's Fiscal Management, Asian Development Bank, Operations and Coordination Division" by Von Seth, Asian Development Bank, February 2003.
223 Rubin, The Fragmentation of Afghanistan: State Formation and Collapse in the International System, 183.
224 Rubin, The Fragmentation of Afghanistan: State Formation and Collapse in the International System, 265.
225 Ibid., 272.
226 Barfield, Afghanistan: A Cultural and Political History, 253.
227 Ibid., 249–50.
228 See Michael Carnahan et al., *Reforming Fiscal and Economic Management in Afghanistan* (Washington: World Bank, 2004), 3–5.
229 Barfield, Afghanistan: A Cultural and Political History, 255.
230 Ibid., 257.
231 See Ahmad Rashid, Taliban: Islam, Oil and the New Great Game in Central Asia (London: I.B. Tauris, 2002).
232 See Barfield, Afghanistan: A Cultural and Political History, 257; Saikal, Modern Afghanistan, 27; and Rashid, Taliban: Islam, Oil and the New Great Game in Central Asia, 2, 29.
233 Islamic Republic of Afghanistan, "Policy Directions and Strategies for Sustainable Sources of Revenue for Afghanistan," 4. See also Barfield, *Afghanistan: A Cultural and Political History*, 1.
234 A Taxpayer, Interview by Author, Kabul, June 15, 2011.
235 Carnahan et al., Reforming Fiscal and Economic Management in Afghanistan, 5.
236 Wahid Muzhda an Afghan writer, who worked under the Taliban regime in Afghanistan, argues that external support was essential in the rise of the Taliban. Wahid Muzhda, *Afghanistan Wa Panj Sal Salta-i Taliban* (Kabul: Maiwand, 1381 *Solār Hijri* Calendar).
237 President Karzai in most of his speeches has stated that Afghanistan has been continuously occupied, referring to the Taliban era as a "hidden occupation" by Pakistan. Even before 2001, the Afghan resistance movement against the Taliban objected to Pakistan's support of the Taliban militias. For example, in 1998 the Afghan Ambassador to Moscow accused Pakistan of the intention to occupy Afghanistan. See Shiping Hua, ed., *Islam and Democratization in Asia* (New York: Cambria Press, 2009); and Saikal, *Modern Afghanistan: A History of Struggle and Survival*, 225.
238 Barfield, Afghanistan: A Cultural and Political History, 264.
239 See Tom Rockmore, Joseph Margolis, and Armen Marsoobian, *The Philosophical Challenge of September 11*, Metaphilosophy Series in Philosophy (Oxford: Blackwell, 2005), 179; and Hua, *Islam and Democratization in Asia*, 78.
240 In 1919, the Afghan government did not receive substantial subsidies or aid. Gankovski, "The Durrani Empire," 88–9; Fry, *The Afghan Economy*, 158–9; Ghubār, *Afghanistan Dar Masyr-i Tārykh*; Hanifi, *Connecting Histories in Afghanistan*, 97–9; and Barnett R. Rubin, *The Search for Peace in Afghanistan: From Buffer State to Failed State* (Karachi: Oxford University Press, 1995), 148–9.

Part III

Post-9/11 state building in Afghanistan

3 Rebuilding an aid-based rentier state

Introduction

After the Taliban regime fell in late 2001, Afghan state building significantly depended on external military and financial support – this dependence was greater than during any other period since 1747 – and the "war on terror" dominated the nature of foreign donors' engagement. Between 2002 and 2009, foreign aid constituted an average of approximately 71 per cent of GDP and financed more than 90 per cent of public expenditures through on- and off-budget mechanisms. Four-fifths of the expenditures, however, bypassed the Afghan state through off-budget mechanisms.

This chapter examines how this aid dependency and the ways that aid was spent reinforced the building of a transitional, yet fragmented, aid-based rentier state. In so doing, the chapter assesses how the new political order and aid dependency shaped the characteristics of the state.

Establishing a new political order

Since the mid-nineteenth century, the US military was the third external force which entered Afghanistan to remove an existing regime so that it could protect its interests in the region and the world. Unlike the previous invasions of the country, the intervention of the US, along with North Atlantic Treaty Organization (NATO) and non-NATO allies, in Afghanistan reconnected the country with the rest of the world. Although the US mainly focused on the "war on terror" and remained reluctant to engage in "nation building" efforts, lasting stability in Afghanistan required rebuilding of state institutions and the economy.

The Karzai government in a document called *Securing Afghanistan's Future* presented a new vision for Afghanistan in Berlin's conference on Afghanistan in 2004 which argues that Afghanistan is pivotal for the stability of its region and the world.

> [The] international assistance to Afghanistan should be looked on as an investment in stability, peace-building, and development at local, regional, and global levels. It is not charity. It will enhance regional stability; reduce the global threats of drugs and terrorism, and lower the associated defence and security-related costs of many nations.[1]

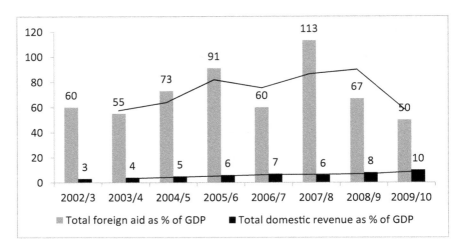

Figure 3.1 Foreign aid and domestic revenue as percentage of GDP in Afghanistan, 2001–2009

Source: Ministry of Finance, Fiscal Policy Unit (FPU), Da Afghanistan Bank and CSO, 2011, Sunley and Gracia, *Afghanistan: Tax Reform–The Next Steps*, 12.

As a result of a prolonged conflict, not only the economy was devastated but the state was also weakened and barely able to collect what domestic revenue that did exist. Thus, Afghanistan relied on foreign military and economic assistance to finance state building and development projects. Figure 3.1 above demonstrates a heavy dependence of the Afghan state on foreign aid, measured by aid and domestic revenue as share of annual GDP, and the existence of very limited domestic revenue.

External revenue in the form of foreign aid comprised the highest percentage of state income of any other period of Afghanistan's modern history in post-2001. However, dependence of the Afghan state on external revenue, as we noted in Chapter 2, was not something new. Aid dependency post-2001 thus reiterated a historical pattern of building the state with significant amounts of external revenue. Karl W. Eikenberry, the former US ambassador to Afghanistan (2009–2010), defined this as an extreme situation and argued that "virtually the Afghan state is on 'life support', provided by the international community, especially the US; therefore the main challenge is how to remove this [aid dependency], which can have a crucial [negative] impact."[2] This fiscal condition had major implications for the state-building efforts and polity.

Building the state institutions

After the Taliban regime fell, representatives of Afghan factions – *mujahidin* commanders, representatives of Afghanistan's different ethnic groups, expatriate Afghans, and representatives of the exiled monarch (Zahir Shah), while excluding the Taliban – met under the auspices of the United Nations (UN) in Bonn to agree on a new political order. They signed the Bonn Agreement on December 5, 2001, emphasizing the right of people to democratically determine their political future according to the principles of Islam and promoting national reconciliation, stability and respect for human rights. The Bonn Agreement focused on the creation of a central authority around which a state could be reconstructed with external military and financial assistance. This agreement urged the UN, the international community[3] and donors to support the rehabilitation of Afghanistan and guarantee its national sovereignty. The deployment of International Security Assistance Force (ISAF) first in Kabul, which the UN Security Council authorized, and the flow of foreign aid that foreign donors pledged at the Tokyo conference in January 2002 further supported the implementation of the Bonn Agreement.[4]

The Bonn Agreement also included provisions for the formation of new Afghan security forces, judicial and legal reforms, the establishment of an independent human rights commission, the formation of a civil service commission and the creation of an independent central bank.[5] However, it did not project timelines for any of these goals. It largely reconciled the Afghans and the international community's interest. Accordingly, the political system was restructured around liberal democracy, while also emphasizing the country's Islamic and traditional values, and replaced the planned economy with a market one.[6] These priorities were later enshrined in the Constitution of 2004.

Subsequently, President Rabanni, head of the *mujahidin* government whose supporters had recaptured Kabul after the fall of the Taliban regime, transferred the power to an interim administration headed by Hamid Karzai (an ethnic Pashtun). Six months later, an emergency *loya jirga* elected Hamid Karzai as the head of state for a period of two years.[7] A Constitution Commission drafted a new Constitution for Afghanistan which a *loya jirga* approved in January 2004. Subsequently, the government held presidential and parliamentary elections in 2004 and 2006 respectively, and Karzai was elected President.

Afghanistan experienced major economic and political transformation, especially as it started from a very low base. Even before 1978, Afghanistan was among the least developed countries in the world, and two decades of armed conflict following the Soviet Union invasion of 1979 added to the country's problems, devastating its institutions and causing a huge humanitarian and economic loss to the country.[8] The total cost over the period of conflict, as measured in terms of lost growth and the cost of humanitarian assistance and military expenditure, was estimated by the World Bank to be US$240 billion.[9] In 2003, with an average per capita income estimated at less than US$200, Afghanistan was among the least developed countries in the world.[10]

The Afghan civil administration was extremely weak. While "many of the formal structures and some of the traditional practices of public administration remained in place, they lacked the human, financial and physical resources to do their job, particularly in modern context".[11] The government thus needed to reform public administration. Some of the immediate tasks included:

> to establish an appropriate legal-rational framework and culturally relevant processes and institutions to ensure the development of a governmental system

and polity, whose operations would be underpinned by principles of public participation, transparency, accountability, administrative-bureaucratic efficiency, social equity, observation of basic human rights, and promotion of merit rather than family connection and ethnic affiliation as the basis for governmental appointments.[12]

Afghanistan has made important progress in building some of the state institutions and expanding education and health services. Alastair McKechnie, the former Word Bank Director for Afghanistan (2001–2008), notes that since Afghanistan began from a very low base the overall impact of foreign aid was positive on service delivery and economic growth, as Figure 3.2 below demonstrates.[13] GDP per capita rose from US$ 119 in 2001 to US$ 459 in 2009,[14] and about 8 million students attended school in 2013 in comparison to less than a million (which by large excluded girls) in 2003.[15]

However, insecurity and poor governance posed a major challenge for Afghan state building. Inefficient use of foreign aid exacerbated these challenges. The Karzai government by large reinforced the politics of patronage. Karzai offered senior public positions in return for political support. To ensure the flow of aid to Afghanistan, the government remained preoccupied with donors. The business of government, to borrow from Paul Collier, became ". . . dominated by the need to satisfy donors, replacing the need to satisfy citizens."[16] While the Karzai government repeatedly emphasized remaining accountable to Afghan citizens and foreign donors, the latter dominated as foreign donors financed a large portion of the Afghan government budget and had a greater leverage. For example, in the 2002 Tokyo conference on reconstruction assistance to Afghanistan, Karzai

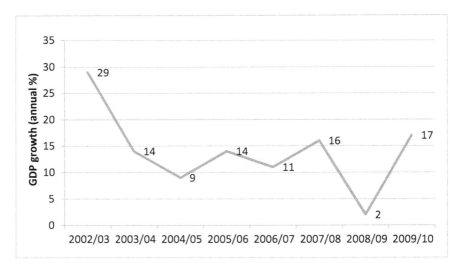

Figure 3.2 GDP growth rate, 2002–2009

Source: Da Afghanistan Bank 2011

stated: "Our vision is of a prosperous, secure Afghanistan . . . our government shall be accountable to its citizens as well as to the international community."[17] As we will consider in Chapters 4, 5 and 6, in practice the government increasingly remained accountable to donors rather than Afghan citizens. This dynamic of aid accountability along with the politics of patronage adversely affected the government accountability to citizens.

Development planning and aid

The government prepared development plans and strategies in response to the flow of aid. Between 2001 and 2009, the government prepared four main strategies and plans: the Afghanistan Development Framework (ADF) in 2002; Securing Afghanistan's Future (SAF), which was presented at the Berlin international conference in 2004; the Interim Afghanistan National Development Strategy (I-ANDS) in 2006; and Afghanistan National Development Strategy (ANDS, 2008–2013), a five-year development plan presented at the Paris Conference on Afghanistan in 2008.[18] These strategies and plans largely identified the government priorities to effectively allocate foreign aid and domestic revenue. Donors for their part were interested to know what the government's priorities were to align their funding where they matched donors' interest. Western donors (such as the US, the UK and Canada), as well as World Bank and the United Nations Development Programme (UNDP) provided financial and technical support to the government to develop plans and strategies.

The Afghan government and foreign donors' relationships changed over time. In 2006 especially, the Afghanistan Compact redefined such relationships and emphasized mutual accountability. The Afghanistan Compact, which succeeded the Bonn Agreement, emerged as a blueprint for cooperation between the international community and the Afghan government.[19] It aimed to improve Afghan living conditions and security by achieving 43 five-year benchmarks (2006–2010) in security, governance, rule of law and human rights, and economics and social development. While the Afghan government committed to the Compact goals, the international community undertook to provide financial support for its implementation.[20] The government and donors established a Joint Coordination and Monitoring Board (JCMB) to oversee the Compact implementation. Forty-five Working Groups, 12 Consultative Groups and six Crosscutting Consultative Groups were established to coordinate and monitor the Afghanistan Compact implementation. The Compact promoted the government and donor relations. Between 2006 and 2009, nine meetings of the JCMB were held; two outside Afghanistan and the rest in Kabul, where the government basically reported to and bargained with donors.[21] The parliament did not have an active oversight role over the Compact implementation. Maybe this was because the Parliament was established only in late 2005, few months before the Compact was endorsed in London Conference in February 2006.[22]

Mostly the planning process was driven by technical considerations and through an extensive consultation between different ministries and departments and the Afghan government and foreign donors. Except for ANDS, consultation did not take place with the public. In 2007, the government launched a "sub-national" consultation with different actors for development of the ANDS document for the first time. This was not institutionalized to promote public participation in the planning process for the future.[23] Hitherto, this was not something new. Even in the past, when the four Five-Year Plans had been developed (1956, 1961, 1967 and 1972),[24] the government in Kabul had prepared the plans alone.

Government proposed the development component and a significant part of operating cost of its strategies for funding to donors. However, donors criticized that these strategies and plans were poorly prioritized and sequenced. In fact because of the protracted conflict and poor investment in the past, the needs were huge and the government aimed to include as many as projects that donors could choose among for funding. The implementation of these plans was only modestly successful. They were neither fully funded nor implemented in full.[25] ANDS, for example, required about US$10 billion a year, a total of US$50 billion for five years. While it was estimated that domestic revenue would provide US$7 billion, US$43 billion was requested from donors in aid for financing the ANDS.[26] Between 2002 and 2009, the average annual foreign aid to Afghanistan stood at US$5.7 billion (see Chapter 4).

Yet donors continued to have their own strategies, policies and even projects which were parallel to those of the government. Donors often justified their off-budget projects on the basis that the Afghan administration was weak and corrupt, something which we discuss in the next chapters. In many cases, especially in the first years of post-2001, instead of deciding which projects to finance, the government had to only track projects financed by donors and include them in the so-called national budget, including on- and off-budgets items. This situation added the pressure on the government to preoccupy with donors concerning aid management and tracking, in addition to, as we noted earlier, negotiating with donors for receiving on-budget aid. For example, out of the five lessons mentioned in the ADF report in April 2002, four were on how to utilize aid and only one was on the importance of market and private sector for sustainable growth in Afghanistan.[27]

However, the Afghan government and donors could not develop a clear development policy, something which South Korea and Taiwan did, for economic self-reliance and for aid-exit.[28] The government perceived fiscal sustainability a situation when domestic revenue finances the government operating budget. The World Bank also had a similar view about Afghanistan's fiscal sustainability. This assumption seems to have adversely impacted on the government's economic and fiscal policies. The strategies projected that the domestic revenue should fund the entire government operating budget within a decade. However, the increase in security expenditure made this target unrealistic within the projected timeframe.[29] While it is a key step for moving towards fiscal sustainability when the government can fully finance its operating budget, it is not an effective strategy to exit from aid dependency.

Managing aid dependency: a challenge for state building

Unlike the Taliban regime which restricted the activities of development agencies in Afghanistan, the Karzai government opened up the space for them.[30] Donor agencies, multilateral financial institutions, the United Nations (UN) development agencies and international NGOs participated widely in development and state-building efforts. Sixty governmental donors, including forty-seven countries contributing military forces, many international organizations and local NGOs (2,000 in 2004) operated in Afghanistan.[31] Since the number of international actors with diverse and even sometimes conflicting interests rapidly increased, coordination of aid became a major problem which was ultimately exacerbated by the use of off-budget mechanisms, bypassing the state and national systems. Major (bilateral) donors, such as the US and Japan, prepared their own strategies, policies and projects. The UN also had its own reconstruction strategy for the country. Many of these strategies and policies were poorly aligned with Afghanistan's needs and the Afghan government priorities.[32]

The excessive number of donors, their diverse interests in dealing with Afghanistan's problems and the aid modality adopted made aid coordination a daunting task. While in theory each international actor had a distinct role to play in Afghanistan, in practice many overlapping systems emerged. Each donor country sponsored a particular sector and programme. The US took the lead in building the Afghan National Army (ANA); Germany led the development of the Afghan National Police (ANP); Italy, the Justice system; and the UK, counter narcotics. The United Nations Children Fund (UNICEF) was engaged in technically supporting primary and secondary education while Japan became the lead donor for Disarmament, Demobilization and Reintegration (DDR) of illegal armed groups. In the meantime, NATO took the lead in the ISAF. In addition, Provincial Reconstruction Teams (PRTs) of concerned donors followed their military presence in the provinces to deliver basic construction projects such as bridges, schools and clinics for local communities to "win the hearts and minds" of the population.[33] The World Bank and IMF worked closely with the Ministry of Finance and the Central Bank of Afghanistan (*Da Afghanistan Bank*), focusing on public financial management and macroeconomic issues. The UN Special Mission for Afghanistan (UNAMA) assisted and monitored the implementation of the Bonn Agreement and took the diplomatic lead.[34] Russia and India readjusted their aid and policy to the post-Taliban order, as did Iran. The US remained the single most important foreign military and economic actor as it contributed about two-thirds of the total aid to Afghanistan between 2002 and 2010 (see Table 3.1).

In addition, international NGOs and international consulting companies and contractors also participated in a range of activities such as implementing projects and assisting the government. When the interim administration was set up in late 2001, some of the consulting companies such as Adam Smith International (ASI), Bearing Point and Crown Agents were contracted to deliver services which included financial management and procurement.[35] These actors worked directly with different ministries and departments, depending on their types of contracts, expertise and interests.

However, the Afghanistan needs and foreign donors' preferences did not easily match. In some cases, donors had conflicting views on how best to approach the post-2001 Afghanistan situation. For example, Iran, the US, India and Pakistan

Table 3.1 Top 30 donors to Afghanistan (in US$ million), 2002–2010

Rank	Donor	2002–2013 Pledge	2002–2011 Commitment	Total disbursement	2002–2010 On-budget disbursement	Off-budget disbursement	2002–2010 On-budget disbursement (as percentage)	Off-budget disbursement (as percentage)
1	United States of America	56,100	44,356	37,118	2,455	34,663	7	93
2	Japan	7,200	3,152	3,152	900	2,252	29	71
3	Germany	5,029	2,130	762	287	475	38	62
4	European Union/European Commission	3,068	2,883	2,594	774	1,820	30	70
5	United Kingdom	2,897	2,222	2,222	861	1,361	39	61
6	World Bank	2,800	2,137	1,700	1,700	0	100	0
7	Asian Development Bank	2,200	2,269	1,005	955	50	95	5
8	Canada	1,769	1,256	1,256	491	765	39	61
9	India	1,200	1,516	759	0	759	0	100
10	Norway	938	775	636	232	404	36	64
11	Netherlands	864	1,015	1,015	426	589	42	58
12	Italy	753	645	540	212	328	39	61
13	Iran	673	399	377	0	377	0	100
14	Denmark	533	438	438	252	186	58	42
15	Sweden	515	635	635	171	464	27	73
16	Australia	369	744	656	112	544	17	83
17	Spain	308	220	194	84	110	43	57
18	United Nations	305	446	182	2	180	1	99
19	Pakistan	289	5	0	0	0	0	0
20	Saudi Arabia	268	140	103	25	78	24	76
21	China	252	139	58	0	58	0	100
22	Russian Federation	239	151	147	4	143	3	97

23	Switzerland	197	118	102	7	95	7	93
24	Agha Khan Development Network	190	140	140	0	140	0	100
25	Finland	152	160	160	48	112	30	70
26	Turkey	143	213	180	0	180	0	100
27	France	134	323	174	62	112	36	64
28	United Arab Emirates	97	134	117	0.4	117	0	100
29	Islamic Development Bank	87	70	17	17	0	100	0
30	South Korea	85	116	83	6	77	7	93
31	Others	327	305	283	59	224	21	79
	Total	**89,981**	**69,252**	**56,805**	**10,142**	**46,663**	**18**	**82**

Source: Ministry of Finance, 2010[36] and calculation by author

were all providing assistance to Afghanistan, while each had its own views and strategies on such issues as the presence of NATO in Afghanistan and the "war on terror."[37] Pakistan was playing a contradictory role because of its past and ongoing support for the Taliban,[38] undermining security and state-building efforts in Afghanistan.

The ways in which each external actor allowed a project to be delivered had a significant impact on its cost. The construction of a national ring road in Afghanistan is an important example. While this was financed by different donors and implemented through different companies, "[s]tandards for different components of the ring road also differ[ed] from each other, and there [were] major variations in costs."[39] Additionally, projects were often subcontracted many times with each subcontractor taking a percentage of the funds for overhead costs, lowering the benefit to direct beneficiaries.[40] Some like technical assistance projects suffered from poor coordination. In 2007, the World Bank found that "the widespread use of uncoordinated and non-strategically targeted technical assistance is neither fiscally nor politically sustainable."[41]

Donors funded projects that they deemed to be important to individual countries. For example, India financed the construction of a 218 km Zaranj to Delaram highway in 2008, facilitating the movements between Afghanistan and Iran,[42] and built the 220 KV DC transmission line in 2009, bringing power from northern border countries such as Uzbekistan to Afghanistan.[43] These projects were likely to decrease the economic dependency of Afghanistan on Pakistan and help further Afghanistan's relations with India via the Chabahar port of Iran. Pakistan's assistance concentrated on the rehabilitation of the Turkham Jalalabad road, thus facilitating movement between Afghanistan and Pakistan, although Islamabad only delivered less than 2 per cent of its aid committed to Afghanistan between 2002 and 2011.[44] The major portion of the US assistance concentrated on building the security sector and infrastructure. Iranian assistance focused on the infrastructure sector in its border area with Afghanistan (Chapter 6).[45]

The government and foreign donors established multiple coordination mechanisms. In 2006, in addition to internal government and donor coordination structures, at least six types of coordination structures existed. These were 12 Consultative Groups (CGs), six Crosscutting Consultative Groups (CCCGs) and 45 Working Groups (at the technical level), Consultative Groups Standing Committee (CGSC, until 2005) – at the policy level, an External Advisory Group (EAG), three Standing Committees under JCMB (established in 2008) and JCMB (established in 2006) – at the policy level.[46] The government would call these meeting on quarterly basis. The government would organize up to 128 meetings of these bodies annually. Government officials, members of aid agencies, international institutions and civil society organizations would attend the CGs and WGs meetings. JCMB members, the ANDS oversight committee and the Cabinet would further consider the WGs and CGs' recommendations for endorsement.[47]

Although these mechanisms to some extent improved aid coordination, they also had their limits. Most of the time coordination was perceived as more of a process of information sharing than a mechanism for policy adjustment and redirection of resources. Donors would hardly share the details of off-budget expenditures and the concerned challenges.[48] These coordination mechanisms substantially increased the internal communication among the government departments, as they needed to regularly report on their achievements and the government responsiveness to donors.[49] But they could not substitute for the inherent problem of institutional and actors fragmentation in Afghanistan and of incoherence in aid modality, which by large bypassed the Afghan state and some flowed secretly to strongmen and militias. Aid modality thus unintentionally undermined the effectiveness of state-building project.

In addition, discontinuity in some policies and changes in the ministries' leadership largely challenged donor and government relationships. The Ministry of Finance especially suffered in this respect due to changes in its leadership and aid policy. The ministry established some principles for donors' investment in Afghanistan in 2002. These included limiting donors' participation to a maximum of three sectors (unless at least US$30 million was allocated to each sector); channelling of aid on-budget; emphasizing the utilization of the national budget as an instrument of policy making; providing timely information on allocations and disbursements and reporting to the Afghan public. While donor compliance with these principles was weak,[50] they were soon abandoned when Anwar-ul Haq Ahady replaced Ghani as the minister of Finance in the new Cabinet of 2005. Additionally, unlike 2003–2004 the government budget committee[51] did not involve donors in the development budget meetings during budget preparation. Although this approach increased the interaction between the Finance Ministry and other government ministries and departments, abandonment of the requirement for donor's engagement allowed donors to attend the many sectors in which they had an interest. This latter had adverse implication on aid coordination.

Access to foreign aid: a prime focus

With a distorted economy and empty treasury, the government was not able to pay its employees and to finance the reconstruction and stabilization efforts. Access to foreign aid thus became a top agenda for the government. In so doing, the government leadership preoccupied itself with issues concerning advocacy, bargaining, management, reporting and monitoring of aid. In 2002, because of inadequate funding in the government treasury to pay public sector employees' wages, the Minister of Finance had to repeatedly approach donors in order to secure payment for government employees. In doing so, the Minister therefore spent nearly half his time approaching donors rather than focusing on the management of internal issues.[52]

In addition, the government organized ten international conferences from 2001 to 2010 – all in donor countries, except for one in Kabul in 2010, in which the government sought to attract international assistance. Despite the pledges that were made by donors,[53] there was a wide gap between what they promised and the actual amount disbursed. As Table 3.1 demonstrates, a total of US$90 billion in aid was pledged for Afghanistan through these conferences and supplementary promises for the period 2002 to 2013. However, less than two-thirds had been disbursed by 2010. A high priority was given to security, which accounted for 51 per cent of the total aid, while the rest supported development efforts.[54]

The state's dependence on aid and external military support rapidly increased over time. This, in fact, reinforced the historical pattern of building an aid-based rentier state. It "discouraged the state from generating domestic revenue and building local administrative capacity."[55] Despite the growth of domestic revenue collection over time, which started from a very low base, it funded only a small portion of public expenditure because of the rapid increase in the public spending and weakness of the economy and tax system.

In addition, foreign military expenditure was increasing along with the "war on terror" and counterinsurgency activities. By 2010, total foreign military operations in Afghanistan had cost in excess of US$243 billion.[56] The US military expenditure comprised the bulk of it. By the end of June 2010, the US Department of Defense reported that the cumulative total of war-related expenditure for Afghanistan was US$217 billion, including funds appropriated for Afghanistan Security Forces.[57] John Spoko, the Special Inspector General for Afghanistan Reconstruction (SIGAR), reported to the US Congress in July 2014 that, after adjusting for inflation, the US$109 billion the US has appropriated since 2002 to reconstruct Afghanistan exceeds the US$103 billion it committed between 1948 and 1952 for the post-World War recovery of the 16 European countries.[58]

Although aid was necessary for institution building and reconstruction of Afghanistan, the ways in which aid was managed and channelled largely undermined the development of effective institutions and accountability. In particular, among others, the Afghan state weakness, politics of patronage and deficit of skills along ineffective aid modality distinguish the two contexts – Afghanistan and Western Europe – as well as the Marshall Plan aid to that of aid to Afghanistan. Four-fifths of foreign aid was spent through "off-budget" mechanisms which bypassed the state by using parallel systems (Table 3.1). In addition, most of the aid did not reach Afghanistan and also the outflow of aid was significant, which we will discuss later. This type of aid, unlike the classic rentier states, deprived the government of full control over the use of aid and constrained its ability to fully use the aid for patronage.[59]

However, the government still retained some influence, for example, over the granting permission to commence some of the off-budget projects. This situation left the government with limited options to buy off adversaries through foreign aid. Karzai instead largely relied on other tactics. He awarded public offices in exchange for political support from strongmen and troublemakers to stay in and consolidate his power. Some donors, as we will note in Chapter 5, also provided Karzai with concealed cash to distribute it among Afghan influential actors, including the insurgents, in exchange for political support. The US also resorted to using its aid as a means of patronage to buy off some of the commanders and local notables (Chapter 5 and 6). Both Karzai and the US approach contradicted institution building and reinforced a patron-client governance system which was inconsistent with the needs of Afghanistan for a rationalized Weberian state, something what Karzai also promised during his presidential campaign in 2004.[60]

Improving fiscal management

With increases in the degree of aid dependency, not only aid but also aid modality became one of the most important aspects of the discourse in Afghan state building.[61] Before examining aid modality and its effects, the following section assesses fiscal management in Afghanistan.

The Budget Law (1983), the Accounting Manual (date is uncertain), the Control and Audit Regulation (issued under the Budget Law in 1985) and the Procurement Regulations (1977) governed Afghanistan's fiscal affairs.[62] Although these laws provided the basic rules and checks and balances for fiscal management, they were out of date and were not suitable in the existing context. The government thus revised the existing laws or replaced them (see Chapter 4).

Although Afghanistan had two levels of government, central and sub-national which were organized by capital and provinces (including districts and municipalities) respectively, fiscal management and administration remained highly centralized. The central government was legally in charge of major public expenditures such as health and education, and the military. It included 25 ministries, 21 independent directorates and two independent commissions.[63] The institutions were inflated and many of them were designed such that they could offer positions to strongmen or influential actors. Such institutional arrangements resulted in or reinforced duplication and institutional rivalry and undermined services delivery to citizens. Many of the ministers and senior executives by large treated the ministries as patronage networks rather than as impartial administrative units of the state. Senior positions with high illegal returns were also offered in exchange for a single time payment in bribe or a continued commitment to pay the patron. A number of senior positions and ministries were created or maintained to accommodate politicians and strongmen to assure their allegiance.[64] Such pro-politics institutional arrangement did not respond to the developmental needs of the people. In post-2001, the government, for example, assigned three ministries (finance, planning and reconstruction) and an independent government authority, Afghanistan Assistance Coordination Authority (AACA), to coordinate and oversee development planning, aid coordination and reconstruction.[65] An internal assessment (2015) found that the role of state institutions overlapped in 21 areas, including financial audit, procurement and licensing and managing investments.[66]

The government at sub-national level was divided into four levels. The first were the *vulāyats* (provinces), which did not have independent legal authority. These were instead the administrative arms of the central government and included the customs houses and *mūstūfiats* (provincial financial directorates) which were part of the central government institutions and collected revenue on behalf of the central government. The number of *vulāyats* increased to 34 over time. The provincial administration was headed by a *vālī* (governor) directly appointed by the President. The second type was *vulūs'valīs* (districts), which mirrored the structure of the provincial departments (although not all of them). There were approximately 364 *vulūsvalīs* around the country (four to 27 in different provinces).[67] The third and fourth types were the provincial and rural municipalities (*shārvālī vulāyatay* and *shārvālī vulūs 'valī*). There was normally one municipality in each province and district. In some cases, however, rural municipalities did not exist in districts.

Unlike the other provincial administrative units, the municipalities were legally authorized to collect revenue in order to provide limited services such as cleaning and greening.[68] But they exercised little autonomy in budget preparation and execution. The Ministry of Interior (before 2007) and then the Independent Directorate of Local Governance (IDLG) had to approve their *tash 'kīl* (staffing establishment and list of sanctioned posts) and budget.[69] Despite the existence of central and sub-national government structures, the administration and fiscal management remained highly centralized. The provincial and district expenditure was made on behalf of the central government. Conversely, outside the central government, the only limited tax autonomy was at the municipal level for funding its expenditures, while the tax rates were set in Kabul.[70]

The Ministry of Finance was in charge of public financial management. It especially looked after revenue collection and the management and execution of the budget as defined in the Budget Law. It also looked after customs, aid management and payments of the government's bills. The Afghanistan Customs Department (ACD) and the General Presidency of Revenue (GPR) at the ministry were charged with the collection of customs duties and management of customs services. The GPR was in charge of domestic taxation policy, with actual collection being dealt with by the *mūstūfiats*. Post-2001, the Ministry of Finance was also tasked twice to develop the national policies (2003–2005, and after 2009), making it a central institution in Afghanistan's state-building process. This was justified by the fact that the Ministry of Economy which ought to have led the planning process did not have sufficient capacity. This became a major area of ongoing dispute between the two institutions at the technical and cabinet levels.[71]

The government administration thus remained highly centralized and 40 per cent of the civil service workforce was concentrated in Kabul. The ministries and departments in Kabul made most of the appointments, including senior provincial officials.[72] The 2004 Constitution reinforced such type of centralization. Thomas Barfield observes that the Constitution:

> created a government barely distinguishable from the centralized monarchies and dictatorships that had characterised earlier regimes. Similarly, notwithstanding discussions about inclusivity and popular participation, neither were allowed at the local level. Provincial governors, police officials, and even schoolteachers would still be appointed exclusively by the central government in Kabul without consultation.[73]

This type of arrangement unintentionally established a centralized patronage system. Karzai extensively used this system to make political alliances and consolidate his power, especially, by offering senior positions. These positions largely included ministers, deputy ministers and other top appointees in Kabul and provincial governors, district heads, provincial and district police chiefs.[74]

Aid modality: undermining institution building

Donors, as we noted earlier, largely bypassed the Afghan government public financial management systems. They used two mechanisms for funding projects: the on- and off-budgets. Two approaches existed for using the on-budget funding. These included direct funding of programmes administered by the Ministry of Finance or funding through Trust Funds which were administered by the World Bank and UNDP before being channelled into the government treasury. The government also referred to these mechanisms as the "core-budget." The government defined on-budget as "the portion of the national budget that [was] controlled by the government . . . and the government [was] accountable for reporting on the expenditure of these funds."[75] Domestic revenue, Trust Funds such as Afghanistan Reconstruction Trust Fund (ARTF) and Law and Order Trust Fund for Afghanistan (LOTFA), and the grants and loans from the World Bank and the Asian Development Bank were on-budget. Some donors such as Denmark spent 58 per cent of its aid on budget (2002–2010). However, only a small portion of aid which came on-budget was discretionary because donors earmarked the bulk of their aid for specific projects or decided where it was to be spent. For example, of the US$70 billion which the US Congress approved for assistance to Afghanistan since 2001, US$2.1 billion was on-budget, of which only US$46 million or less than 1 per cent was at the discretion of the Afghan government.[76]

Off-budget aid was channelled to projects managed directly by UN agencies, NGOs and private contractors. A great portion of aid by major bilateral donors, like the US and Japan, and humanitarian assistance were spent off-budget.[77] The government called this mechanism an "external budget." Off-budget aid was defined as "the portion of the budget that flow[ed] outside of the government accounts." Donors saw the off-budget aid as a mechanism to substitute for the Afghan government limited capacity and to avoid the risk of waste due to corruption in the Afghan public sector. The government thus neither had fiscal control over and nor considered itself accountable for off-budget expenditure.[78] This aid modality even deprived the Afghan Parliament of its "power of purse" over projects financed off-budget. Even the government, as it occasionally claimed, did not have sufficient information on off-budget expenditure.

> Aid created confusion since we became dependent on aid money, in particular since the government was not involved in spending the money (external budget). When I was a minister, a lady in the US announced a US$5 million by the US government to support Afghan women, in a meeting where Karzai was also present. But later when Karzai asked where the money has gone, we did not get the information where the money has gone.[79]

In addition, the use of off-budget channels for aid minimized the input of the Afghan government and Parliament in the development of state institutions. The Afghan National Army (ANA) is a notable example. The Parliament and the government had little say and oversight on how it was compensated and paid for, as it was mainly funded off-budget by the US.

This type of aid while constraining the government to use aid as patronage, as Ashraf Ghani argued, had adverse impact on state building.[80] As the share of off-budget spending was large, it created a "dual public sector" and drained some of the skilled employees of the government or encouraged the potential employees, who would otherwise join the government, to join this dual or parallel public sector.[81] This was run parallel to, and often in competition with, the state structures.[82] Of the US$57 billion aid disbursed between 2002 and 2010, only US$10.15 billion (18 per cent) was provided through the on-budget (see Table 3.1).[83] It also, as we will note in Chapter 6, largely made the societal actors, who received direct funding from donors, accountable to donors.

However, donors underestimated the capacity which existed in the public sector and neglected the degree of corruption which could result from channelling the significant portion of their aid off-budget. This policy largely undermined continuity in what capacity might have existed in the public administration. Off-budget aid, in the words of McKechnie, contributed to corruption and cronyism in Afghanistan.[84] The US Special Inspector General for Afghanistan Reconstruction (SIGAR) has documented the waste and corruption involved in the US off-budget projects.[85] In 2002, for example, the donors pledged only US$20 million to finance 260,000 civil servants for one year. They, however, provided US$1.8 billion to UN agencies and NGOs for reconstruction efforts in Afghanistan. During this time, the state had representation in all provinces and "a fairly robust and resilient legal system and knowledge of the rules." On the other, while many UN agencies were running programmes inside Afghanistan, no UN agency had a head office inside Afghanistan as they were operating from outside Afghanistan, mainly Islamabad.[86]

Many of the donors, especially the US, Japan and the UN, focused their attention on establishing parallel systems, each having their own procurement, management, reporting and monitoring requirements. Donors were also legally constrained in using on-budget channels. The US Congress, for example, took the view that if control of the US taxpayers' money was given to the recipient country, it would undermine the constitutional fiduciary responsibilities of the Congress.[87] On many occasions, although donors refused to finance a government proposal for funding the construction of public buildings, the UN was able to use the aid funds for constructing and renting elaborate networks of buildings for their offices.[88]

While off-budget spending to some extent fostered project implementation in Afghanistan's rigid fiscal regime, its implications on accountability, institution building and the state–society relations were erosive. "Despite the large volume of aid, most international spending 'on' Afghanistan [was] not spent 'in' Afghanistan, as it [left] the economy through imports, expatriated profits of contractors, and outward remittances."[89]

The local content, when using local goods and services, of on-budget aid is estimated by the World Bank about 70–95 per cent, compared to 10–25 per cent for off-budget aid. On-budget aid, therefore, in addition to a positive impact on state capacity, had a greater economic impact.[90] Aid directly impacted about 6–10 per cent of the working population, most of them short-term (six months). The World Bank estimates that "a US$500 million decline in aid delivered outside Afghanistan's budget could directly affect 11,000–18,000 six-month jobs."[91]

Most of the informants that the author interviewed noted that aid modality was important in the process of state building. For them off-budget aid largely undermined institution building. This type of aid reinforced political and institutional fragmentation. The environment remained contested as to who should control the resources. The government tried to secure a "greater share of external funds [off-budget] and decision rights" which was supported by the World Bank.[92] The donors' claim for limited capacity in government was valid to the extent that the execution rate of the development budget, which the government spent on-budget, was low. Between 2004 and 2010, on average the government spent 43 per cent of its approved development budget.[93]

Government preoccupation with foreign donors

The donor relationship with the Afghan government concentrated first on the "war on terror" and then state building. While the flow of aid to Afghanistan prompted the expansion of basic services, such as education and health and road building, which expanded the state's reach, it, as we noted earlier, created a parallel public sector because of the flow of a greater portion of aid off-budget. Donors unintentionally competed with the government in implementing projects, especially by offering higher wages to their employees.[94] This challenged the building of state permanent institutions.[95]

The government made repeated demands for increases in on-budget funding, but the issue sometimes became politicized, depending on relations between the Afghan government and donors. In 2012, for example, while President Karzai was under increasing donor pressure to reduce widespread corruption within his government, he argued that the nature of the international engagement contributed to violence and corruption. Karzai stated "[t]he bigger corruption is the corruption in contracts. The contracts are not issued by the Afghan government. The contracts are issued by the international community, mainly by the [US]."[96] This highlights a lack of consensus between the government and donors on how to channel aid and shows the level of distrust in government-donor relations regarding aid modality.

Despite the importance of off-budget aid for state building, only the Afghan government and donors debated whether donors should use on-budget or off-budget mechanisms for delivering aid. For the Afghan public and societal actors the main concern was not whether aid was spent on-budget or off-budget, but whether they received benefits from the programmes. No strong reaction from the societal actors, asking for shifts from off-budget funding to on-budget, is recorded. This might be attributed to the fact that the people were not aware of the donor-government relationship and, even if they were so, might have had little confidence in the government due to high levels of corruption and its limited implementation capacity.[97]

Relations at the administration level

Donors in the first years of their engagement in Afghanistan largely neglected to invest in civil administration. But gradually they changed their policy and financed programmes aiming to build the civil administration capacity. However, such attempts were not effective:

> [They] Launched a range of schemes to provide technical assistance and expand [the government] capacity. But those schemes have largely substituted for – rather than built – regular civil service capacity, relying on foreign expertise and, increasingly, on Afghan externally funded staff (EFS), who receive[d] higher salaries than regular civil servants, or top-ups through various government or donor-funded initiatives. Most of these capacity-substituting schemes involve[d] funding channelled outside the budget, fragmenting efforts and reducing transparency about the real cost of running the government and delivering services.[98]

By 2010, the total number of consultants stood at 7,000 (200 international and the rest national) in state civilian ministries and agencies. These were referred as the "second civil service."[99] The number of international consultants working through external budget projects could significantly increase this number but it is hard to confirm them due to lack of data. By comparison with the total number of civil servants, the mentioned number of consultants was small. But they played a most important role in shaping policies and managing implementation processes. In 2007, there were 307,288 public servants of whom 18 per cent were women and only 16 per cent had education above high school, including a small number with bachelors and master's degrees.[100]

The Ministry of Finance managed the on-budget aid and therefore it remained the key institution for Afghan government-donor relations. The Ministry received more international technical assistance than any other civilian government institution and was fundamentally reformed (see Chapters 3, 4 and 5). However, other ministries, such as the Ministry of Border, Tribal and Ethnic Affairs, which focused on domestic issues, attracted little donor support and remained almost undeveloped. This trend shows that institutional development was selectively implemented.

A large number of parallel structures and units were created. Only 35 Project Implementation Units, Grant Management Units, Project Management Units and Project Management Offices were established by donors across the ministries to distribute aid and implement projects.[101] In addition, donors established many parallel structures outside the government departments which are hard to estimate. The second civil service in the absence of adequate capacity helped with management of the implementation process. However, this kind of intervention divided the civil servants into an "ordinary civil service" and a "second civil service." Unlike the former, the latter was recruited on short-term contracts. They were bound to achieve predetermined project outcomes. The second civil service did not have job security and other benefits which the ordinary civil servants had, though very little according to the market value. Hence, the second civil servants would prefer to change their jobs depending on the nature of the contract offered to them.

The consultants, at least in theory, were recruited through a competitive process which was less affected by local politics than was the case with the process of ordinary civil servant recruitment. The national consultants mainly comprised a class of young Afghan professionals with university degrees from inside and outside Afghanistan, who spoke English and were computer literate. National and foreign consultants in some cases reported on a monthly basis on their performance to foreign consulting firms.

Foreign consultants (advisors) had diverse skills and knowledge, although they had only limited understanding of the complex political settings of Afghanistan and limited working experience with government. They mainly came from academies, NGO and aid agency backgrounds. They were engaged in areas such as public financial management, policy development and programme implementation, especially in Kabul.[102] However, the foreign consultants, as a senior government official noted, "were preoccupied with issues concerning donors, including project report writing and exchanging English emails with donors."[103] They had better access to information, sometimes playing the role of intermediary between ministry leaderships, government managers and the donors. The government became more dependent on the consultants over time.[104] Through advisors, donors established a direct relationship with government ministries and departments, although it varied between institutions. Some donors appointed and funded the consultants as well as the projects they worked for, fiscally retaining greater leverage over the second civil service.

In this setting, the ordinary civil servants (especially the older generation) were suspicious of changes in administration and reluctant to pursue reforms. They were acutely aware of the politics of survival and how a reform could disappear along with its creator in the Afghanistan context. A new minister, for example, would come with a new mind-set and a reform package, or a new regime would totally abandon the programmes of its predecessor. The civil servants had learned this from experience under the previous rule of the People's Democratic Party of Afghanistan (PDPA, 1978–1992), the *mujahidin* (1992–1996) and the Taliban (1996–2001).

In addition, the protracted armed conflicts in the country and sudden policy shifts had prevented them from developing skills. As a matter of pragmatism and for the sake of their survival, some of the civil servants had preferred to develop linkages with strongmen and to engage in local rivalries. This compromised their commitment to public service, weakened state institutions and had a negative impact on service delivery.

The emergence of the two elements of civil service eventually affected the integrity of public administration. Although the use of consultants helped to some extent to overcome the problems arising from administrative weakness in the short-run, it discouraged ordinary civil servants who felt marginalized. The second civil servants resented their lower salary and the lack of attention they received in their administrative units. For example, an internal government assessment, which followed a Presidential decree in 2012, found that the dual approach to building the administrative capacity undermined the development of the permanent government structures.[105] Although the government attempted to integrate the consultants into its budget, it was not successful because the civil service law was still too inflexible and there were insufficient on-budget funds to finance them. The inflexibility of the civil service law after 2001 was a major obstacle. "It was so difficult in the public sector to increase the salary from US$60 to above that level – that seemed illegal, while it was legal for the staff to move from a ministry to work with a donor agency and receive US$600 or above that amount."[106]

Relations in regard to senior appointments

Funding more than 90 per cent of the on-and off-budget public expenditure (see Chapter 4), donors were inclined to intervene in senior political appointments made by Karzai. Occasionally, this brought Karzai and Afghanistan's major donors into conflict, especially when Karzai made most of the senior appointments based on prior political commitments and in return for the loyalty of strongmen and commanders. His appointment of governors was highly criticized as most of them did not meet the requirements of the Afghan civil administration and lacked the ability to meet provincial challenges. The fragile situation of Afghanistan might have required appointing the senior government official in a way that would address sensitive political and ethnic issues. But Karzai extensively relied on such an approach which had adverse implications for state building. The Killid Group, a local radio station, reported in 2010, that out of 34 provincial governors, 30 were appointed because of their affiliation with the *mujahidin tanzīms* (organizations), influential politicians and powerbrokers.[107] With this type of appointment, Karzai weakened the state institutions and undermined service delivery. In addition, Karzai often replaced his ministers, creating a sense of instability in the institutions. The Ministry of Finance suffered the most from lack of continuity in its leadership. Between 2001 and 2009, four finance ministers were appointed (Hedayat Amin Arsala, 2002; Ashraf Ghani, 2002–2004; Anwar-ul Haq Ahadi, 2005–2008 and Omar Zakhilwal, 2009–2014). Each minister had a different way of operating and set of priorities. In 2005, because of the change of the Finance Minister, the entire leadership of the ministry left (or resigned) from their positions.[108]

Subsequently, the government and donors agreed on new measures to improve the senior appointment mechanism in January 2006 at the London Conference.

> A clear and transparent national appointments mechanism will be established within 6 months, applied within 12 months and fully implemented within 24 months for all senior level appointments to the central government and the judiciary, as well as for provincial governors, chiefs of police, district administrators and provincial heads of security.[109]

However, progress in establishing a senior national appointments mechanism was slow. Karzai only signed the terms of reference for the senior appointments in April 2008.[110] Western diplomats expressed frustration with Karzai not only in relation to his appointments but also in the way he was managing the appointment process. In 2009, the Guardian reported:

> Karzai is in the habit of getting involved in the appointment of junior officials and relatively lowly [*sic*] [*vulūs 'vals* or district officers] of some of the country's 360 or so districts, rather than spending his time on bigger issues. But while Afghanistan's highly centralized system allows for presidential micro-management it is not very good at delivering services to ordinary Afghans.[111]

The US and Europeans closely watched the senior appointment process. This does not indicate that other foreign actors, especially Afghanistan neighbours, did not have interest. They lobbied and reacted in meetings in response to Karzai's decisions and his exclusion of the so-called "reform minded" ministers from his Cabinet and marginalization of others. In 2005, when Ali Ahmad Jalali, the Interior Minister, resigned, the US, Canadian and UK aid agencies all withdrew their funding from the Afghanistan Stabilization Programme (ASP), led by the Ministry of Interior.[112] Although their decision to terminate the funding was not officially linked with Jalali's resignation, most people believed it was.[113] Moreover, following the vote of no confidence in Foreign Minister R. Dadfar Spanta on May 10, 2007, the US Ambassador, William B. Wood, alerted Yonus Qanoni, speaker of the *wolūsī jirga* (lower house) that Western donors were concerned about the outcome. He stated that:

> He fully respected the Parliament's rights under the Constitution; he also flagged that the removal of the Foreign Minister would increase confusion in the international community regarding Afghanistan at a time when Afghanistan does not need to send any more confusing signals.[114]

Donor-government relations were forged through individuals. As noted earlier, the degree of support by an institution could obtain was largely linked to the credibility of such relations and the donors' priority. This approach polarized leadership and was largely counterproductive. Donor support based on individuals unintentionally set the *mujahidin* leaders and commanders against Afghan expatriate officials. Even Karzai was jokingly calling some of the expatriates "agents of foreigners" in Cabinet meetings, a sensitive expression in Afghanistan to undermine one's credibility.[115] For expatriates who did not have popular support and a power base inside Afghanistan, the donors' backing made them mere technical actors dependent on state institutions which minimized their role in Afghan politics.

Conclusion

Aid dependency post-2001 reinforced the building of a transitional, yet fragmented, rentier state in Afghanistan. However, aid had contradictory effects. On the one hand, aid contributed to economic growth, the promotion of education and the expansion of health services. On the other hand, aid dependency and the nature of the aid produced adverse political pathologies. It created parallel institutions competing with those of the state, as donors spent more than four-fifths of their aid outside the government budget and made the government increasingly accountable to donors.

Therefore, aid and the ways in which the international community participated in the post-2001 period largely shaped the characteristics of the Afghan state. Although aid contributed to the reconstruction of the country and the building of state intuitions, the ways in which aid was delivered and managed resulted in a number of political pathologies. Structural problems in state institutions and the politics of patronage, the complex nature of aid through off-budget mechanisms, and the deficit of coordination between donors had adverse consequences for state building. This situation prompted the government to concentrate its political and administrative efforts on improving government-donor relationships. The government's preoccupation with donors and the politics of patronage made it unable to overcome domestic problems and to foster government accountability.

Notes

1 Transitional Government of Afghanistan, "Securing Afghanistan's Future: Accomplishments and the Strategic Path Forward," (March 2004), 12.
2 Karl Eikenberry, "Former US Ambassador to Afghanistan (2009–2010). Interview by Author, Canberra, 25 October 2011."
3 The states and aid agencies engaged with the government of Afghanistan were generally called the international community.
4 See United Nations Security Council, "Agreement on Provisional Arrangements in Afghanistan Pending the Re-establishment of Permanent Government Institutions," (December 5, 2011); and Asrhaf Ghani et al., "The Budget as the Linchpin of the State," in *Peace and the Public Purse: Economic Policies for Postwar Statebuilding*, ed. James K. Boyce and Madalene O'Donnell (London: Lynne Rienner Publishers, 2007), 155–6.
5 Although Afghanistan already had a Central Bank (Da Afghanistan Bank), the Bonn Agreement envisaged reorganizing it as an independent state organization.
6 Ministry of Justice of Afghanistan, "Qānoni Asāsī Afghanistan," http://moj.gov.af/fa/page/1684.
7 The perception was that the former King Zahir Shah would nominate himself as head of the state. While he to a large extent had the support of some tribal elders (traditional actors), the so called *mujahidin* leaders and the US did not support him.
8 UNHCR, "Human Rights Dimension of Poverty in Afghanistan," (Kabul: UNHCR, 2010), 1–3.
9 World Bank, "Two Decades of Conflict Cost US$240 Billion: Now Afghanistan Will Need US$27.5 Billion to Recover," http://web.worldbank.org/WBSITE/EXTERNAL/NEWS/0,,contentMDK:20186600~menuPK:34463~pagePK:34370~piPK:34424~theSitePK:4607,00.html.
10 Islamic Republic of Afghanistan, "Afghanistan National Development Strategy: An Interim Strategy for Security, Governance, Economic Growth and Povery Reduction," (n.d.), 34. In 2001, the Afghanistan Human Development Index (HDI) rank was 89, the last after Niger. UNDP, *Human Development Report 2001, Making New Technologies Work for Human Development* (New York: Oxford University Press, 2011), 151. In 2002, the 225 members of the constitutional *Loya Jirga* expressed their demands for reconstruction of Afghanistan which (according to estimation by the

Finance Minister) amounted to around US$80 billion. This in comparison to US$240 billion, the cost of destroyed infrastructure as well as the lost opportunities due to the decades of war, did not seem to have been ambitious.

11 World Bank, Context and Prospects for Reform (n.d.), 3.

12 Amin Saikal, Modern Afghanistan: A History of Struggle and Survival (London: I.B. Tauris, 2004), 238.

13 McKechnie, Alastair, Former World Bank Country Director for Afghanistan (2001–2008), Interview by Author, Bethesda, April 17, 2013.

14 World Bank, "World Development Indicators," (2014).

15 USAID, "Afghanistan: Education," www.usaid.gov/afghanistan/education. However, recently it was revealed that the actual number of students attending school is much lower than this number.

16 Paul Collier, "Aid Dependency: A Critique," *Journal of African Economies* 8, no. 4 (1999): 530.

17 Hamid Karzai, "A Vision for Afghanistan: Statement of the Chairman of the Interim Administration of Afghanistan in Tokyo Conference," (Tokyo, January 2002).

18 In July 2002, the World Bank made the development of Poverty Reduction Strategy Paper (PRSP) conditional to low-income countries in order to receive the Word Bank assistance. See World Bank, "Poverty Reduction Strategy Papers," http://web.world bank.org/WBSITE/EXTERNAL/PROJECTS/0,,contentMDK:20120705~menuPK:5155 7~pagePK:41367~piPK:51533~theSitePK:40941,00.html. The Afghanistan National Development Strategy (ANDS) served as the country's PRSP. However, it was more comprehensive than a PRSP that also included measures to improve security and governance.

19 The Bonn Agreement benchmarks were concluded with the opening of the National Assembly in 2005. More than 60 governments and international organizations participated in the London Conference of 2006 and agreed on the Afghanistan Compact. ANDS Secretariat, "The London Conference on Afghanistan: The Afghanistan Compact," (JCMB Secretariat, Kabul 2007).

20 See UNSC, "Report of the Security Council Mission to Afghanistan, 11 to 16 November 2006 (S/2006/935)," (New York: UNSC, December 4, 2006); and ANDS Secretariat, "The London Conference on Afghanistan: The Afghanistan Compact."

21 ANDS and JCMB Secretariat, "Joint Coordination and Monitoring Board (JCMB) Reports," (2006–2008).

22 The London Conference which endorsed the Afghanistan Compact was organized on January 31 and February 1, 2006. The communiqué of the conference was released in the second day of the conference.

23 For details on ANDS consultation at the provincial level, see the Islamic Republic of Afghanistan, "Afghanistan National Development Strategy (ANDS), 1387–1391 (2008–2013)," (Kabul: ANDS Secretariat, n.d.), 17–26.

24 See Maxwell J. Fry, The Afghan Economy: Money, Finance, and the Critical Constraints to Economic Development (Leiden: Brill, 1974), 70.

25 For details, see the Islamic Republic of Afghanistan, "Afghanistan National Development Strategy: An Interim Strategy for Security, Governance, Economic Growth and Poverty Reduction, Summary Report," (Afghanistan National Development Strategy [ANDS] Secretariat, n.d.); Transitional Government of Afghanistan, "Securing Afghanistan's Future: Accomplishments and the Strategic Path Forward"; Islamic Republic of Afghanistan, "Afghanistan National Development Strategy (ANDS), 1387–1391 (2008–2013)"; and "Afghanistan National Development Strategy: An Interim Strategy for Security, Governance, Economic Growth and Poverty Reduction, Summary Report."

26 Islamic Republic of Afghanistan, "Afghanistan National Development Strategy (ANDS), 1387–1391 (2008–2013)," 51.

27 Interim Administration of Afghanistan, "National Development Framework (Draft for Consultation)," (Kabul: Afghanistan Assistance Coordination Authority [AACA], April 2002), 5–6.

28 Nematullah Bizhan, "Continuity, Aid and Revival: State Building in South Korea, Taiwan, Iraq and Afghanistan," (Working Paper 2015/109, the Global Economic Governance Programme, Oxford: University of Oxford, 2015).

29 ANDS projected that by 2012/2013 domestic revenue could fully fund the state's operating budget. However, in 2010, the government and donors agreed to increase the number of Afghan security forces to 352,000 by 2014, replacing the US and the NATO combat forces who planned to leave Afghanistan by 2014. This further delayed the projected target until 2030. See Islamic Republic of Afghanistan, "Afghanistan National Development Strategy (ANDS), 1387–1391 (2008–2013)," 48; Transitional Government of Afghanistan, "Securing Afghanistan's Future: Accomplishments and the Strategic Path Forward," 103; and Government of Islamic Republic of Afghanistan, "Public Finance Framework, Annex 2, Kabul Process: Building Afghanistan from Within," (Kabul, 2011).

30 See Islamic Republic of Afghanistan, "Development Cooperation Report," (Kabul: Ministry of Finance, 2010).

31 Asrti Surhke, *When More Is Less: The International Project in Afghanistan* (London: Hurst and Company, 2011), 1; IRIN, "Afghanistan: Concern at Ministerial Proposal to Dissolve 2,000 NGOs," (December 14, 2004); and ANDS Secretariat, "The London Conference on Afghanistan: The Afghanistan Compact."

32 Clare Lockhart, "The Aid Relationship in Afghanistan: Struggling for Government Leadership," (Oxford Global Economic Governance Programme, Managing Aid Dependency Project, GEG Working Paper, Oxford, 2007), 20–2.

33 See for example Paul Fishstein and Andrew Wilder, "Winning Hearts and Minds? Examining the Relationship between Aid and Security in Afghanistan," (Boston: Feinstein International Center, 2012).

34 Astri Suhrke, ed., *The Dangers of a Tight Embrace: Externally Assisted Statebuilding in Afghanistan*, The Dilemmas of Statebuilding: Confronting the Contradictions of Postwar Peace Operations (London: Taylor and Francis, 2009), 230–1.

35 See Seema Ghani and Nematullah Bizhan, "Contracting out Core Government Functions and Services in Afghanistan," in *Contracting out Government Functions and Services: Emerging Lessons from Post-Conflict and Fragile Situations*, ed. OECD, 97–113, (Paris: OECD, 2009).

36 Islamic Republic of Afghanistan, "Development Cooperation Report," 115, 123.

37 Iran in a number of the multilateral meetings on Afghanistan raised its concern on the presence of NATO and the US forces in Afghanistan by calling them a destabilizing force in the region. Pakistan also in many occasions remained distrustful of Indian growing influence in Afghanistan. Fieldwork Interviews by Author, Kabul, March–August 2011.

38 Dashiel Bennett, "Report: Pakistan Is Supporting the Taliban in Afghanistan," *The Atlantic*, February 1, 2012.

39 Ashraf Ghani and Clare Lockhart, *Fixing Failed States: A Framework for Rebuilding a Fractured World* (New York: Oxford University Press, 2008), 218.

40 Ashraf Ghani, "A Ten-Year Framework for Afghanistan: Executing the Obama Plan and Beyond," (Washington: The Atlantic Council of the United States, 2009), 7–8.

41 World Bank, "Review of Technical Assistance and Capacity Building in Afghanistan: Discussion Paper for the Afghanistan Development Forum," (April 26, 2007), 2.

42 One India News, "India Completes Zaranj-Delaram Highway in Afghanistan," (August 4, 2008).

43 Sachdeva, Gulshan, "Rethinking Reconstruction," *Geopolitics* 1, no. xii (April 2011): 58–60.

44 See Islamic Republic of Afganistan, "Pakistan's Participation in the Construction of Afghanistan: Progress Report," (Kabul: Ministry of Finance, n.d.).

45 See Islamic Republic of Afghanistan, "Development Cooperation Report," 84, 107–8, 117.

46 See ANDS Secretariat, "The London Conference on Afghanistan: The Afghanistan Compact."

47 Islamic Republic of Afghanistan, "Afghanistan National Development Strategy Progress Report 2006/07," (Kabul: ANDS Secretariat, 2007).

48 Fieldwork Interviews by Author.

49 See for example JCMB Secretariat, "Joint Coordination and Monitoring Board, Annual Report, March 2007–March 2008," (Kabul: JCMB Secretariat, 2008).

50 Lockhart, "The Aid Relationship in Afghanistan: Struggling for Government Leadership," 15.

51 The budget committee was chaired by finance minister and the ministers for foreign affairs, planning and reconstructions, and the head of the *tashkīl* (staffing establishment or list of sanctioned posts) of the "Office of Administrative Affairs" were members.

52 See Ghani et al., "The Budget as the Linchpin of the State," 158; and Michael Carnahan et al., *Reforming Fiscal and Economic Management in Afghanistan* (Washington: World Bank, 2004).

53 Islamic Republic of Afghanistan, "Development Cooperation Report," 18–19.

54 See ibid., 31.

55 See for example Suhrke, The Dangers of a Tight Embrace: Externally Assisted Statebuilding in Afghanistan, 15.

56 Lydia Poole, "Afghanistan: Tracking Major Resource Flows, 2002–2010," (Global Humanitarian Assistance, A Development Initiative, January 2011), 2.

57 Amy Belasco, "The Cost of Iraq, Afghanistan, and Other Global War on Terror Operations since 9/11," (Washington: Congressional Research Service, March 29, 2011).

58 SIGAR, "Quarterly Report to the United States Congress," (Arlington: July 30, 2014); and Nematullah Bizhan, "The Limits of U.S. Aid in Afghanistan," *Foreign Policy*, September 4, 2014.

59 For further discussion also see Thomas Barfield, *Afghanistan: A Cultural and Political History* (Princeton: Princeton University Press, 2010), 315.

60 In 2004, Karzai, in his Presidential campaign, promised the continuation of the public administration reforms and proposed a new national programme called "accountability and support to law enforcement" in Afghanistan. See Mūj'tami'ay' Jāmi'ay' Madanī' Afghanistan (Afghanistan Civil Society Forum), *Khat' Mashī Nukhūstīn Nāmzadān-i Riāsat' Jamhūr-i Afghanistan (Afghanistan First Presidential Candidates Manifestos)* (Kabul, 1384 Solār Hijri Calendar [2005]), 30–48.

61 See Ghani et al., "The Budget as the Linchpin of the State"; Islamic Republic of Afghanistan and Baawar Consulting Group, "Joint Evaluation of the Paris Declaration Phase 2," (Kabul: Ministry of Finance and Baawar Consulting Group, 2010); and Fishstein and Wilder, "Winning Hearts and Minds? Examining the Relationship between Aid and Security in Afghanistan."

62 Anne Evans et al., *A Guide to Government in Afghanistan* (Washington: World Bank and the Afghanistan Research and Evaluation Unit, 2004), 22–3.

63 Islamic Republic of Afghanistan, "Da Afghanistan Kalanay," (1388 Solār Hijra Calendar [2009]). In the 1970s, the government had 15 ministries. This number increased to 29 by 2003; however, after the first Presidential election in 2004 the ministries were reduced to 25.

64 Fieldwork Interviews by Author.

65 In 2004, the Ministries of Planning and Reconstruction were merged to form the Ministry of Economy.

66 Government of Afghansitan, "List of Working Overlaps among State Institutions," (n.d.).

67 See Islamic Republic of Afghanistan, *Afghanistan Statistical Yearbook (2007/8)* (Kabul: Central Statistics Organization [CSO], 2008), 5–6. By 2016, the total number of districts in Afghanistan increased to 376 (364 formal districts and 12 temporary districts).

68 Nematullah Bizhan, Emil Ferhat, and Haroon Nayebkhil, "Bringing the State Closer to the People: Deconcentrating Planning and Budgeting in Afghanistan," (Kabul: AREU and GIZ, 2016), 29.
69 See Evans et al., A Guide to Government in Afghanistan, 8, 10; and Carnahan et al., Reforming Fiscal and Economic Management in Afghanistan, 6. See Evans et al., A Guide to Government in Afghanistan, 22–3.
70 For a detailed discussion of fiscal management in Afghanistan, see Evans et al., *A Guide to Government in Afghanistan*, 70. The IMF country report also highlights the fact that fiscal system in Afghanistan was very centralized. See IMF, "Islamic State of Afghanistan: Selected Issues and Statistical Appendix (IMF Country Report No. 05/34)," (Washington: IMF, 2005), 27.
71 A senior government official, Communication by Author, Canberra, August 7, 2011.
72 For details on fiscal centralization, see Evans et al., *A Guide to Government in Afghanistan*, 9; and World Bank, "Governance: Governance in Afghanistan," http://go.worldbank.org/N41DIJDKG0. For discussion on administrative centralization, see World Bank, "Afghanistan-State Building, Sustaining Growth, and Reducing Poverty," (Washington: World Bank 2005), 46.
73 Barfield, Afghanistan: A Cultural and Political History, 7–8.
74 See William Byrd, "Changing Financial Flows During Afghanistan's Transition: The Political Economy Fallout," United States Institute of Peace, Washington, September 11, 2013).
75 Transitional Government of Afghanistan, "Financial Report, 4th Quarter 1380–2nd Quarter 1383 (21 January 2001–20 September 2004)," (Kabul: Ministry of Finance, October 2004), 4.
76 Ministry of Finance of Afghanistan, "Press Release (Clarification of the Special Inspector General for Afghanistan Reconstruction [Sigar] Report)," (Kabul: Media Department, July 26, 2011).
77 Lockhart, "The Aid Relationship in Afghanistan: Struggling for Government Leadership," 20–2.
78 Transitional Government of Afghanistan, "Financial Report, 4th Quarter 1380–2nd Quarter 1383 (21 January 2001–20 September 2004)," 4. Also see Nematullah Bizhan, "Re-Engaging in a Fragmented Context: Development Approaches and Aid Modalities in Afghanistan, 2001–2004," in *Failed, Fragile and Pariah States: Development in Difficult Socio-Political Contexts* ed. Anthony Ware (London: Palgrave, 2014).
79 A Former Afghan Minister, Interview by Author, Kabul, July 17, 2011.
80 Ashraf Ghani, Former Afghan Finance Minister, Interview by Author, Kabul, August 4, 2011.
81 Ghani et al., "The Budget as the Linchpin of the State," 157.
82 See OECD, Do No Harm: International Support for State Building (Paris: OECD, 2009), 15.
83 See Islamic Republic of Afghanistan, "Development Cooperation Report," 25–40.
84 McKechnie, "Senior Research Associate at Oversees Development Institute (ODI) and Former World Bank Country Director for Afghanistan (2001–2008)."
85 For SIGAR reports see www.sigar.mil/. Also see Deb Riechmann and Richard Lardner, "Taliban, Criminals Get $360 Million from US Taxes," Associated Press, www.nbcnews.com/id/44171605/ns/politics/t/taliban-criminals-get-million-us-taxes/#.Ub5K4Zw1d8F.
86 Lockhart, "The Aid Relationship in Afghanistan: Struggling for Government Leadership," 8–11.
87 Michael Dauderstadt and Arne Schildberg, *Dead Ends of Transition: Rentier Economies and Protectorates* (Frankfurt: Campus Verlag, 2006), 34.
88 Lockhart, "The Aid Relationship in Afghanistan: Struggling for Government Leadership," 8–11.
89 World Bank, "Afghanistan in Transition: Looking beyond 2014," (2012), 2.

90 World Bank, "Afghanistan in Transition," 8.
91 World Bank, "Afghanistan in Transition," 2.
92 Ghani et al., "The Budget as the Linchpin of the State," 157.
93 Data from the Ministry of Finance on the core development budget execution rate and calculation by author, 2011.
94 See Toby Poston, "The Battle to Rebuild Afghanistan," *BBC News* February 26, 2006.
95 Mustafa Mastoor, "Deputy Finance Minister," Interview by Author, Kabul, July 4, 2011.
96 RT (Russia Today), "Karzai Blames the US for Afghan Corruption," (December 7, 2012), http://rt.com/usa/news/karzai-us-afghan-president-546/.
97 Fieldwork Interviews by Author, March– August 2011.
98 World Bank, "Afghanistan in Transition: Looking beyond 2014," 12.
99 Ibid., 13; Also see World Bank, "Afghanistan: Building an Effective State, Priorities for Public Administration Reform," (Kabul: AINA Media and Culture Center, 2007), xvi.
100 Islamic Republic of Afghanistan, *Afghanistan Statistical Yearbook (2007/8)*, 10, 15.
101 Commisiun Mu'zaf Ba Artibat' Juz' (14) Mādah Aval' Farmān Shūmārah (45) Mu'rikh 1391/05/05 Mūqam' Riāsat' Jamhūrī Aislāmī Afghanistan, "Gūzarish Commisiun (the Commission Report)," (Kabul: Islamic Republic of Afghanistan n.d.).
102 Between 2007 and 2008, the ANDS oversight committee identified policy, planning, procurement and budgeting as priority areas for capacity building in the public sector. The Joint Coordination and Monitoring Board (JCMB) archive, ANDS Oversight Committee meeting minutes, 2006–2008.
103 An Afghan Deputy Minister, Interview by Author, Kabul, June 26, 2011.
104 An Afghan Deputy Minister.
105 Commisiun Mu'zaf Ba Artibat' Juz' (14) Mādah Aval' Farmān Shūmārah (45) Mu'rikh 1391/05/05 Mūqam' Riāsat' Jamhūrī Aislāmī Afghanistan, "Gūzarish Commisiun (the Commission Report)."
106 Ashraf Ghani, "Former Finance Minister (2002–2004) and a Presidential Candidate (2009), Interview by Author, Kabul, August 4, 2011"; for details also see Poston, "The Battle to Rebuild Afghanistan"; Carnahan et al., *Reforming Fiscal and Economic Management in Afghanistan*, 118; and Tim Bird and Alex Marshall, *Afghanistan: How the West Lost Its Way* (New Haven: Yale University Press, 2011), 120.
107 Malyar Sadiq, "Ra'Zi Taqarur-I Vāli Ha: Gūzarish Vīzha (the Secret of Governors Appointments: Special Report)," (Kabul: The Killid Group, December 9, 2010).
108 When Ashraf Ghani the Finance Minister left the new cabinet, his three deputy ministers, director of budget, treasury, state-owned enterprise and internal audit already had left or resigned from their positions. A senior government official.
109 See ANDS Secretariat, "The London Conference on Afghanistan: The Afghanistan Compact," 7.
110 JCMB Secretariat, "Joint Coordination and Monitoring Board, Annual Report, March 2007–March 2008," 7.
111 Jon Boone, "Hamid Karzai: Too Nice, Too Weak–How West's Own Man Fell out of Favour," *The Guardian* March 23, 2009.
112 See Shahmahmood Miakhel, "The Afghanistan Stabilisation Program (ASP): A National Programme to Improve Security and Governance," (Middle East Institute, June 19, 2012), available at www.mei.edu/content/afghanistan-stabilisation-program-asp-national-program-improve-security-and-governance.
113 Fieldwork Interviews by Author.
114 The US Embassy, "Afghan Parliament Flexes Its Muscules: [Foreign Minister] Spanta Loses No-Confidence Vote, Supreme Court to Review Decision (07kabul1605)," (Kabul: Wikileaks, May 14, 2007).
115 A Senior Government Official, Interview by Author, Kabul, June 11, 2011.

4 Reforms and setbacks

Rebuilding the revenue system

Introduction

The new Afghan government inherited an empty treasury in December 2001. The Afghanistan Interim Administration (December 2001-July 2002) and the subsequent Transitional Government (July 2002-December 2004) did not have adequate income to finance their operational costs and to pay the wages of government employees. The economy was devastated because of a protracted conflict that had been occurring since 1978. Local commanders and strongmen controlled border customs and other provincial revenue sources. Donors were reluctant to fund Afghan government employees' wages and operational costs. Meanwhile, the flow of aid to Afghanistan was uncertain.

The government had to meet annual revenue targets, agreed upon with major foreign donors, to become eligible for certain types of aid. This type of aid conditionality and the need to pay government employees' wages increased pressure on the government to improve the revenue system. In response, the government highly recentralized its revenue collection – to a more extreme degree than in the predecessors' regimes – and reformed the revenue system. The flow of military and economic aid expanded economic activities, which enabled the government to collect more revenue. A great portion of the government revenue derived from customs tariffs. However, domestic revenue financed only a small portion of the government budget, which increased significantly in response to the worsening security situation after 2005.

This chapter argues that aid had mixed impacts on the taxation system. While aid helped to partially reform the taxation system, such efforts were full of inherent contradictions and were limited. Overreliance on customs tariffs, the neglect of politics of taxation to build a fiscal social contract between the state and taxpayers, tax extortions and tax exemptions, among other factors, impeded the building of a unified and effective taxation system to sustain the state-building process.

Donors largely shaped these reforms. The influence of merchants was minimal and *ad hoc*. The domination of the economy by agriculture and an informal sector, tax extortion by Taliban insurgents and militias, and corruption in revenue institutions have further hindered the revenue system. Special tax exemptions to Afghans and to aid-related projects and imports undermined the creation of a harmonized taxation system. The Karzai government could not significantly reduce aid dependency, establish a social contract for taxes and prevent tax extortion and the fragmentation of the tax system.

Chapter 4 explores the taxation effects of aid. It examines the revenue reforms; discusses their complexities and inherent contradictions; and explores how internal pressure, aid conditionality and political incentives shaped the development of the taxation system. The chapter first explores Afghan state revenue sources post-2001 and then discusses the major revenue reforms and setbacks.

State revenue sources

Afghanistan's annual domestic revenue and the share of such revenue as percentage of GDP indicate a weak state capacity and poor economy. The country had a low revenue base and certain tax categories such as excise taxes did not exist. A worsening security situation post-2005 has also exacerbated the revenue system weakness.[1] The revenue collection as a percentage share of GDP remained among the lowest in the world between 2003 and 2009. It was only a third of that collected by low-income countries (7 per cent of GDP compared to 21 per cent) and about half of that of post-conflict countries between 2006 and 2009.[2] Moreover, the reliance of Afghanistan on trade-related taxes was substantial and at least 10 percentage points higher than other comparable countries such as Burundi, Central African Republic, Republic of Congo, Ethiopia, Guinea Bissau, Rwanda and Sierra Leone.[3]

Afghanistan relied on imported goods for its consumption and on taxes collected at borders for a large part of its domestic revenue.[4] These included customs duties, fixed taxes on imports and exports and administrative fees.[5] The revenue system also included income taxes withheld from wages, rents, dividends, interest and royalties.[6] These taxes eased revenue collection.

Domestic revenue and public expenditure increased by the end of decade. Figure 4.1 below shows that domestic revenue rose to 10 per cent of GDP in 2009 from 3 per cent in 2002. Also, public expenditure increased dramatically responding the reconstruction needs and a deteriorating security. The total public expenditure – core-and external-budgets – increased to US$7.6 billion in 2009/10 from US$2.7 billion in 2002/3. Although domestic revenue steadily increased, it did not reach a level sufficient to lessen significantly the degree of aid dependency (Figure 4.1). The government failed to fully finance its operating and development budgets from domestic revenue. Hence, aid on average has financed 45 per cent of the operating budget and 98 per cent of the development budget from 2003 to 2010.[7] If we assess the nature of taxation, as a measure to assess the state capacity, as we discussed in Chapter 1, in that case the Afghan state capacity seems very low. For example, while revenue from personal and corporate income taxes increased, the total personal and corporate income taxes income as share of GDP remained stable at 3 per cent in 2003 and 2009 (see Figure 4.1).

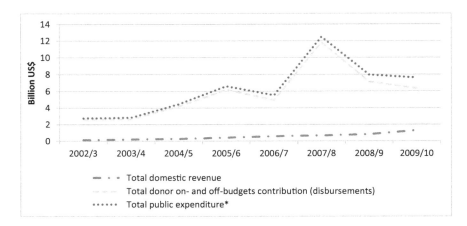

Figure 4.1   Public expenditure, aid and domestic revenue, 2002–2009

Source: See Table 4.1

*Public expenditure is calculated based on annual aid disbursement and domestic revenue allocation. This method provides more precise information than the total budget of a year because often donors' commitments based on formulation of the annual budget were not disbursed and translated into real implementation of projects.

The tax system weakness was multifaceted. Protracted conflict since 1978 as well as political and economic instability have had exacerbated the tax system weakness. The IMF noted in 2004 that the country needed adequate time and comprehensive efforts to realize tax reforms. Some of the IMF recommendations included:

> rewriting tax laws, building institutional structures, developing and executing organizational strategies, designing work processes and information systems, repairing physical infrastructure, strengthening human resource capacity and improving staff conditions, overcoming widespread corruption, and developing relationships with a community that has a weak culture with regard to paying tax. It requires a long-term effort, involving implementation in manageable stages over many years.[8]

A number of factors have undermined revenue mobilization. These were a narrow tax base, associated with a very low level of development, a large informal sector, and dominance of the economy by agriculture (which had suffered from years of drought and conflict), along with a weak tax administration.[9] The opium economy, which was about half of the legal GDP in 2006,[10] further complicated revenue mobilization. The government did not tax the opium business directly. The opium economy instead provided large amounts of revenue to the Taliban insurgents, local strongmen and corrupt officials.

Aiding the revenue reforms

Aid, which on average annually comprised 71 per cent share of gross domestic product (GDP) between 2002 and 2009 (Table 4.1), mainly affected the revenue system in three ways. First, the flow of aid considerably increased public expenditure and private consumption in Afghanistan, thereby contributing to the expansion of taxable activities. It also enhanced the volume of imports because the country was dependent for most of its consumption on imported goods, which resulted in the passage of taxable goods through customs. The availability of such aid-related taxable activities in the economy prompted the government to strengthen its taxation capacity. Military imports, however, by such entities as North Atlantic Treaty Organization (NATO) and the US were exempt from tax.

Second, the Finance Ministry received technical assistance from international monetary fund (IMF), World Bank and bilateral donors to develop new revenue systems and policies.[11] The ministry received 60 foreign advisors – the largest number of international technical assistants by 2011 among the state civilian institutions.[12] The technical assistants included foreign and local consultants. Foreign consultants helped to draft new revenue policies and laws. The national consultants would get the civil servants' input and then translate policies and laws from English into Dari and Pashtu.[13]

The ministry dependence on technical assistance improved the speed of reforms. It, however, created perverse incentives and led to an unintentional neglect of the ordinary civil servants. The ordinary civil servants felt isolated. They remained reluctant to implement the reforms. Especially as they did not see a better career in the long run, nor did they expect better compensation in higher wages or fair opportunities for promotion. Carnahan *et al.* argue:

> The problems of resentment are exacerbated by the fact that most international staff providing technical assistance in the Ministry of Finance have support staff working for them either as translators or for data entry or general office support. These staff are also paid considerably more than the counterparts of the international staff. Anecdotal evidence suggests that the wages paid to the assistants of international staff outstrip the wages paid to senior civil servants well after a country moves out of the post-conflict limelight![14]

Although the reforms aimed to increase the wages of ordinary civil servants, they were implemented ineffectively with a slow pace. President Hamid Karzai ratified the new Civil Servant law only in 2007. This law replaced the 1–12 grades system with a minimum salary of $40 and a maximum of $80 per month by the 1–8 grades system with a minimum salary of $100 and a maximum of $650 per month.[15] A senior Finance Ministry tax official noted:

> Low wages made the revenue and tax departments less attractive for skilled employees. The cases where the applicants aimed to use the expected positions as a way of extracting illegal income are the exception. In such cases, they would even pay bribes and use political pressure to get the position.[16]

Table 4.1 Domestic revenue, foreign aid and public expenditure (in US$ million), 2001–2009

Source of revenue	1380	1381	1382	1383	1384	1385	1386	1387	1388
	2001/2	2002/3	2003/4	2004/5	2005/6	2006/7	2007/8	2008/9	2009/10
Nominal GDP*	—	4,376	4,761	5,706	6,821	8,167	10,410	10,620	12,736
Total domestic revenue	—	**131**	**208**	**268**	**416**	**580**	**673**	**812**	**1290**
Total domestic revenue as % of GDP	—	3	4	5	6	7	6	8	10
Tax revenue	—	—	128	200	283	438	492	612	1046
Tax revenue as % of GDP	—	—	3	4	4	5	5	6	8
Personal income tax	—	—	4	7	10	18	25	39	73
Personal income tax as % of GDP	—	—	0	0	0	0	0	0	1
Corporate income tax	—	—	3	13	43	117	125	128	244
Corporate income tax as % of GDP	—	—	0	0	1	1	1	1	2
Business receipt tax	—	—	6	23	36	48	69	133	250
Business receipt tax as % of GDP	—	—	0	0	1	1	1	1	2
Custom duties	—	—	110	152	190	232	253	281	442
Custom duties as % of GDP	—	—	2	3	3	3	2	3	3
Other taxes	—	—	5	4	4	24	18	31	37
Other taxes as % of GDP	—	—	0	0	0	0	0	0	0
Social Security contributions	—	—	1	7	4	7	8	16	22
Social Security contributions as % of GDP	—	—	0	0	0	0	0	0	0
Non-tax revenue	—	—	78	62	129	135	173	184	222
Non-tax revenue as % of GDP	—	—	2	1	2	2	2	2	2
Total donor on- and off-budgets contribution (disbursements)**	—	**2,614**	**2,615**	**4,170**	**6,182**	**4,931**	**11,789**	**7,133**	**6,319**
Total donor on- and off-budgets contribution as % of GDP	—	60	55	73	91	60	113	67	50
Total public expenditure	—	**2,745**	**2,823**	**4,438**	**6,598**	**5,511**	**1,2462**	**7,945**	**7,609**
Total public expenditure as % of GDP	—	63	59	78	97	67	120	75	60

Source: Ministry of Finance; Fiscal Policy Unit (FPU); Da Afghanistan Bank (Central Bank of Afghanistan) and Central Statistics Organisation (CSO), 2011
Sunley and Gracia, *Afghanistan: Tax Reform-The Next Steps*, 12. * Nominal GDP excludes the illegal economy.
** The data on aid disbursements are used in the table instead of donors' commitments because these show the real expenditure.

The IMF missions seem to have shaped significantly the design of the revenue reforms. They came to Afghanistan on a regular and *ad hoc* basis to assess the revenue system and advise the Afghan government on how to improve it. These missions worked with the Finance Ministry and other relevant institutions such as the *Da Afghanistan Bank* (the Central Bank). They prepared various reports like the IMF Staff Monitored Programme reports and provided the government with specific recommendations on tax and revenue reforms.[17] These mainly laid the foundation for the design of revenue reforms especially because they made available the sole technical analyses and by large focused on universal best practices and on pro-revenue measures.

Finally, aid was conditional on the achievement of the revenue reform agenda agreed upon between the government and key donors. This external accountability to donors put considerable pressure on the government to increase its domestic revenue. The IMF and the Afghan government would agree on annual minimum revenue targets and institutional reforms in the Ministry of Finance to measure the government's compliance with the reforms.[18] This process became a vehicle for shaping the government's revenue efforts. In 2009, under the Afghanistan Reconstruction Trust Fund (ARTF), the World Bank also proposed a 25 per cent Revenue Matching Grant Scheme for four years to provide further incentives for domestic revenue collection.[19]

The Ministry of Finance regarded the minimum revenue targets as maximum.[20] It maintained a good record of compliance with the IMF revenue targets which played a role as a "credibility stamp" for the government to secure the flow of major donor funding, especially through the Trust Funds. Despite improved compliance at the policy level, at the implementation level the reforms barely reached outside the central administration. The government, as a number of tax experts at the Ministry of Finance claimed, paid minimal attention to maximizing its revenue mobilization efforts and lacked a long-term vision to end aid dependency.[21]

Additionally, internal pressures fostered the revenue reforms. The urgency to pay the government employees' wages and salaries compounded the external pressure to boost the tax reforms. The government was acutely aware of the discontent caused when predecessor regimes (the Taliban and *mujahidin*) had failed to pay the civil servants. In the first years after the fall of the Taliban, border customs, which generated the bulk of domestic revenue, was under the control of the regional strongmen. Donors were reluctant to finance the government operating costs. The government was thus under a mounting pressure to pay the civil servants regularly. Already in 2004, disabled and martyrs' families and decommissioned army officers and soldiers had demonstrated in front of the Ministry of Finance near the Presidential Palace, demanding timely payments of their benefits.[22]

The Finance Ministry had limited continuity in the area of revenue reforms because of change in leadership, especially in 2005. In addition officials in Kabul and provinces had little incentive to implement the reforms. Donors, at least in theory, by large used their leverage on the projects and senior public servants, whose wages came directly from donor-funded projects, by linking the reform outputs with the project appraisal.[23] The success of these measures, among others, depended on factors such as the leadership commitment, influence of the Finance Ministry in Kabul and provinces. Furthermore, the donors' influence, the capacity of government departments and will of the ministers and governors, including the incentives and disincentives created by the reforms were all crucial.[24]

Reforming revenue policy and laws

In 2004, the new Constitution redefined the relationship between the government and the legislature in the area of economic management and accountability of the government to the legislature. It obliged the government to report to the legislature the tasks accomplished and the main plans for the new fiscal year (Article 75). However, it significantly limited the power of the legislature to intervene in government financial affairs because the strong presidential system established under the constitution gave little amendment power to the legislature, especially in relation to the budget.[25] The Constitution required the government to submit the state budget and development programmes for the approval of the legislature stating, "[i]f for some reasons the budget is not approved before the beginning of the new fiscal year, the budget of the year before shall be applied pending the passage of the new budget."[26]

The inherited revenue system was out of date and difficult to administer. Tax administration was short of skills. Tax officials poorly assessed the taxpayers and kept the records manually and arbitrarily. Some 113 out-of-date laws and regulations, which regulated taxation, existed. Multiples laws and regulation complicated the system and confused taxpayers and tax collectors. The system was inefficient and costly.[27]

The government revised its revenue policy in 2003 and enacted a new Income Tax Law (2005). A tax manual also followed. These attempts aimed to simplify and modernize the tax system. The Income Tax Law included personal and corporate income taxes and a fixed tax. The latter was applied to businesses usually associated with the informal economy instead of the standard for taxing incomes.[28] To encourage businesses to provide their accounting records to the government, different rates were applied to registered and unregistered businesses. A higher tax rate was levied against businesses with no accounting records, while a lower tax rate was imposed on the ones with partial accounting records.[29] Personal income tax, a progressive tax imposed on incomes derived from salaries and wages, self-employment and investment had a top rate of 20 per cent for high-income earners and smaller rates for low-income earners.[30] The corporate tax rate was also set at 20 per cent, which was relatively low by international standards.[31] Although Afghanistan did not adopt Value Added Tax (VAT) due to weak tax administration, it aimed to implement it by 2014.[32] The Income Tax Law did not make mention of agricultural lands, gardens and livestock taxes; these historically were important sources of domestic revenue (see Chapter 2). It indicated, however, that a separate law would identify them.[33] The Cabinet granted a tax exemption on agricultural lands and gardens between 2001 and 2006 because of continuous drought and the two decades of war which had badly damaged agriculture.[34]

To improve productive investment in Afghanistan, the government pursued a policy of granting tax holidays to temporarily eliminate tax for four years. In 2005, donor pressure led to the elimination of this policy. The IMF argued that corruption and abuse existed in granting tax holidays.[35] It claimed that tax holidays would encourage tax avoidance and short-term investment in the country, and benefit investors with a high rate of return in the country.[36] Under the Income Tax Law of 2002, for instance, the Ministry of Commerce and Industries (MoCI) issued around 6,000 business licences before 2004 and the government subsequently granted tax holidays with little scrutiny. However, of the total tax holidays granted, 40 per cent were granted to unqualified construction companies. Some ministries also arbitrarily granted tax exemptions under "ministerial agreements,"[37] without Ministry of Finance's approval. The Income Tax Law of 2005 also deprived ministries of the right to grant tax exemptions. Instead of tax holidays, the law provided registered enterprises with much improved depreciation conditions so that "for investment undertaken in the year of registration and the subsequent two years such enterprises may write off the cost on a straight-line basis over four years (for buildings) and two years (for other assets)."[38]

The Law, however, did not precisely specify whether tax payment was compulsory or voluntary.[39] The tax officials deemed that tax payment was voluntary and they were not obliged to apply tough measures against tax evaders, especially as it would prove counterproductive for the personal relationship of the tax officials where the culture of tax payment was weak. This made the tax officials less motivated to enforce the evaders.[40] In 2009, the law was amended to emphasize the compulsory nature of tax payments. It stated

> tax is a compulsory payment collected from natural and legal persons in accordance with the provisions of this Law for the purposes of financing of government and social welfare without the taxpayer receiving any direct goods or services from the government.[41]

This provided tax officials with more enforcement power,[42] and added nine additional articles about enforcement, anti-avoidance and tax penalties.[43]

However, the law still remained unclear in some areas, giving tax collectors the discretion to manipulate the system and shift the power "balance" from taxpayer to tax collectors. For example, a major area of dispute concerned the discretion of tax officials to appraise house rental taxes and the shopkeepers' taxable income. Shopkeepers with a lower income often paid higher taxes than those who had a much higher income. This was because the latter were paying bribes to the tax collectors to be appraised lower.[44] This created a sense of unfairness and, in the words of Habiba Sorabi, the governor of Bamyan, a feeling of "why should I pay tax if my neighbour is not paying it?"[45] In addition, the law neither mentioned the obligations of the government to provide better services for taxpayers, nor made provision for obliging the government for increased accountability and transparency in collecting the taxpayers' money. The donors also neglected this issue because they largely focused on increasing the government revenue rather than strengthening revenue transparency.[46]

As a matter of urgency in 2003, new tariff rates were set and the artificial exchange rates were replaced with market ones.[47] Arbitrary use of weight as a measure for the rate of customs duty was replaced by a value-based system. The new tariff rates included a top rate of 16 per cent, while the majority of goods were subject to a tariff rate of 8 per cent or below.[48] A new Public Finance and Expenditure Management Law, earlier known as the Budget Law, was also enacted in 2005, defining the government's role in raising revenue, incurring expenditure, raising loans or issuing guarantees.[49] Accordingly, all revenue and expenditure of state was to be presented on a gross basis. Furthermore, in 2005, a new Customs' Act was enacted, accompanied by a new Customs Code. In 2008, the government indicated in the Afghanistan National Development Strategy (ANDS) that it would consider introducing *zakāt* (an obligatory Islamic tax, one of the five pillars of Islam),[50] to be used to finance social protection programmes, such as preventing malnutrition, but at the end there was neither a public debate on this nor did the government come up with a concrete policy.[51]

Reforming revenue administration

Although the amendment of laws and policies was a lengthy process, some of which were adopted in 2005, administrative reforms started earlier and were funded and technically supported by donors. Important administrative reforms included reorganization of revenue authorities and improvement of the revenue collection process.

The government recentralized revenue collection and allocation. Previously, the loss of revenue from provinces to central government was significant as most of the revenue was spent locally without approval by Kabul through the national budget process. These were Herat, Ningarhar, Balkh and Kandahar. Strongmen like Ismail Khan, Abdul Qadir's family, Atta Muhammad Noor, and Gul Agha Shirzai governed or had extensive influence in these provinces. In August 2003, different bank accounts of the provincial *mūstūfiats* were frozen (see Chapter 3). The government then established two new accounts, for revenue and expenditure. This reform resulted in a significant increase in the flow of income from the provincial customs revenue to Kabul.[52] By 2004, provincial revenues were centralized through the political and legal process.

The expansion of economic activities offered the strongmen to benefit from alternative sources such as private businesses and aid projects. Their presence and the greater political influence in provinces relatively put them in a more advantageous position.[53] The recentralization of revenue was not easy and straightforward, however – an issue which will be discussed later.

In addition, the government prepared a Five-Year Revenue Plan in 2003. The plan emphasized a number of measures to improve revenue collection such as:

> improving clearance times; bringing customs tariff, exchange rates, and valuation in line with internationally accepted practices; enabling remittance of all customs revenues collected in the regions to the central treasury; improving

the key customs infrastructure; reorganizing and rebuilding capacity of the Kabul and regional offices; building a stable and comprehensive legal framework for customs; and establishing effective enforcement controls.[54]

A new deputy minister for revenue, a director general for customs, as well as directors for airport customs and the Kabul customs house were appointed. In addition, most provincial directors of customs were replaced.[55] Each donor funded a specific area of the reforms. For example, USAID supported the reformation of the customs procedures and management, DFID (Department for International Development) provided technical assistance for organizational development and staff trainings[56] and the World Bank assisted the development of the customs physical infrastructure and communication.[57] However, there was a deficit of coordination among government departments and among donors. Donors did not embrace a holistic strategy to strengthen the tax system. They increasingly focused on projects that they funded and deemed priority. Different government institutions, as we will discuss later, suffered from deficit of trust and coordination.

In conjunction with these, the government simplified customs procedures and introduced an internationally recognized document called the "single administrative document." This reform, which was first implemented in Kabul and then replicated in other customs houses, replaced the lengthy and old process of documentation. Earlier, one had to pay US$8 in bribes (almost half of the monthly wage of a public servant) for the "pleasure" of paying a US$2 customs fee. One also had to wait, if lucky, for a week to obtain the twenty signatures required from different departments spread out across the city, as well as filling out some twenty-four pages of documentation.[58]

The relationship between decision makers and clients were redefined to minimize the chances of corruption. The decision makers were separated from clients. Hence, one who needed to apply for a government decision on issues such as clearance of goods in a customs house had to submit the application to someone who could not make a decision. Although this approach could help to keep decision makers separate from clients, the possibility of collusion between the different parties existed.[59]

Capacity building of the revenue and tax department staffs was also prioritized. The development of the Ministry of Finance *tashkīl* was given priority under the Priority Reforms and Restructuring (PRR) programme of the Independent Administrative Reform and Civil Service Commission (IARCSC). This reform had a slow pace and the remuneration offered, in comparison to what the international and donor organizations were offering for their project staff, was low.[60] The ministry largely relied on national and international consultants who were recruited through projects financed by donors.

By 2009, the customs and revenue departments had 750 employees in Kabul recruited by government, and had 27 international advisors and 76 national experts recruited through projects financed by aid, the highest number of any department of the ministry.[61] Yet the revenue and tax departments had weak capacity to collect revenue and to prevent tax extortion. However, increases in the salary of the staff and the replacement of some senior managers, which each Finance Minister argued was necessary for lowering corruption, had minimal impact. The firing and hiring of the tax officials were largely political. Graft, especially in customs, became more serious and systemic.[62] Neither President Karzai nor ministers took firm measures against corruption in customs. Absence of proper oversight mechanisms exacerbated such a problem.

The government established the Large, Medium and Small Taxpayers Offices (LTO, MTO and STO) within the Revenue Directorate of the Ministry of Finance in Kabul in 2004 to enhance revenue collection and improve tax compliance. In 2008, the LTO units were expanded into Herat (which covered 13 large taxpayers), Ningarhar (19 large taxpayers) and Balkh (14 large taxpayers).[63] The LTO covered around 300 large taxpayers and collected about one-third of the total income tax in 2007/8.[64] The MTOs were established first in Kabul and then in Herat, Ningarhar and Balkh by mid-2007, covering around 4,000 taxpayers.[65] The STOs collected taxes from around 130,000 registered taxpayers in 2010, of which 30,000 were small businesses.[66] In 2008, the government established an Inter-Ministerial Revenue Board. Five ministers, the chief economic advisor to President Karzai and revenue and customs department representatives were selected as members of the board. The Chief Executive Officer of the Afghanistan Chamber of Commerce and Industries (ACCI) was also invited to the board as an observer.[67] The board, however, did not function systematically to assess the revenue system, and reports on the conduct of the Board were not accessible to the public.[68]

Improving revenue infrastructure

Even before the armed conflict erupted in 1978, Afghanistan had a poorly developed revenue infrastructure. It lacked proper buildings and modern equipment. Decades of armed conflict had damaged the existing infrastructures and undermined their maintenance. In post-2001 modernization of the customs buildings and equipment was planned. It was included in a Five-Year Plan (2003–2007)[69] with a budget of around US$99.75 million. The World Bank provided US$29.93 million for improving the revenue physical infrastructure at broader stations, inland depots and transit checking-points, and training facilities in Kabul.[70] Some customhouses were equipped and their physical infrastructure renovated and upgraded – as in Tourkham (Ningarhar), Kabul, Tourghundi (Kandahar), Hairatan (Balkh), Sher Khan Bandar (Kunduz), Ghulam Khan (Khost), Islam Qala (Herat) and Nimroz.[71]

The World Bank also funded an Automated System for Customs Data (ASYCUDA) in 2007. This project was first implemented at Kabul Inland Customs Depot (ICD) and was then rolled out to Jalalabad, Herat and Kabul Airport ICDs. By 2010, it was replicated in seven customs houses. The ASYCUDA aimed to tighten controls and remove the human interface in customs transactions, expediting clearance and reducing the opportunities for corruption.[72] According to the Ministry of Finance, the system streamlined customs procedures and improved the management of interactions between traders and customs officials.[73] However, inadequate

Internet bandwidth and lack of customs staff familiarity with English were two challenges which constrained the implementation.[74] Political interference by politicians and influential individuals, including rehiring dismissed staff, undermined modernizing the information technology of customs.[75]

The implementation of the revenue reforms helped to raise substantially the domestic revenue because it started from a very low base. However, they had limits. The reforms were driven by technical considerations. The government did not establish monopoly over revenue collection and failed to prevent tax extortion by a range of sub-state actors. Tax extortion became widespread, especially when the Taliban organized a shadow taxation system in some areas under their influence, something which will be discussed in the next section.

Confrontation and consultation

The state did not conduct systematic bargaining with citizen taxpayers and interest groups. When Karzai government wanted to recentralize revenue collection in the immediate fall of the Taliban regime, it consulted with strongmen, who controlled border customs and provincial revenues, and the business community consisting of a large group of traders who were mainly importing goods to Afghanistan. Despite the fact that, as a number of the fieldwork interviewees argued, there was a strong desire for promotion of a social contract around taxation in Afghanistan, taxpayers were not able to influence tax policies. A businessman put it, "we are happy to pay higher tax in return for public services than filling the coffer of corrupt government officials."[76] Particularly, the income taxpayers were sensitive about how the government was spending their tax money.[77] Their reluctance to press the government collectively, which could potentially enhance accountability, limited their influence.

The absence of a public debate on tax through media further undermined the citizens and government interaction. On the other hand, as income tax contributed a small portion of the total revenue, income taxpayers captured little attention of the government. Between 2003/4 and 2009/10, income and corporate taxes on average consisted of about 4 per cent and 16 per cent of total revenue respectively (see Table 4.1). The reliance of the government on customs revenue by taxing goods indirectly eased the collection of revenue. However, this policy hit the poor hardest and undermined the emergence of a fiscal social contract between the taxpayers and the state because the consumers, who indirectly paid taxes through inflated prices in the market, were not sensitive about how their tax money was spent and were largely unaware of the implications of the government tax policies. Mahmmud Saikal, a political activist and former Deputy Minister of Foreign Affairs, argued "in fact, the proportion of increase in customs revenue comes from the public pockets indirectly, but they do not feel it."[78] A lack of demand for accountability perpetuated the graft in customs during revenue collection.[79]

There was even lack of continuity in government bargaining with business community and strongmen, however. The degree of bargaining had changed according to the balance of power between them and the state and their share of contribution to domestic revenue. When the strongmen had control over provincial revenue, they were increasingly consulted but once the central government's control extended to the provinces, the consultation process eventually waned. The role of businessmen instead increased along with their share of contribution to the domestic revenue.

Revenue collection was complex. The government did not have full control over collection of provincial revenue between (late) 2001 and 2002. Recentralization of revenue collection took place through a complex process that included consultation and imposition of legal rules. Strongmen had control of Herat, Ningarhar, Balkh and Kandahar provinces which generated a greater share of domestic revenue. Provincial revenue was used to finance the local administration wages and for funding of local militias outside of the national budget process. It also, in some cases, funded provincial infrastructure. This process of revenue allocation helped the development of Herat's infrastructure the most because of the high yield of Herat's customs revenue and relative stability that was achieved under Ismail Khan who consolidated his power in the province.

However, provinces with limited income such as Badakhshan and Bamyan suffered from lack of funds and repeatedly failed to pay the wages of local government employees on time or at all.[80] Provincial revenue collection and allocation was not accounted properly to the central government and to the public. Governors and revenue officials easily could use the revenue for personal benefits. Often collusion among governors and *mūstūfīs* (provincial financial directors) was important to ease misappropriation of the revenue.

The government officially recentralized the revenue collection in 2003. This was achieved through a consensus building process rather than imposition of formal rules on the regional strongmen. Karzai asked the government National Security Council (NSC) and then the Cabinet to discuss and build consensus on the need for recentralization of revenue collection and allocation. This, however, could not be done without the compliance of the strongmen and commanders who controlled the provincial revenue. Thus, Karzai called a meeting of the *u'lamā* (Islamic religious scholars) and made his position clear about the centralization of revenue. This put social pressure on the strongmen, and after making a public declaration on centralization of the revenue, Karzai held a four-day meeting of all the provincial governors and commanders (strongmen) to discuss the issue. As a result, they signed off on the policy and subsequently a presidential decree was issued making centralization of revenue a public policy.[81] The donors welcomed this approach because, especially, it would reduce the pressure on donors for funding of government budget by increasing the central government revenue.

The formal rules were constrained, however. First, in some key customs checkpoints a "double booking system" emerged. One was submitted to Kabul, a document recording less revenue than the actual one, while the second one registered the actual revenue but was not officially reported. Second, ten border crossings became points of entry for very large quantities of goods without being recognized as customs posts. This generated revenue for strongmen and their militias in the areas concerned. By the end of the decade the role of strongmen in appropriation of customs revenue was marginalized. It is hard to confirm the exact data on this due to lack of information. Third, at the local level the strongmen were arbitrarily applying different policies, favouring merchants based on diverse considerations. This approach hindered fair competition among the merchants,[82] and resulted in a loss of revenue and deterioration in economic activities.

Customs thus attracted the attention of the government, strongmen and officials, representing a power struggle between them to control customs which generated a greater portion of revenue. Civil society and media in Afghanistan remained critical of customs corruption which acquired a bad reputation. Donors also increasingly stressed the need to reform the customs. Increased control from the Ministry of Finance over customs had minimal impact on preventing corruption and the misconduct. Alliance of some *mūstūfīs* and directors of customs with politicians in Kabul and provincial governors reinforced misuse of revenue in customs. They, therefore, had impunity from prosecution and administrative discipline. A senior advisor to President Karzai informed the author that he found that a number of customs directors made regular financial transfers – and purchased houses in few cases – to their political patrons in Kabul and strongmen in the provinces in 2010.[83]

Despite the fact that provision of effective services and government accountability was important in order to foster businesses, the business community interaction with the government mainly concentrated on customs tariffs.[84] When in 2003 the government introduced the new tariff rates which ranged from 7 per cent to 150 per cent, (including 25 tariff bands), a small but politically influential group of merchants protested against it. They refused to comply with the new tariff rates and ultimately the attempts to implement the new customs tariffs failed.[85] This forced the government to come up with new but lower rates, comprising 6 tariff bands: 2.5 per cent (essential products), 4 per cent and 5 per cent (raw materials and capital goods), 8 per cent (gasoline and diesel fuel), 10 per cent (semi-manufactured goods), and 16 per cent (non-priority).[86] This process delayed the introduction of the new rates until March 21, 2004 (the beginning of the new fiscal year).[87] The new rates were eventually implemented, although there was a minor protest in Khost, which lost special concessions that had been granted under the People's Democratic Party of Afghanistan (PDPA) 1978–1992 regime.[88]

Although the government strengthened ACCI to encourage businesses and promote trade and investment,[89] it failed, as noted earlier, to systematically consult with the business community on tax policies.[90] The ACCI became an independent entity and was reorganized by electing a board of directors. However, it largely remained dominated by major importers and key politicians.[91] In 2004, the Afghanistan International Chamber of Commerce (AICC) was merged with the ACCI. The ACCI represented only 37,000 out of 87,621 businesses and entrepreneurs registered through ACCI, Afghanistan Investment and Support Agency (AISA) and the Ministry of Commerce and Industry (MoCI).[92]

The business class remained fragmented in bargaining with the government. An elected representative of the business community argued that the government used a policy of "divide and rule" in negotiating with influential taxpayers. This undermined transparency and the emergence of a coherent resistance against government tax policies. The government maintained a good relationship with strong and influential large taxpayers, who had the potential to challenge its policies. Even such a relationship was not institutional, rather depending on whom the Finance Minister was or who was influential in the President's Office. This situation enabled a number of businessmen to buy off political support by offering donations to politicians. Kabul Bank, a large private bank, for instance, donated to the election campaign of individual politicians and President Karzai in 2009. It also provided loans to some politicians and regional strongmen, which were not repaid, and invested in dubious projects. Such a mismanagement and abuse resulted in the loss of about US$900 million, the biggest ever in the history of the country.[93]

Failing to enforce tax compliance

Tax compliance remained extremely low.[94] The compliance rate against withholding and business receipt (BRT) tax was below 50 per cent in 2009.[95] Five different but interconnected factors undermined the compliance. These were: a weak culture of the society in paying taxes, ambiguity in tax laws (though updated), widespread corruption, a weak administrative capacity to collect taxes and poor enforcement mechanisms. The government relied on revenue collections in customs and where possible relied on a withholding tax system, and the LTO, MTO and STO to ease the cost of collection to compensate weak tax compliance.

Three groups of taxpayers existed concerning compliance. As noted by a *mūstūfī* (provincial financial director), the first one paid their taxes and complied with the tax policy. The second group wanted to pay their taxes, but they did not have a proper knowledge of the system. The third group included those who did not comply and evaded to pay their taxes, although they were aware of tax laws and policies. The last group mostly consisted of influential individuals.[96]

The compliance also had a cost, however. The people who complied with tax policy sometimes had to carry the burden of the additional cost arising from unfair treatment by tax officials because those who were paying informal fees were treated much better than them. This further discouraged the compliance of otherwise honest taxpayers. Several interviewees noted that on many occasions taxpayers paid an informal fee to receive legal receipts on time, otherwise, they could face irregularities and delays in processing their payments, which could cost them fines and penalties in the event of making late payments. Tax officials behaved aggressively instead of appreciating the taxpayers' contribution. A field interviewee said when he paid his tax dues he felt guilt instead of pride. One of the main reasons behind this was the way in which the tax officials treated him. There was, however, a strong feeling among taxpayers to pay for services. A business community representative argued, "the businessmen just wanted to get rid of the government headache, while they were happy to pay more taxes to contribute for public services instead of filling the pockets of corrupt officials."[97] The informal fee sometimes could surpass the actual tax due. "Sometimes people had to pay twice as much as the actual tax due."[98] It was even noted that a few senior government officials paid informal fees in order to receive the receipts of their tax payments on time.[99]

Low levels of taxpayers' literacy and poor understanding of the taxation system hindered tax compliance. Many small businesses were unable to pay their taxes on time. According to the Ministry of Finance out of some 5,000 taxpayers/clients, almost 70 per cent of them were "illiterate in tax matters."[100] Even in such a context that quality government services were crucial for improving the effectiveness of the taxation system, the government provided poor services and there were:

> arbitrary tax assessments; excessive waiting time when attending the STO; often the need to return multiple times to resolve issues; weeks delay for answers to basic questions about obligations; inappropriate auditing of businesses . . . and significant opportunities for corrupt behaviour in speeding customers assessments and/or inappropriately modifying their tax liabilities.[101]

A daily penalty of Afs1,000 for a business and Afs200 for an individual were imposed for late tax payment. The penalty rate was reduced to Afs500 and Afs100 respectively in 2008. However, this policy did not foster the compliance of businesses.[102] Most businesses preferred to reregister under a different name rather than pay their tax dues and penalties.[103] A high penalty rate and weak enforcement on the one hand, and the incentive to avoid the renewal of the annual business licences on the other, were some reasons to avoid renewal of a business registration.[104]

The large taxpayers acted differently. Private telecommunication companies kept their tax payments up to date, although some others, such as airline companies, had a strong incentive to evade paying their taxes. A major obstacle in this process, as noted from the author's field interviews, was political interference from the President's Office and other senior government officials.[105] In the case of the airline sector, regardless of the efforts by the Ministry of Finance to gain compliance by methods such as garnishing money from airline bank accounts or preventing them from flying, most of the airlines did not pay their taxes regularly.[106] The ministry also cancelled a 10 per cent BRT for the airlines for 2006/7 and the earlier BRT liabilities on condition they kept their tax payments up-to-date. Despite such a concession, the airlines still did not keep their tax payment up to date.[107]

In addition, the local employees of foreign embassies and aid agencies, according to the Afghan government, had a poor compliance. The Ministry of Finance noted in 2011 that the Afghan employees of USAID and the British, German and Canadian Embassies did not pay income tax. While some of the embassies such as the British claimed that it transferred its local employees' income taxes to the Ministry's account, government officials rejected the claim.[108]

Failing to prevent illegal taxation and extortion

The Taliban, local militias, tax collectors and corrupt government officials extracted illegal taxes and informal fees from the people. Illegal taxation and informal fees posed major constraints to state-building process and, especially, building of an effective revenue system. People burdened the cost as extortion and illegal taxation inflated the cost of goods and services. Despite growing evidence of extortion and corruption, the government did not implement measures to stop them. The government was preoccupied with donors and was afraid of confronting the strongmen and corrupt officials who were the main allies of President Karzai.

Foreign experts who helped to design the revenue reforms had limited access outside Kabul to understand the complexities of Afghanistan's revenue system. Because of insecurity, they were hardly able to go outside Kabul and do proper field assessments. The problem of tax extortion has been raised on *ad hoc* manners without proper follow up. Tax extortion was raised by the Ministry of Finance and was discussed in the Cabinet and Economic Council of the ministers without much success to prevent the extortion. A disconnect between the policy makers in Kabul and implementers in provinces further complicated the process. This was especially a major issue in the initial process of the revenue system reforms. Despite the introduction of new tariff rates, for instance, some of the government departments imposed taxes based on the old tax rates. An IMF team found in 2004 that customs and other agencies collected the fees and taxes which had already been legally eliminated:[109]

> In some cases officials do not provide official receipts, particularly for fees and charges that have been officially eliminated with the new tariff. For example, in the North, a 3 per cent extra duty is imposed on gasoline and diesel products over and above 8 per cent duty.[110]

In the early years after the fall of the Taliban, armed groups, military factions and local commanders set up roadblocks in Kabul and some other provinces and demanded taxes.[111] Between US$100 to US$200 per truck was collected as informal fees.[112] The excessive number of tariffs, fees and commissions (which was above 25 by 2005) justified the establishment of several collection points for authorized officials to collect taxes. The tax collectors could keep a share of the taxes for themselves without reporting it.[113]

Some senior officials also used their positions to exact taxes. For example, Gul Agha Shirzai, the governor of Kandahar (2002–2003) and then Ningarhar (2004–2014) imposed a reconstruction levy on trucks. The revenue and expenditure collected through the levy was not reported to the government.[114] Others imposed illegal taxation in the name of government departments and ministries. In 2009, because of the rise of extortion, some businessmen complained to the Parliament. The *wolūsī jirga* (lower house) Commission on the National Economy asked the representatives of the Ministries of Commerce and Industries, Finance, Transport and Interior to prevent the extortion and subsequently sent them an official letter, warning that if the situation continued they would be summoned by the Parliament.[115] However, no record is available if the progress in this area was monitored.

Different government departments needed to cooperate to improve the revenue system but they failed to build trust among themselves and reinforce the building of an effective revenue system. The major institutions included the President's Office which did not provide adequate political support for tax collection and enforcement. Instead, on many occasions, it hindered the process. Afghanistan's politics and taxation were at odds, making politicians reluctant to help build an effective taxation system.[116]

People paid informal fees and bribes on the top of the actual cost of government services. In 2009, a survey by the Asia Foundation found that people most frequently faced corruption as an obligation to pay bribes when:

> [R]eceiving documents (30%), applying for jobs (27%), and dealing with the judiciary/courts (26%). However, around one in five respondents report encountering corruption in receiving public healthcare services (21%), dealing with officials in the municipality (21%), getting admissions to schools or universities (20%), dealing with the ANP (Afghan National Police) (19%) and dealing with state electricity supply (19%) or the customs office (19%).[117]

Except for customs, other institutions were not directly dealing with revenue, while they were funded from domestic revenue. This way people were also indirectly taxed that filled the coffers of corrupt officials. A survey by the United Nations Office on Drugs and Crime in 2009 examined the incidences of bribery and perception of corruption by interviewing 7,600 people from 12 towns and 1,600 villages. This survey found that Afghans paid approximately US$2.5 billion in bribes to access public services.[118] This was equivalent to 23 per cent of the country's legal GDP and almost twice the total annual revenue of the country in the same year (Table 4.1).[119]

The existence of a parallel taxation system was another challenge. The Taliban operated a parallel tax system and imposed in-kind and in-cash tax on businesses and villages, increasing the burden on the people. They had a strong and predictable taxation system in the areas under their control.[120] An official of Afghanistan Peace Council noted that the compliance rate of the local communities was higher with the Taliban's tax policy in comparison to that of the Karzai government because of the fear of the Taliban's harsh punishment.[121]

The Taliban imposed taxes on the opium trade, charged "protection fees" on trucks carrying cargo through the territories under their influence and demanded fees from local businesses, including construction projects financed by donors. In return, the Taliban would not attack the trucks and the projects. The international community and their contracting partners called such type of payments "protection fees" as a matter of convenience. The Taliban also taxed telecommunication companies and, in some cases, the beneficiaries of electricity, and occasionally issued simple receipts to them. Although the Taliban did not provide any services, they were able to cut off services such as electricity or destroy telecommunication towers.[122] Due to a lack of data on the Taliban's revenue, it is hard to make an estimate of their annual tax extortion.

Ambiguity to end aid dependency

Afghan politicians failed to develop a clear vision on how to end aid dependency and ensure a self-reliant state-building process. This could be seen in the manifestos of the first presidential candidates in 2004, which were dominated by the assumption that foreign aid would pay for their development promises. The candidates disregarded the importance of domestic revenue for state building and they anticipated that there would be adequate aid available for this purpose. Although all 18 presidential candidates included ambitious development programmes in their campaign agenda, none of them explicitly mentioned the cost of their programmes and how they would finance them.[123] They mostly ignored the fact that without adequate revenue, whether from domestic or foreign sources, the state could not function.[124]

Most of the taxpayers and tax officials interviewed during the author's fieldwork criticized the Karzai government and the influential politicians for their reluctance to strengthen the tax system. The politicians, especially, were trying to evade paying their taxes where possible.[125] A senior tax official, who worked in the 1970s under Daud Khan's Presidency, compared Daud Khan's government with that of Karzai and claimed that the latter was not an appropriate model for taxpayers:

> When President Daud Khan assessed his salary form to learn how much he had contributed to the government revenue through taxation, he found an error in his tax receipt. He therefore sent a letter to the Minister of Finance and asked him to assess his salary form. The tax officers at the Ministry of Finance found that his tax due was assessed Afs16 less than the exact amount. Though very sceptical of the President's reaction, they included this amount and also charged him Afs3 as a penalty for the late tax payment. Accordingly, the President had to pay Afs19 to the government. The tax officers expected a harsh reaction from the Presidential Palace, but instead they were rewarded, while the officer, who made the error in calculating the President's tax due, was replaced.[126]

While for Karzai and Daud Khan governments aid was an important source of revenue, the leadership commitment in complying with tax policies encouraged tax officials to enforce tax policies and built the confidence of taxpayers. Daud Khan's stand is an important example of how a politicians' commitment to paying their taxes can promote culture of taxation. "When people realise that their leaders pay their [fair share of] taxes and that they are honest, it also encourages them to pay their taxes."[127] For public awareness about taxation, it is therefore necessary to publicize words and actions especially from the top leadership.

The Karzai government failed to encourage taxpayers, especially as people do not know whether top officials had paid their tax dues. The leadership reluctant in promoting culture of taxation also undermined institutional cooperation for implementing tax reforms. Instead, interference by different state oversight and monitoring institutions, such as the Attorney General's Office (AGO), the

Directorate of Intelligence and government auditors, complicated the Finance Ministry's tax efforts. The representatives of these institutions occasionally could threaten tax collectors and force them to work according to their personal will to expedite some cases or block others. The intervention by AGO and police in customs houses was mostly criticized as an impeding factor for revenue collection.[128]

Fragmenting the tax system

Tax exemptions of aid projects complicated the system. A parallel mechanism of tax administration was created which eventually encouraged other actors to seek tax exemption, undermining the establishment of a harmonized system. The tax exemption policy for aid suffered from a lack of consensus between the government and donors. It also shows the limits of donor interest in building a harmonized tax system.

The 2004 Income Tax Law granted tax exemptions to donors, multilateral financial institutions and multilateral organizations, based on their agreement with the Afghan government. Although NGOs were not automatically exempted from tax, they had to meet the requirements established in Article 10 of the law.[129] Tax exemptions for contractors implementing aid programmes had a negative impact on the system. Carnahan *et al.* observe some of the contradictions in the donors' approach in building the tax system:

> the response of most international development partners who insiste[d] that the government of Afghanistan must increase its domestic revenue collection as a condition for the ongoing receipt of assistance [remained a challenge]. Their vehemence in arguing for this [was] only overshadowed by their insistence that the contractors who [were] implementing their aid programmes not be subject to any taxes or duties. In many cases, they also argue[d] that non-development-related businesses also [would] be given generous concessions from taxes – as an encouragement to these firms. This result[ed] in complexity for the tax administration, which [was] already stretched in such a post-conflict setting, and financial losses for the government.[130]

Most of the taxpayers did not understand the complexity of the international aid system and thus exemption of aid projects created a sense of unfairness among them.[131] Especially the sentiment was strong among taxpayers who were working under the same roof but while one had to pay taxes the other did not, depending on their sources of funding (despite having the same qualifications or delivering the same task).[132] The exemption led to a misunderstanding between the Afghan government and donors. The Minister of Finance Anwar-ul Haq Ahadi's letter to USAID in 2005 and subsequent policy notes from the Ministry of Finance show such disagreements. The letter confirmed that the Ministry of Finance would grant USAID tax exemptions based on their earlier agreements (signed between USAID and the Afghan government).[133] The ministry, however, later released a circular which aimed to bring clarity on taxation of NGOs and aid funded projects.[134]

The ministry also issued a press release stating, "all contractors would be subject to tax on their profits," despite whether the contractor was working on a donor-funded contract or not. That is, construction companies performing work in Afghanistan, funded by the World Bank or Asian Development Bank (ADB), would be subject to the Income Tax Law, just as those contractors that provided goods and services to private companies.[135] The circular also reiterated that the Afghan employees of donors and international financial institutions had to pay income tax.[136] The tax exemption policy also indicated that the government would try to "avoid any and all clauses in its agreements with donor countries, international financial institutions, and multilateral organizations that seek to exempt contractors or Afghan individual residents from income tax."[137] Although the exemption policy clarified the Afghan government position, it did not satisfy the donors. A lack of consensus between donors and the government on the exemption policy made compliance of the aid-funded contractors with the tax policy unlikely.

The Finance Ministry issued tax notices to the contractors to pay their taxes. However, the donors resisted and did not allow the contractor to pay their taxes. They argued that as foreign aid was tax exempt, this had to be applied to aid-funded contractors. The government failed to unilaterally enforce the contractors to pay their taxes. This became a source of conflict between the government and donors, especially with USAID which contracted out most of its projects to international contractors.

The problem of expatriate taxation was easier and resolved in three ways. First, the United Nations (UN) was not taxed at all according to its treaty-based exemption. Second, tax exemption with bilateral donors was negotiated separately in order to ensure consistency across tax regimes.[138] Third, in 2005, the World Bank offered an option to the Ministry of Finance on the available funds that they could agree to tax or not. The Ministry chose to tax. While this reduced the funds available to development, the taxable portion ought to be channelled on-budget and would effectively expand the tax base.[139]

The separate rules on taxation placed extra burdens on tax administration and encouraged other taxpayers to lobby for exemption.[140] Goods, while exempt from tax, entered Afghanistan under one category and were sold under another.[141] This undermined fair competition in the market. In 2010, on a daily basis the Department of Tax Exemption had to process around 300 to 350 tax exemption forms (mainly related to aid projects and military imports). Each form was assessed in four stages: when registered; when submitted to the department; when the information was entered into the exemption database; and a final check.[142] It opened up the system to abuse. Although a database was established to track the exemptions granted under the Income Tax Law, it did not record the tax exemptions which President Karzai granted.[143]

The exploitation of the tax exemption system was often reported. In 2011, for example, 184 containers of imported goods (with an estimated value of US$9.2 million) were processed in a customs house under the name of International Security Assistance Forces (ISAF) to be exempted from tax. However, later it was found that the containers did not belong to ISAF; instead, they were intended to be sold in the local market.[144] In addition, organizations which were tax exempt would provide cash called *bakhshishī* (bonus) to customs officers to speed up their work which undermined the provision of fair services to the actual taxpayers. They sometimes gave up to US$300[145] to customs officers encouraging them to quickly and favourably process their goods and documents. This weakened the officers' will to treat fairly clients, especially those who were not exempted from tax and did not make a donation.

Donors argued that if tax was imposed on aid projects it would increase the cost of the projects.[146] Even if aid projects were taxed, they would not have been permanent sources of revenue, as with a decline in the size of aid the state would not only lose its income from foreign aid, but also from projects which were taxed by the government. It, however, could have helped to build the taxation system and allow the government to learn by doing. By taxing aid contractors there would be a long-term benefit of state building by enhancing the taxation system and allowing increased donor pressure on the government for improving the taxation system.

Conclusion

Foreign aid helped to modernize the taxation system and improve revenue collection in Afghanistan, but the efforts were limited, neglecting the politics of taxation and the context that could reinforce state building. The government did not embrace the notion of promoting a fiscal social contract among taxpayers and failed to prevent tax extortion and corruption, while donors constrained the building of a harmonized taxation system. Domestic revenue significantly increased from its low baseline over time; however, it remained dependent on customs and financed only a small portion of government expenditure. Thus, domestic revenue did not substantially reduce aid dependency, given the increases in government expenditures, the poor economy that did not generate sufficient revenue and ineffective government efforts to maximize revenue collection.

The government and donors shaped the taxation system, representing a technical process without systematic input from taxpayers. Provincial actors including commanders and strongmen were consulted regarding the recentralization of revenue, and businessmen were consulted about the changes in tariff rates. There was an absence of systematic consultation and cooperation to improve the revenue system overall. The government responded positively to meeting the annual revenue targets agreed upon with the IMF; however, it failed to use taxation as an instrument of state building and improving public confidence in the state. The government neglected the need to be accountable to the public and taxpayers on how revenue was collected. Corruption and misuse, especially in border customs, and reliance on indirect taxation undermined the emergence of a fiscal social contract that could promote government accountability in the long term.

Not only did donors lack a coherent strategy for strengthening the revenue system, but government leadership had limited commitment. The new tax system was not welcomed by everyone, as it would challenge people who had exploited the old system. Ultimately, the government did not convince taxpayers of the fairness of the system. The growing insecurity eased tax extortion, which reinforced the weakness of the taxation system.

Notes

1 Emil M. Sunley and Borja Gracia, "Afghanistan: Tax Reform – the Next Steps," (IMF, Fiscal Affairs Department, November 2010), 11.
2 Ibid., 13; and World Bank, "Global Development Finance," http://data.worldbank. org/data-catalog/global-financial-development.
3 See Sunley and Gracia, "Afghanistan: Tax Reform – the Next Steps," 13, 15.
4 See ibid., 12.
5 Islamic Republic of Afghanistan, "Policy Directions and Strategies for Sustainable Sources of Revenue for Afghanistan: Official Tax Policy Framework and Revenue System Strategy," (Kabul: Ministry of Finance, 2007), 9.
6 Ibid., 50. The withholding tax system has become an important revenue collection method in developing countries, lowering the cost of tax administration and reducing the chances of tax evasion. Ibid., 48.
7 Islamic Republic of Afghanistan, "Development Cooperation Report," (Kabul: Ministry of Finance, 2010), 103.
8 Russell Krelove and Graham Harrison, "Building a Strong Foundation for Domestic Taxation," (IMF, June 2004), 4.
9 For more information see World Bank, "Afghanistan: Managing Public Finances for Development, Main Report," (World Bank, 2005), 32.
10 The Daily Beast, "A Harvest of Treachery," (January 8, 2006).
11 Michael Carnahan et al., *Reforming Fiscal and Economic Management in Afghanistan* (Washington: World Bank, 2004), 11.
12 World Bank, "Issues and Challenges for Economic Growth and Sustainability in Afghanistan after 2014," (Kabul, July 16, 2011).
13 Only a very small number of civil servants spoke English, such as some of the managers and senior officials mainly recruited through donor-funded projects and government programmes which aimed to build the capacity of the civil service.
14 Carnahan et al., Reforming Fiscal and Economic Management in Afghanistan, 146.
15 UNITAR, "Implementation of the Afghanistan Civil Service New Pay and Grade Reform: Case Study," (n.d.).
16 A senior tax official, Interview by Author, Kabul, June 15, 2011.
17 The IMF Staff Monitored Programme is "an informal and flexible instrument for dialogue between the IMF staff and a member on its economic policies." However, it is not supported by the use of IMF financial resources, nor is it subject to the endorsement of the Executive Board of the IMF. See IMF, "Islamic State of Afghanistan: Letter of Intent, Memorandum of Economic and Financial Policies, and Technical Memorandum of Understanding," (September 6, 2004).
18 See for example Asrhaf Ghani et al., "The Budget as the Linchpin of the State," in *Peace and the Public Purse: Economic Policies for Postwar Statebuilding*, ed. James K. Boyce and Madalene O'Donnell (London: Lynne Rienner, 2007), 162.
19 See ARTF, "ARTF Incentive Program and SY1388 (2009/10) Benchmarks: Memorandum of Understanding," (ARTF, 2009).
20 A senior tax official.
21 Fieldwork Interviews by Author, Kabul, March–August 2011.
22 A senior government official.
23 Donors did not have much direct influence on the contract of senior civil servants if funded by them but they had the discretion to sustain or terminate a project.

24 Fieldwork Interviews by Author.
25 See Islamic Republic of Afghanistan, "The Constitution of Afghanistan," (2004); and Carnahan et al., *Reforming Fiscal and Economic Management in Afghanistan*, 91–2.
26 Islamic Republic of Afghanistan, "The Constitution of Afghanistan," 28.
27 Ghani et al., "The Budget as the Linchpin of the State," 173.
28 Islamic Republic of Afghanistan, "Policy Directions and Strategies for Sustainable Sources of Revenue for Afghanistan: Official Tax Policy Framework and Revenue System Strategy," 36. The government charged between 2 and 3 per cent of fixed taxes on the total cost (including custom duties) on goods imported of licensed businesses and businesses with interim licence and without it respectively. The tax was used as a credit in one's annual income tax assessment. See Islamic Republic of Afganistan, "The Income Tax Law," in *Official Gazette* (Kabul: Ministry of Justice, 2009), Article 68–72.
29 Islamic Republic of Afghanistan, "Policy Directions and Strategies for Sustainable Sources of Revenue for Afghanistan: Official Tax Policy Framework and Revenue System Strategy," 36.
30 Ibid.
31 Steven Symansky et al., "Selected Issues and Statistical Appendix: IMF Country Report No. 06/114," (Washington: IMF, 2006), 29.
32 In 2010, the IMF mission recommended that Afghanistan should implement 10 per cent VAT in 2012 with a high threshold for registration to control for 250 to 400 domestic VAT taxpayers. However, later the implementation date extended to 2014. See Sunley and Gracia, "Afghanistan: Tax Reform – the Next Steps," 7. IMF, "Islamic Republic of Afghanistan: First Review under the Extended Credit Facility Arrangement, Request for Waiver of Nonobservance of a Performance Criterion, Modification of Performance Criteria, and Rephasing of Disbursements," (Washington: IMF 2012), 10.
33 See Islamic Republic of Afghanistan, "The Income Tax Law," in *Official Gazette*, (Kabul: Ministry of Justice 2005), 20.
34 Islamic Republic of Afghanistan, "Policy Directions and Strategies for Sustainable Sources of Revenue for Afghanistan: Official Tax Policy Framework and Revenue System Strategy," 54–6.
35 Symansky et al., "Selected Issues and Statistical Appendix: IMF Country Report No. 06/114," 35.
36 Ibid.
37 Ibid.
38 Emil Sunley, John Isaac, and Thomas Story, "Afghanistan: Tax Reform-Selected Issues," (IMF, 2006), 31. Also, see Islamic Republic of Afghanistan, "The Income Tax Law."
39 Islamic Republic of Afghanistan, "The Income Tax Law."
40 Fieldwork Interviews by Author.
41 Islamic Republic of Afganistan, "The Income Tax Law," 1.
42 A senior tax official.
43 See Islamic Republic of Afganistan, "The Income Tax Law."
44 Fieldwork Interviews by Author.
45 Sorabi, Habiba, Governor of Bamyan, Interview by Author, Kabul, July 17, 2011.
46 Fieldwork Interviews by Author.
47 Carnahan et al., Reforming Fiscal and Economic Management in Afghanistan, 10.
48 Ibid.
49 For details see Islamic Republic of Afghanistan, "Official Gazette (Extraordinary Issue): Public Finance Management and Expenditure Law," (Kabul: Ministry of Justice, June 27, 2005). The law indicates that all revenue and receipts are public assets. These includes taxes, fees, interest received by administrations, dividends, income from sales or leasing of state's property, royalties, fines, grants received by the state,

128 *Post-9/11 state building in Afghanistan*

debt due to the state, money transfers corresponding to credit taken by state and as well as issuance of national and international security.

50 Encyclopedia Britannica. "Zakat." In Encyclopedia Britannica May 7, 2007. Available at www.britannica.com/topic/zakat-Islamic-tax

51 Islamic Republic of Afghanistan, "Afghanistan National Development Strategy (ANDS), 1387–1391 (2008–2013)," (Kabul: ANDS Secretariat, n.d.), 35, 71. The government argued that "the religion of Islam requires all Muslims to support the poor and vulnerable in society [through *zakāt*]. . . ." It asserted that *zakāt* promotes the idea of social solidarity and actively encourages charity and hence creation of a *zakāt* Administration in the government could help to collect donations and redistribute them in an organized manner among the neediest. Ibid., 69.

52 Carnahan et al., *Reforming Fiscal and Economic Management in Afghanistan*, 9; and Yoichiro Ishihara, "Public Expenditure Trends and Fiscal Sustainability," in Working Paper 2 for Afghanistan Public Expenditure Review 2010 Second Generation of Public Expenditure Reform (World Bank and DFID, 2010), 5.

53 Fieldwork Interviews by Author.

54 Carnahan et al., Reforming Fiscal and Economic Management in Afghanistan, 8.

55 Ibid.

56 Gilles Montagnat-Rentier and William E. LeDrew, "Islamic State of Afghanistan: Strategy and Priorities for Customs Administration Modernization," (IMF, 2004), 4.

57 Ibid., 4, 6.

58 Ashraf Ghani and Clare Lockhart, *Fixing Failed States: A Framework for Rebuilding a Fractured World* (New York: Oxford University Press, 2008), 21.

59 Carnahan et al., Reforming Fiscal and Economic Management in Afghanistan, 8–9.

60 A senior tax official-B, Interview by Author, Kabul, May 10, 2011; Sailendra Pattanayak, "Sustainability in PFM Capacity-Building in Post-Conflict Countries-Afghanistan's Experience," Public Financial Management Blog, IMF, http://blog-pfm.imf.org/pfmblog/2009/08/sustainability-in-pfm-capacitybuilding-in-postconflict-countries-afghanistans-experience.html#comment-captcha. Also, see Islamic Republic of Afghanistan, "HRMD Annual Achievements Report 1390," (Kabul: Human Resource Directorate, Ministry of Finance, 1390 [2012]).

61 Islamic Republic of Afganistan, "Technical Assistance Summary Report," (Office of the Deputy Minister for Administration Reform Implementation and Management Unit, Kabul, August 2009), 3.

62 Fieldwork Interviews by Author.

63 Thomas Story, Frank Bosch and Darryn Jenkins, "Afghanistan: Reforming Tax and Customs Administration," (IMF, 2009), 10.

64 Ishihara, "Public Expenditure Trends and Fiscal Sustainability," 5; and Subhan Fahimi, "LTO Strategy for Year 1390," (Director of Large Taxpayers Office [LTO] of Afghanistan's Ministry of Finance, April 2, 2010).

65 Story, "Afghanistan: Reforming Tax and Customs Administration," 10.

66 Harakat, "Current Activities: Featured Project, Small Taxpayers Office Reform Project (November 2010–November 2013)," www.harakat.af/index.php?page=en_Our+Activities. Enterprises paid their taxes through LTO, MTO and STO based on specification of industry, size of business, and profile. The size of business was a major criterion for registration. A business with an annual turnover of Afs75 million (or more) or a capital of Afs150 million was registered under the LTO. However, all telecommunication, airlines, state-owned enterprises (SOEs), foreign owned oil and gas companies, as well as banks, were handled by LTO irrespective of their size of business. For other enterprises, if the size of a business was less than Afs75 million but greater than Afs3 million, it could come under the management of the MTO. STO managed businesses with an annual turnover of less than Afs3 million, or if the original business capital was less than Afs3 million. See Islamic Republic of Afghanistan, "Fact Sheet: Taxpayer Selection Criteria" (Kabul: Ministry of Finance, 2010); and Ishihara, "Public Expenditure Trends and Fiscal Sustainability," 5.

67 Ministry of Finance, "Corrective Actions for Revenue Collection," (Kabul: Revenue Department, n.d.).
68 There is no public record available on how this committee functioned.
69 Montagnat-Rentier and LeDrew, "Islamic State of Afghanistan: Strategy and Priorities for Customs Administration Modernization," 4.
70 Ibid.
71 Story, "Afghanistan: Reforming Tax and Customs Administration," 33.
72 World Bank, "Afghanistan: Modernizing Customs Control," (2009).
73 Story, "Afghanistan: Reforming Tax and Customs Administration," 9; and Islamic Republic of Afghanistan, "Afghanistan National Development Strategy (ANDS), 1387–1391 (2008–2013)," 96.
74 See World Bank, "Afghanistan: Managing Public Finances for Development, Main Report," 57.
75 See World Bank, "Afghanistan: Modernizing Customs Control."
76 Khanjan Alikozai, Deputy Chairman of the Afghanistan Chamber of Commerce and Industries (ACCI), Interview by Author, Kabul, July 6, 2011.
77 Fieldwork Interviews by Author.
78 Mahmoud Saikal, "Former Deputy Foreign Minister (2005–2006)."
79 Fieldwork Interviews by Author.
80 A senior tax expert, Interview by Author, Kabul, May 15, 2011.
81 Ghani et al., "The Budget as the Linchpin of the State," 169; and Mūsharikat Millī Weekly, "Kharj' Jib' Qumandānān Kam Mīshawad," June 1, 2003.
82 See Ghani et al., "The Budget as the Linchpin of the State," 170.
83 Fieldwork Interviews by Author.
84 Islamic Republic of Afghanistan, "Revenues Forgone as a Result of Tax Exemptions in Afghanistan," (Kabul: Ministry of Finance, 2006), 3.
85 Montagnat-Rentier and LeDrew, "Islamic State of Afghanistan: Strategy and Priorities for Customs Administration Modernization," 13. Also for more information see Ghani et al., "The Budget as the Linchpin of the State," 171.
86 Montagnat-Rentier and LeDrew, "Islamic State of Afghanistan: Strategy and Priorities for Customs Administration Modernization," 13.
87 Carnahan et al., *Reforming Fiscal and Economic Management in Afghanistan*, 10; and Ghani et al., "The Budget as the Linchpin of the State," 170–1.
88 Ghani et al., "The Budget as the Linchpin of the State," 171.
89 Afghanistan Chamber of Commerce and Industries (ACCI), "About ACCI: Background," www.acci.org.af/about-us/about-acci.html.
90 US Embassy Kabul, "Duelling Afghan Chamber of Commerce," Wikileaks, http://wikileaks.org/cable/2005/12/05KABUL5118.html.
91 The most influential members of the ACCI were those merchants who were importing goods from neighbouring countries to Afghanistan.
92 As of 2011, 59,815 businesses were registered with ACCI, 8,168 with the Ministry of Commerce and Industries and 19,638 with AISA. Source ACCI (February 21, 2012). Also see Afghanistan Chamber of Commerce and Industries (ACCI), "About ACCI: Background," ACCI, www.acci.org.af/about-us/about-acci.html. ACCI derived its income from membership fees, and its rental properties and donors such as the German Technical Cooperation (GTZ), USAID and DFID.
93 The Kabul Bank audit report (2011). Kabul Bank paid the salaries of the Afghan National Army and Police, which amounted to US$1.5 billion per year. However, frequently the bank delayed these payments to make money through overnight interest rates. A cable which was leaked on February 13, 2010, illustrated that Kabul Bank was "the least liquid bank operating in Afghanistan," constrained in raising cash such that it would take more than two days to process withdrawals. It has also delayed paying government employee salaries by two weeks "in order to place those funds in overnight accounts to collect interest." Under the IMF and the US pressure, the Afghan government dissolved Kabul Bank and put it under Da Afghanistan Bank

receivership. See for details Alissa J. Rubin and James Risen, "Losses at Afghan Bank Could Be $900 Million," *The New York Times* January 30, 2011; and Ernesto Londono, "Afghanistan Officials Agree to Dissolve Kabul Bank under Pressure from US and IMF," *The Washington Post* March 27, 2011.

94 Symansky et al., "Selected Issues and Statistical Appendix: IMF Country Report No. 06/114," 26.
95 Fahimi, "LTO Strategy for Year 1390."
96 A mūstūfī (provincial financial director), Personal Communication with Author, Kabul, April 23, 2011.
97 Alikozai.
98 Rafie Aziz, "Director of Afghan Civil Society Forum (ACSF)."
99 A senior government official.
100 Islamic Republic of Afghanistan, "An Internal Memo on the Client Assistance Option," (Kabul: Afghanistan Revenue Department, 2008).
101 Harakat, "Current Activities: Featured Project, Small Taxpayers Office Reform Project (November 2010–November 2013)."
102 See Ghanizada, "Afghanistan Reduce Penalties for Failure to Pay Taxes," *Khāmah Press* January 2, 2012; and a senior tax expert.
103 Ibid.; Kabir Haqjo, Chief Executive Officer (CEO), Afghanistan Chamber of Commerce and Industries (ACCI), Interview by Author, Kabul, July 11, 2011.
104 The renewal of the annual business licences was conditional on keeping tax dues up to date.
105 Ministry of Finance of Afghanistan, "Tackling Airline's Unpaid Taxes and Fees," (Kabul: Revenue Department, n.d.).
106 Three private airlines (Kam Air, Pamir and Safi) and a state-owned airline (Ariana) did not keep their tax dues up to date.
107 Ministry of Finance of Afghanistan, "Tackling Airline's Unpaid Taxes and Fees."
108 Khalil Noori, "Kashmakashi Afghanistan Wa Safāratkhāna Ha Bar Sari Maliati Karmandān," *BBC Persian* May 23, 2011. The US Embassy recruited the largest number of local staff (1200) among other embassies in Afghanistan who lagged behind to pay their income tax. Ibid.
109 Montagnat-Rentier and LeDrew, "Islamic State of Afghanistan: Strategy and Priorities for Customs Administration Modernization," 14.
110 Ibid. 14.
111 Neamatollah Nojumi, Dyan Mazurana, and Elizabeth Stites, *After the Taliban: Life and Security in Rural Afghanistan* (Lanham: Rowman and Littlefield, 2009), 176–7.
112 Robert Myers, "Tax Collectors, Appendix C," (Ministry of Finance of Afghanistan Archive, August 14, 2005).
113 Ibid.
114 Fieldwork Interviews by Author; ibid.
115 Rāhī Nijāt Daily, "Wolūsī Jirga Dar Tala'Sh Bāraī Kāhish' Akhāzī Ha Az Tājiran: Mūshkil Aqtisād' Afghanistan Bay Qānoni 'Ast (the Lower House Seeks to Address Illegal Extortion: The Economic Problem of Afghanistan Is Absence of the Rule of Law)," *Rahe Nejat Daily* Hamal 31, 1388 *Solār Hijra* Calendar (April 20, 2009).
116 Ashraf Ghani, "Former Finance Minister (2002–2004) and a Presidential Candidate (2009)."
117 The Asia Foundation, *Afghanistan in 2009: A Survey of Afghan People* (Kabul: The Asia Foundation, 2009), 71.
118 UNODC, "Corruption in Afghanistan: Bribery as Reported by the Victims," (2010).
119 Ibid., 9.
120 See David Kilcullen, *Counterinsurgency* (New York: Oxford University Press, 2010), 61.
121 An Advisor to the High Peace Council Secretariat, Communication by Author, Kabul, June 30, 2011.

122 Ibid., also for details see *Tolo News*, "Taliban Destroy 7 Communication Antennas in Helmand," (March 29, 2011); and Journeyman Pictures, *A Decaying State, Afghanistan (a Documentary Film)* (Journeyman Pictures).

123 For details see Mūj'tami'ay' Jāmi'ay' Madanī' Afghanistan (Afghanistan Civil Society Forum), *Khat' Mashī Nukhūstīn Nāmzadān-I Riāsat' Jamhūr-I Afghanistan (Afghanistan First Presidential Candidates Manifestos)* (Kabul, 1384 *Solār Hijri* Calendar [2005]). Among the Presidential Candidates, only eight of the candidates briefly mentioned foreign aid and tax revenue as potential sources of income to pursue their goals. However, these statements were vague and no more than a few paragraphs, lacking a clear picture of how they would finance their programmes after being elected. Among them, Latif Pedram highlighted the need for the reform of the tax system; Hamid Karzai emphasized the centralization of domestic revenue; Ahmad Shah Ahmadzai emphasized both centralization of domestic revenue and finding new sources of revenue; and Ibrahim Rashid mentioned the realization of changes in Afghanistan through foreign aid and extraction of natural resources. Yonus Qanoni's agenda highlighted further attention to the state's revenue and proper use of foreign aid. Masouda Jalal mentioned a fiscal policy of self-sufficiency in her campaign by finding new sources of revenue and relying more on direct taxation; while another presidential candidate, Abdul Hadi Dabir promised that he would create a unified custom system and would gradually increase taxes. Ibid.

124 Ibid., 1–29, 30–48, 238–53, 332–8, 39–63, 64–89, 90–407.

125 A senior tax expert, Interview by Author, Kabul, May 15, 2011.

126 Although Daud Khan during his term as prime minister did not much focus on building the tax capacity of the state, during his presidency he initiated some reforms to improve his government domestic revenue base. Ibid.

127 A senior tax expert.

128 A government tax expert, Interview by Author, Kabul, May 10, 2011.

129 Ministry of Finance of Afghanistan, "Ministerial Circular: Tax Exemption Policy for Donor Countries, International Financial Institutions, Non-Governmental Organizations, and Their Contractors Operating within Afghanistan," (Kabul: Revenue Department, n.d.), 2. The revised Income Tax Law in 2009 also provided similar provisions. Islamic Republic of Afganistan, "The Income Tax Law."

130 Carnahan et al., *Reforming Fiscal and Economic Management in Afghanistan*, 12. For example, in 2003/4(1382), due to concessions to international development partners the revenue loss was estimated as high as US$200 million. Ibid.

131 Fieldwork Interviews by Author.

132 Ibid.

133 In 2005, the Minister of Finance instructed the Revenue Department to apply the interpretation of the 1951 treaty between the US government and Royal Government of Afghanistan for the "Strategic Grant Agreement" which was signed in 2005. He stated "the Ministry of Finance's position is that, until the 1951 Treaty [Technical Cooperation Agreement] is renegotiated, the 1951 Treaty applies to all taxes and duties imposed by the Afghan national or local government. In particular, the 1951 Treaty does apply to exempt taxpayers from income tax and business receipt tax if they are using funds, materials, and equipment in Afghanistan pursuant to a USAID-funded project." Ministry of Finance, "Proposal for Clarification of Tax and Duties of the Usaid under Technical Cooperation Agreement of 1951," (Kabul: Director General of LTO (Large Taxpayers Office), 2005).

134 Islamic Republic of Afghanistan, "Ministerial Circular: Tax Exemption Policy for Donor Countries, International Financial Institutions, Non-Governmental Organizations, and Their Contractors Operating within Afghanistan," (Kabul: Ministry of Finance, n.d.).

135 Islamic Republic of Afghanistan, "Ministry of Finance Releases New Circular Regarding the Taxation of NGOs and Donor-Funded Projects," (Kabul: Ministry of Finance Archive, n.d.).

136 Ministry of Finance of Afghanistan, "Ministerial Circular: Tax Exemption Policy for Donor Countries, International Financial Institutions, Non-Governmental Organizations, and Their Contractors Operating within Afghanistan."
137 Ibid., 6.
138 OECD, Do No Harm: International Support for State Building (Paris: OECD, 2009), 106.
139 Ibid.
140 Ghani et al., "The Budget as the Linchpin of the State," 174.
141 A government tax expert.
142 In 1389 (2010/11), the tax exemption department processed about 82,000 exemption forms, mostly belonged to the military imports and aid projects. A government revenue official, Interview by Author, Kabul, May 4, 2011.
143 A foreign tax advisor, Ministry of Finance, Interview by Author, Kabul, June 12, 2011.
144 A government revenue department official, Interview by Author, May 4, 2011.
145 Ibid.
146 Fieldwork Interviews by Author.

5 Budget spending

Fiscal fragmentation and patronage

Introduction

Another important aspect of post-2001 state building in Afghanistan included public spending and transparency. Although the Karzai government after 2001 became fiscally more open than its predecessors, the overall budget was divided between on- and off-budget items and suffered from poor transparency, and cash transfers to strongmen and the President Office remained secret. While off-budget aid constrained the government in spending aid funds on patronage, the government resorted to other means, such as offering senior positions and spending some domestic revenue on patronage. Although donors demanded increasing openness from the government, very little information about off-budget spending was made public. As such, fragmentation in fiscal management and poor transparency severely undermined the Afghans' perception of the credibility of the Afghan state and of donors.

This chapter examines the government budgetary process and budget transparency and explores whether the government and foreign donors adequately informed Afghan citizens of their fiscal activities. The chapter first examines budget reforms and transparency and then explores the degree of transparency in on- and off-budget spending.

Some improvements in government budget transparency

As Afghanistan emerged out of the devastating conflict after 2001, the government largely focused on implementing budget reforms and building state institutions until 2004. The citizen's engagement, however, in the budget process was not a priority at this stage. This situation slightly improved after 2005 when Parliament was elected.

While budgets included operating and development components, the division across on- and off-budgets had critical impact on fiscal management and transparency. After 2001, the budget process and laws were reformed to improve fiduciary control of the financial management system. However, the fragmentation in the budget structure undermined budget transparency towards the Afghan citizens. The government budget (on-budget) did not comprehensively represent overall public expenditure – though off-budget projects titles and total budget were included in it and referred to as "national budget" – because the greater amount of aid was spent outside the government budget. Even some on-budget items, such as the President's special fund and *dasterkhvān pūli* (table money or business allowance), remained underreported to the Afghan Parliament.

Overall, the flow of foreign aid to the government budget had a positive impact. By conditioning their aid on on-budget reforms, donors pressed the government to improve the budget process and produce comprehensive budgetary documents which donors and the Afghan policy makers needed. Despite some major improvement, overall budget transparency in Afghanistan was one of the lowest in the world in 2008 according to the Open Budget Survey, an independent measure of budget transparency and accountability around the world.[1] Among the 85 countries surveyed, Afghanistan scored 8 out of 100 where a higher score indicates greater budget transparency.[2]

To meet one of the main preconditions to receive on-budget aid, it was imperative for the government to develop a complete and realistic annual budget based on international standards.[3] In 2004, for example, the International Monetary Fund (IMF) explicitly advised the Afghan government to improve its budget legal and institutional frameworks, budget preparation and execution processes. Donors such as the Japan, Canada, Germany, DFID and UNDP financed and provided technical assistance to the government to reform the budget process and develop new laws.[4]

Between 2002 and 2005, the Ministry of Finance implemented a policy of no deficit funding of the budget. It also largely verified the actual number of government employees, established a Donor Assistance Database, outsourced procurement of development projects to an international company (Crown Agents) and then established an independent procurement unit (Afghanistan Reconstruction and Development Services), under the Ministry of Economy in 2003. Finally, it adopted a new budget law (Public Finance and Expenditure Management Law). It also kept the Cabinet up to date on the fiscal conditions of the country, while some information was made public through the Ministry of Finance's website.[5]

The budget reforms, however, largely concentrated on internal documentation to improve fiduciary control and provide access of donors and Afghan policy makers to relevant data, thus promoting horizontal accountability. The reforms were conducive to budget transparency by improving internal budget procedures.[6] This approach was imperative for institution building in the first years after the fall of the Taliban regime. The World Bank and IMF support also concentrated on the fiduciary control of financial management and increasing role of the executive.[7] This approach, as Sediq Ahmad Osmani, a member of the Budget Committee of the Lower House, noted, created an imbalance in capacity between the executive and the Parliament after 2005. Osmani argues that unlike the generous support given to improving the executive's analytical capacity,[8] donors neglected the Parliament's request for support and provided it with minimal technical assistance.

Because of dependence on aid for its day-to-day operations and development expenditure, the government became preoccupied with winning the confidence of donors. Thus, it was fiscally more transparent and accountable to donors than to its citizens, who did not have equal access to financial information. Thus, to borrow from a donor agency official, this type of arrangement created a situation whereby the government treated the Afghan legislature and citizens as second-class citizens.[9] It was also evident that when international organizations and the media demanded information from the government, they would get detailed information in a timely manner, but this was not the case if local organizations and media would make a similar demand.[10]

As a result of the reforms, the budget process improved after starting from a very low base. The Ministry of Finance already established a good reputation among the donors and, to some extent, the public.[11] However, the state of budget transparency to the public was not monitored against firm measures until 2008. In 2008, Afghanistan for the first time was included in the Open Budget Survey. The survey analyzed 123 observable features of the budget in Afghanistan. The measures included the frequency with which the government disclosed its budget documents, the comprehensiveness of the documents, and the role played by government auditors.[12] As shown in Table 5.1, the survey found that although the Afghan government was producing most of the necessary budget documents, it

Table 5.1 Availability of key budget documents, 2008

Budget documents	Status	Availability to public	Comment
Pre-budget statement	Prepared	No	
Executive's budget	Not Prepared	No	It was not made public prior to legislature approval and lacked important details.
Citizens budget	Not Prepared	No	A summary of the national budget to reach and be understood by public.
Enacted budget	Prepared	Yes	It was difficult to assess budget performance once the fiscal year was over.
In-year reports	Prepared	Yes	It lacked important details.
Mid-year Review	Prepared	Yes	Did not provide very detailed information.
Year-end Reports	Prepared	No	Although this provided information about what was budgeted and what was implemented, it lacked explanation about these differences.
Audit report	Prepared	No	The government did not provide information if audit report recommendations were implemented.

Source: International Budget Partnership (IBP), Afghanistan: Open Budget Index 2008

made public very little budgetary information during the year.[13] Out of the eight key budget documents, only the enacted budget, the mid-year budget review, the year-end report and the in-year reports were made public through the Ministry of Finance's website.[14] Although the survey suffered from a number of contextual shortcomings, it established a credible baseline to measure budget transparency in Afghanistan. For example, the survey concentrated on on-budget and measured the dissemination of the budgetary information through the Ministry of Finance website. It neglected Afghanistan's reality such as a low level of literacy (about 28 per cent)[15] and existence of very small number of computer literate people.[16] In addition, it did not assess off-budget transparency.

The Open Budget Survey finding impaired the reputation of the Ministry of Finance among donors and therefore the ministry implemented some measures to improve its budget transparency. The Open Budget Survey had already provided a simple and easy strategy for improving budget transparency, as well as a means of assessing progress. The government identified the budget documents, which it had to publish, and the key deadlines for making them public. It also improved the content of these documents, and established an internal monitoring process at the Ministry of Finance.[17] Thereafter, Afghanistan made important progress in increasing its budget transparency as measured by the increase in its Open Budget Index[18] score from 8 in 2008 to 21 in 2010. Yet the score was below the average.[19] Overall, access to detailed budget information regarding the government's progress in carrying out a particular project or activity, especially at the local level, was limited.[20] The absence of a Law on Access to Information reinforced the situation.[21] Because of this and a culture of secrecy which existed among public servants, government officials had discretion over whether to make information public or not. They were not legally obliged to do so. This situation made it hard for the public to participate in the budget process and hold the government to account for management of the public money.[22]

In addition, the mining sector was even less transparent but the Open Budget Survey did not focus on it. The Resource Governance Index which measures transparency and accountability in the oil, gas and mining sectors among 85 countries, in 2013 rated Afghanistan as failing in overall resource governance.[23] In 2009, the Afghan government committed to implementing the Extractive Industries Transparency Initiative (EITI).[24] The Ministry of Mines and Petroleum (MoMP) disclosed 200 contracts in 2012 which had been signed earlier.[25] However, despite these late developments, the sector lagged behind in transparency between 2001 and 2009. Information was not disclosed on the bidding process, while the mining contracts were kept out of public scrutiny. This contributed to a lack of trust in the government. The social impact projects, which the mining companies would finance based on their contractual agreement, were also negotiated outside the government budget between the government and the companies with no involvement of the people concerned.[26] This type of bargaining deprived the Parliament of the opportunity to engage in approval and oversight of the projects as well as the public to enter into a political dialogue.

The citizens' role

The public was not well aware of the budget process and the complex international aid system. However, as many of the interviewees observed, the public were acutely aware of the fact that a project could severely affect their lives. They were therefore motivated to engage in monitoring the outcomes.[27] Moreover, widespread corruption made the public intensely suspicious of fiscal management in Afghanistan and aware of the need for fiscal transparency.[28] However, they did not have access to information such as project budgets and performance reports to hold implementers and local government to account. This was exacerbated by the absence of consolidated provincial budgets and the lack of details on provincial projects in the national budget.[29]

The government's aid dependency and how it dealt with donors further constrained the timely availability of fiscal information to the Afghan public and media. The government prepared budget documents in English so it could easily bargain with donors. Once they were finalized they had to be translated in Dari and Pashtu.[30] Provincial budgets did not exist; the public were not able to track the budget of a school or clinic or to hold the local government to account.[31] Even an audit report, which was made public only in 2009, lacked important details and focused mainly on the central government financial statements, neglecting the local implementation.[32] Lack of transparency in large project contracts, especially in the areas of construction and security, increased the vulnerability of these projects to corruption,[33] undermining the credibility of the governance system.

In this context, the beneficiaries of projects and government services had little chance to raise their voice and shape government and donor policies. Even though Provincial Councils were elected in 2005, they did not have the right to decide on local priorities or approve the provincial budgets. Nor did they have a clear mandate to approve or disapprove the provincial appointments. These were the sole responsibility of the executive, especially in Kabul. The Constitution and the Provincial Councils Law envisaged an advisory role for them in dealing with local authorities.[34] Article 139 of the Constitution states:

> The provincial council takes part in securing the developmental targets of the state and improving its affairs in a way stated in the law, and gives advice on important issues falling within the domain of the province. Provincial councils perform their duties in cooperation with the provincial administration.[35]

While the provincial council's roles and responsibilities remained unclear concerning powers and resources,[36] the Karzai government also postponed the District Council elections, which ought to happen in 2010.[37] The absence of District Councils undermined the completion of the *Loya Jirga*[38] which was defined as the highest manifestation of the people of Afghanistan in the Constitution, and deprived them of the opportunity to decide on major national issues.

Some NGOs such as the Afghanistan Integrity Watch[39] became increasingly active to promote transparency. Others took a role to coordinate civil society organizations, such as the Afghan Civil Society Forum Organization to advocate for a greater role for the civil society in Afghanistan.[40] They organized public meetings and conferences, initiated policy dialogues and prepared advocacy papers. These activities, however, were focused on major urban centres and remained dependent on donors for funding. The CSOs and NGOs like the Afghanistan Integrity Watch with better organization capacity and awareness of the budget process, which focused on targeted areas, made an important contribution to lobbying for greater budget transparency.

The media and public discontent against corruption in project implementation, service delivery, and poor performance of the government pressed Karzai to take some measures to increase government transparency. The media and public became "vocal critics of the government and its lack of commitment in fighting corruption."[41] In 2005, in order to address these complaints, President Karzai created "accountability week" – a week in November every year during which members of the Cabinet would report to the public on their achievements. This was, however, somewhat political, symbolic and inadequate in its nature to address the problem of corruption. Many observers found that the week was treated more as a "reporting week" than an "accountability week."[42] The process also lacked a systematic approach in sharing the information with media and the public. The ministers and senior government officials were not sharing information in advance with the media, undermining any objective oversight of the government performance. Additionally, the information, which was shared in these meetings, was generalized and did not include details on actual budgets and expenditures.[43]

Underreported on-budget items

Under the budget, the President had preserved a discretionary fund which he could use for immediate allocation in case of "emergencies." These included a Presidential Discretionary Fund under Contingency Fund for Emergencies in the budget. A Policy Fund was also under the discretion of the President. Ministers, governors and heads of independent directorates also received *dasterkhvān pūli* (table money or business allowance) on a monthly basis. These expenditures not only remained unavailable to the public, but were also underreported to the state oversight mechanisms, such as the Parliament. In 2008, the Presidential Discretionary Fund amounted to US$20 million and the Policy Fund was US$8 million respectively – 2 per cent of the total government operating budget.[44] The monthly amount of the *dasterkhvān pūli* for the ministers was Afs60,000 (US$1,200) until 2005 which then increased to Afs80,000 (US$1,600).[45]

The expenditures of the Presidential Discretionary Fund were neither transparently reported to the Afghan legislature nor were they made public. A senior government official noted that Karzai used the fund to send several senior government officials and Members of the Parliament (MPs), including their family members, for medical treatment outside Afghanistan, granting them up to a US$4,000 medical allowance per person. This concession was available only to those who were favoured by the president's office or what the field interviewees called the "palace circle."[46] The fund was also used to top up the salary of president's office employees. Shukria Barukzai, a member of lower house, argued that the government did not have the political will to share the details of the funds with the legislature.[47] Although the government claimed that it sent the expenditure reports to the legislature, she rejected this claim, indicating lack of transparency on how and where the fund was spent.

Additionally, *dasterkhvān pūli* was paid on the top of the senior officials' salaries on which they had full discretion. However, they were not obliged to account for it. Neither the legislature nor the public could track where the *dasterkhvān pūli* was spent. The members of the Parliament also criticized the government for spending large amounts on business allowances.[48] However, the media was not able to track whether the business allowances were spent for political networking or official gatherings related to government businesses. In the absence of a list of participants, dates and other details, it is challenging to make such a conclusion. Likewise, the *dasterkhvān pūli* was virtually treated as a salary top up without any record of the spending, with one exception when the Planning Minister, Ramazan Bashardoost, in 2004 decided to spend his *dasterkhvān pūli* to pay for his ministry's staff lunch.[49]

Poor off-budget transparency

The off-budget offers a different view of transparency. The off-budget flow of a greater amount of aid made the off-budget aid role exceptionally important for development and institution building. There was, however, a severe "transparency gap,"[50] especially as the government refused to account for off-budget expenditure because it did not have discretion and control over it.[51] Off-budget fiscal transparency was therefore a donor responsibility. The donors, however, were more concerned to account to their legislatures than to the Afghan people, and shared little information with the Afghan government and the Parliament.

An assessment by the Integrity Watch Afghanistan (IWA) shows that off-budget transactions were less transparent than the on-budget ones and that donors shared less than 35 per cent of their information with the Afghan people and government.[52] The assessment claims that donors did not share project documents, making oversight of the projects through pubic engagement difficult and undermining the principles of transparency.[53] Only in 2008 did the Afghan government indicate that it did not "have information on how one-third of all assistance since 2001 was spent."[54] In the subsequent year, it claimed that "as far as geographical allocation of aid in Afghanistan is concerned, the government does not have a very clear picture due to lack of information."[55] In addition, sometimes a project could end up with an excellent implementation report, while in fact the project could be a complete failure. A local businessman noted, even some small projects with a value of about US$100,000 might only exist on papers because of collusion between contractors and implementing agencies to pocket the project funds. Although donors fired a number of their employees because of such misconduct, they neither made such information public nor prosecuted their corrupt employees/contractors.[56] When, except, the US Special Inspector General for Afghanistan Reconstruction made public the name of some corrupt individuals after 2008.

The degree of fiscal transparency differed among various donors, depending on their nature of engagement in Afghanistan. However, generally the off-budget military and reconstruction projects, especially those in insecure provinces and largely funded by the US, were less transparent. Many donors, with various reporting, procurement and monitoring requirements to inform their legislatures, tended to micro-manage their aid at project level, undermining off-budget transparency.[57] This approach to off-budget and especially security spending, to borrow from Alastair McKechnie, the former country director of World Bank for Afghanistan (2001–2008), fuelled corruption.[58]

Accessing construction and logistic projects most often had a price tag. One would have to have a connection with a donor agency, a senior government official, or be willing to pay a share of the profit in return for obtaining a contract.[59] Such misconduct compromised the quality of some projects. Poor donor coordination and their incoherent strategies in supporting programmes and projects (see Chapter 3) exacerbated the off-budget transparency gap, making it hard to get a clear picture of the fiscal situation in the country and the development outcomes.[60]

Although the government established the Donor Assistance Database in order to track and report on aid, most donors neither shared their information on time, nor did they properly report their off-budget expenditures. The Ministry of Finance therefore occasionally criticized the donors for their lack of cooperation in data sharing.[61] Despite several attempts, such as conducting annual Donor Financial Reviews, donors lagged behind in keeping the government up to date on their off-budget expenditure.[62]

The International Crises Groups noted that "donor countries spen[t] a significant proportion of assistance on administrative costs and purchasing goods and services, as well as on highly paid foreign advisors."[63] The advisors assisted different ministries and departments, and were available according to donors' priority. Some ministries did not receive technical support to adjust to the new institutional environment. In 2006, the government attempted to survey the availability of the advisors and their performance. However, this initiative failed because of lack of availability of information on the advisors and limited cooperation by donors.[64]

The advisors were accountable to their funding agencies not the recipient government institutions. It was observed from fieldwork interviews that some of the advisors did not regularly come to the office nor did they report on their performance to the concerned Afghan government institutions. They would often prefer to work from their "guesthouses," disconnecting them from their Afghan counterparts with whom they were supposed to work. It was noted by several senior government officials that a number of advisors made comments to their Afghan supervisors, such as "you are not my boss and you do not have to know what and how I perform my duty."[65] At the Interior Ministry, out of 282 foreign advisors who assisted the ministry, 120 were contractors. Their annual cost was US$36 million a year. In the logistics department, the international staff outnumbered their Afghan counterparts by 45 to 14.[66] Despite this level of support, the Ministry had been highly criticized for lack of transparency and for corruption. The advisors, however, were not accountable to the Ministry. Occasionally some senior government officials objected to this type of arrangement, but overall there was an understanding among them about the government's financial limitations. It was no surprise to them if an advisor ignored them as the government itself remained largely accountable to the donors. However, when ministry leadership was competent, it had an important role in utilizing technical assistance. Ministries with strong leadership often used technical assistance efficiently and put pressure on donor agencies.[67]

In 2006, Jean Mazurelle, World Bank manager for Afghanistan, observed that "in Afghanistan the wastage of aid is sky-high: there is real looting going on, mainly by private enterprises. It is a scandal." He estimated that about 35 to 40 per cent of the aid was "badly spent."[68] Donors were reluctant to criticize their own programmes. They would only evaluate those projects that did not expose their fundamental shortcomings.[69] Even then the outcome of the evaluations were rarely shared with the government or made public. Since off-budget project contracts were often complex and written in English, it was almost impossible for the Afghan public to use them even if they were available in such forms.

After 2005, however, the rise of Taliban activities, such as suicide bombings, intimidations and targeting of the government, NGOs and aid agencies employees, further weakened off-budget transparency, as contractors and donors would prefer to keep their information as confidential as possible to safeguard the safety of their staff.[70] This situation became an excuse for concealing contractual arrangements in insecure provinces and bred corruption, damaging the perception of aid and the government in society.

Secret cash payments

While off-budget funding overall suffered from a transparency gap, cash payments to strongmen (commanders) and to the president's office remained hidden from government oversight mechanisms and the Afghan public. The US and Iran made the major payments to Karzai's office. This type of income indicates a close similarity between Afghanistan and some oil-dependent states which suffer from fiscal secrecy. The cash payments were aimed at defeating Al-Qaeda and the Taliban and to buy off adversaries, enhancing the patronage capacity of the recipients. Once the information was leaked, these payments were criticized by the media and political activists in Afghanistan and in donor capitals. They mostly argued that the cash – especially granted to the president's office – should have been channelled through the Ministry of Finance.[71] The term *naqd'salār* (cash-lord) was used by a few civil society activists and politicians to define the politicians' attitude in relation to fiscal affairs.[72]

Since 2001, the US Central Intelligence Agency (CIA) relied heavily on cash distributions to make alliances with local strongmen and commanders, in the "war on terror." These transfers were *concealed* from the Afghan public. Due to lack of reliable data, it is hard to make a quantitative analysis. Alexander Polikoff notes that only two months after the US military intervention in Afghanistan, the CIA distributed some US$70 million to different actors.[73] This process continued throughout the "war on terror" and counterinsurgency campaign in subsequent years. The concealed cash payments distorted the direct relationship of the state and society by empowering strongmen at the local and national level (see Chapter 6).

The cash payments to President Karzai's office were off-budget and remained concealed. This significantly damaged the image of Karzai. In 2010, due to continued criticism by the media and the public, Karzai confirmed the flow of cash to his office.[74] An observer close to Karzai argued that the cash was used to pay Afghan lawmakers, tribal elders and even the Taliban commanders to secure their loyalty.[75] In 2013, the *New York Times* also revealed that Karzai's office received tens of millions of dollars in cash from the CIA. The cash was delivered for more than a decade on a monthly basis and was top secret.[76] Neither the Afghan state oversight mechanisms knew about it nor did the US Congress oversee it. On May 6, 2013, Aimal Faizi, President Karzai's spokesperson, refused to talk about the amount of cash received. However, he argued that the president's office accounted for "each dollar" to the CIA.[77] The hidden flow of cash highlights how the government leadership and donors neglected state institutions and the principles of accountability. According to Karzai's statement, the fund was used to buy off adversaries and to win political influence. This type of payment allowed Karzai to draw ". . . strength largely from its ability to buy off warlords, lawmakers and other prominent – potentially troublesome – Afghans."[78]

A poor state of transparency of off-budget expenditures had multiple impacts on how the Afghan public perceived donors and the Afghan government. Firstly, in the absence of information it was difficult for the Afghan public to understand the complexity of aid architecture and the wide gap which existed between donor pledges and commitments (see Chapter 3). The majority of Afghans largely assumed that once aid was pledged, the government had it in hand to spend. This raised the public expectation of the government and lowered their confidence when the government failed to meet these expectations. Secondly, the small segment of Afghans in urban centres with better knowledge of aid architecture was increasingly losing confidence in donors as they observed the waste in expenditure. They became largely cautious and sceptical of the good intentions of foreign donors in Afghanistan. The Oversees Development Institute (ODI) observes in this regard that "in the current aid system, recipients are highly accountable to donors, but donors are seldom accountable to recipients."[79]

Conclusion

This chapter revealed that in contrast to oil-based rentier states that suffer from "fiscal secrecy," the case of Afghanistan shows a complex pattern. Although the Karzai government has become fiscally more open than its predecessors, Afghanistan has still suffered from a low state of budget transparency. However, the degree of fiscal openness differed between on- and off-budget expenditures. Although the government shared comprehensive fiscal information with donors, it made little budget information available to citizens. While the increasing pressure of donors increased government fiduciary control, it shifted government transparency to donors. Off-budget expenditures were less transparent than on-budget expenditures. Not only did the Afghan public have very limited access to off-budget expenditures, but Afghan government access was also restricted. The on- and off-budget expenditures included unreported items and secret payments, respectively. As such, poor fiscal transparency prevented the public from participating in and monitoring project outcomes at the local level, while secrecy strengthened the politics of patronage, which undermined the credibility of the state-building process. The secret cash payments were an issue that indicates similarities between Afghanistan and oil-dependent states with regard to fiscal management. Fragmentation in fiscal management and poor transparency severely undermined Afghans' perception of the credibility of the Afghan state and of donors.

Notes

1 The "Open Budget Survey" was launched in 2006. It is an independent, comparative and regular assessment of government budget transparency and accountability around the world. The Survey is produced every two years in collaboration with civil society researchers. "The Survey assesses how much timely and useful budget information governments make publicly available and how accountable budget systems are in terms of the strength of official oversight institutions and levels of public participation." Nematullah Bizhan, "Budget Transparency in Afghanistan: A Pathway to Building Public Trust in the State," (Washington: International Budget Partnership, 2013), 1.
2 International Budget Partnership (IBP), "Open Budget Transform Lives: The Open Budget Survey 2008," (Washington: IBP 2008).
3 Eivind Tandberg et al., "Afghanistan: Consolidating Budget Management Systems," (IMF, Washington December 2003).
4 See UNDP, "Project in Spotlight: Making Budgets and Aid Work Project," (Kabul, October 2012).
5 Asrhaf Ghani et al., "The Budget as the Linchpin of the State," 175–80. Crown Agents, a British organization, was contracted to assist the government to handle the procurement of development projects in the first years after the fall of the Taliban regime. The management of this function was then given to a newly established unit under the Ministry of Reconstruction and then was transferred to the Ministry of Economy. See Crown Agents, "Where We Work: Afghanistan," Crown Agents, www.crownagents.com/Afghanistan.aspx; and Afghanistan Reconstruction and Development Services (ARDS), "Who We Are?," ARDS, www.ards.gov.af/index.php.
6 Bizhan, "Budget Transparency in Afghanistan," 5.
7 See Yoichiro Ishihara et al., "Afghanistan: Public Financial Management Performance Assesment, Executive Summary," (May 2008), 8.
8 Osmani, Sediq Ahmand, MP, Interview by Author via Phone, December 18, 2011.
9 A donor agency official, Interview by Author via Skype, Washington, November 25, 2011.
10 An independent journalist, Interview by Author via Phone, Kabul, January 6, 2012.
11 In 2009, an assessment by USAID found that the Ministry of Finance of Afghanistan had the "adequate financial management capacity to effectively and efficiently record,

account for and report on funds that may be provided directly by USAID to the GIRoA (Government of the Islamic Republic of Afghanistan) through direct budget support." USAID Afghanistan, "Report on the Assessment of the Capability of the Ministry of Finance (MoF), Da Afghanistan Bank (DAB) and the Control and Audit Office (CAO) in Regard to Managing Direct Donor Assistance," (July 27, 2009), 3.

12 See International Budget Partnership (IBP), "Open Budget Questionnaire: Afghanistan," (Washington: IBP 2007).
13 International Budget Partnership (IBP), "Open Budget Transform Lives: The Open Budget Survey 2008," 1.
14 The executive's budget proposal, containing plans for the upcoming year and the associated costs was not made public. This had to be made accessible to the legislature and the public at least three months before the beginning of the fiscal year, allowing sufficient time for review and public debate. In addition, the contents of in-year reports and a mid-year review were not comprehensive enough to explain how the budget was being implemented during the year. Similarly, the year-end report did not contain enough information for a comparison to be made between what was budgeted and what was actually collected and spent during the year. Furthermore, because the audit report of the budget was not made public, the public was not able to access information on whether the measures proposed by the report were successfully implemented. See Abdul Waheb Faramarz, "Afghanistan More Open about Finances," (Institute for War and Peace Reporting, February 10, 2011), available at https://iwpr.net/global-voices/afghanistan-more-open-about-finances; and IBP, "Open Budget Index 2010: Afghanistan," (OBI, 2010).
15 The World Factbook, "Afghanistan: People and Society," CIA, www.cia.gov/library/publications/the-world-factbook/geos/af.html.
16 Bizhan, "Budget Transparency in Afghanistan," 7.
17 Ibid., 8.
18 "Open Budget Index" and "Open Budget Survey" are simultaneously used.
19 Afghanistan's budget transparency has dramatically increased to 59 in 2012, mainly because of the reforms being implemented in the first years after the fall of the Taliban regime. However, the study of this period is beyond the scope of this chapter.
20 Bizhan, "Budget Transparency in Afghanistan: A Pathway to Building Public Trust in the State," 6.
21 International Budget Partnership (IBP), "Open Budget Transform Lives: The Open Budget Survey 2008."
22 Ibid., 1.
23 Revenue Watch Institute, "The 2013 Resource Governance Index: A Measure of Transparency and Accountability in the Oil, Gas and Mining Sector," (New York: Revenue Watch Institute, 2013), 11.
24 According to Extractive Industries Transparency Initiative (EITI), the government would publish all payments of taxes, royalties and fees it has received from its extractive sector. Extractive companies operating in Afghanistan would also publish what they have paid to the government. These figures would be overseen by a multi-stakeholder group with representatives from the government, companies and civil society, and then reconciled and published in the Afghanistan EITI Report. Moore Stephens, "Afghanistan First Eiti Reconciliation Report: 1387 and 1388," (Afghanistan Extractive Industries Transparency Initiative [AEITI], 2012).
25 Graham Bowley and Matthew Rosenberg, "Mining Contract Details Disclosed in Afghanistan," *The New York Times* October 15, 2012.
26 Director of an NGO, Interview by Author via Skype, Kabul, November 28, 2011.
27 Bizhan, "Budget Transparency in Afghanistan," 6.
28 Fieldwork Interviews by Author.
29 See Islamic Republic of Afghanistan, "1387–90 National Budget (s)," (Kabul: Ministry of Finance, 1387–90 [2008–2011]); and Bizhan, "Budget Transparency in Afghanistan," 5.

30 See Bizhan, "Budget Transparency in Afghanistan."

31 See ibid. Islamic Republic of Afghanistan, "National Budget 1387–8 Mid Year Review(s)," (Kabul: Ministry of Finance, 1387–8 [2008–2009]).

32 See Bizhan, "Budget Transparency in Afghanistan."

33 See for example Said Ismail Jahangir, "Bastah-I Paīshnihādī Musawīdah-I Qānūnī HaqʻĪ Dastrasī Ba ʻAtlāt Ba Wuzāratī Adliah Sipūrdah Shūd (the Draft of Access to Information Law Was Sent to the Justice Ministry)," *Jumhūr News*, August 29, 2012.

34 BBC Persian, "Matn-I Qānūn-I ShurāʼHa-I Vulāyaty-I Afghanistan (Afghanistan's Provincial Councils Law Text)," August 29, 2005.

35 Islamic Republic of Afghanistan, "The Constitution of Afghanistan," (2004), Ch. 8, Art. 4.

36 Sarah Lister and Hamish Nixon, "Provincial Governance Structures in Afghanistan: From Confusion to Vision?," (Kabul: AREU, May 2006), 3.

37 Kenneth Katzman, "Afghanistan: Politics, Elections, and Government Performance," (Congressional Research Service, April 18, 2013), 9.

38 According to the Afghan Constitution, the *Loya Jirga* consists of members of the national assembly (upper and lower houses) and presidents of the provincial as well as district assemblies. See Islamic Republic of Afghanistan, "The Constitution of Afghanistan."

39 Afghanistan Integrity Watch (IWA) was established in 2005. It aimed to evolve as a reference actor related to understanding, analyzing, and acting for transparency, accountability and anti-corruption issues. IWA (Afghanistan Integrity Watch), "About IWA," www.iwaweb.org/about_iwa.html.

40 ACSFO, "About ACSFO: Background," www.acsf.af/english/index.php?option=com_content&view=article&id=1:background&catid=29&Itemid=3.

41 Bizhan, "Budget Transparency in Afghanistan," 12.

42 BBC Persian, "Hafta' Hasābdihay Dawlat' Afghanistan (Accountability Week of the Afghan State)," (November 26, 2005); and Asma Habib, "Awalīn Rūzi "Hafta' Hasābdihay" Dawlat' Afghanistan (the First Day of 'Accountability Week' of the Afghan State)," *BBC Persian*, November 20, 2005.

43 For more information see Riāʻsat-i ʻAumumī Aidārah-i Aumūr Va Dār al-ainshā-yi Shorā-yi Vazirān (Office of Administrative Affairs and Cabinet Secretariat), "Dast Āward'Hā-Yi Ūmda-Yi Hukūmat Dar Haft Sāli Guzashta Wa Barnāmah'Hā-Yi Panj Sāli Āinda (the Last Seven Years Government Achievments and the Next Five Years Programms)," (Kabul: Aidārah-ʻi Aumūr Va Arziābay, 1388 *Solār Hijra* Calendar [2009]).

44 Islamic Republic of Afghanistan, "1387 (2008/09) National Budget," (Kabul: Ministry of Finance), 101–2.

45 A Director General, Afghan Government, Personal Communication by Author, Kabul, July 4, 2012.

46 Fieldwork Interviews by Author. In the absence of a solid report it is difficult to claim whether the medical allowance was paid from the President's Discretionary Fund or the cash which was given by donors to the president's office. Some members of the Parliament believed that the president used his discretional fund for such allocations. See Tolo News, "Kankāsh: Approval of 1391 (2012/13) Budget (a Roundtable Discussion with Shukraia Barakzai and Sediq Ahmad Osmani Members of Lower House, and Hamidullah Farooqi Professor at Kabul University)," (Kabul, April 22, 2012).

47 Ibid.

48 See Jumhūr News, "Pasūkh' Majlīs' Ba Wūzārat' Māliah: Būdīja-I Bīdun' Taghīr (the Legislature Response to the Ministry of Finance: Budget without Change)," June 27, 2012.

49 A director general, Afghan Government.

50 See for example Paolo de Renzio and Diego Angemi, "Comrades or Culprits? Donor Engagement and Budget Transparency in Aid Dependent Countries," (Institut Barcelona D'Estudid Internationals (IBEI), Barcelona, 2011), 21.
51 For more information see Transitional Government of Afghanistan, "Financial Report, 4th Quarter 1380–2nd Quarter 1383 (21 January 2001–20 September 2004)," (Kabul: Ministry of Finance, October 2004).
52 BBC Persian-Afghanistan, "Fālīāt Hā-I Nehād Hai' Kūmak Dihindah Dar Afghanistan Shīfaf Nīst (Donor Activities Are Not Transparent in Afghanistan)," (November 21, 2011).
53 Director of a NGO.
54 Matt Waldman, "Falling Short: Aid Effectivness in Afghanistan," (Kabul: Agency Coordinating Body for Afghan Relief [ACBAR], March 2008), 17.
55 Islamic Republic of Afghanistan, "Donor Financial Review: Report 1388," (Kabul: Ministry of Finance, 2009), 12.
56 An Afghan Contractor, Interview by Author, Kabul, April 6, 2011.
57 Fieldwork Interviews by Author.
58 McKechnie, Alastair, Former World Bank Country Director for Afghanistan (2001–2008), Interview by Author via Skype, Canberra, April 17, 2013.
59 Fieldwork Interviews by Author.
60 Even the Afghan government occasionally complained because of its limited access to information concerning off-budget projects. See for example Islamic Republic of Afghanistan, "Development Cooperation Report," (Kabul: Ministry of Finance, 2010); and "Donor Financial Review: Report 1388."
61 See Islamic Republic of Afghanistan, "Donor Financial Review: Report 1388," 12, 28–9, 32, 37.
62 See ibid.; and "Development Cooperation Report."
63 International Crises Group, "Aid and Conflict in Afghanistan: Asia Report No 210–4 August 2011," (International Crises Group, 2011), 14.
64 An Afghan Deputy Minister, Interview by Author, Kabul, June 26, 2011.
65 Fieldwork Interviews by Author.
66 International Crises Group, "Aid and Conflict in Afghanistan: Asia Report No 210–4 August 2011," 14.
67 A donor agency official.
68 For more information on contractors and the effectiveness of project implementation see Waldman, "Falling Short: Aid Effectivness in Afghanistan," 18–19.
69 Director of a NGO.
70 The Taliban and other anti-government militants executed a number of NGOs and aid agencies employees and contractors. See, for example, Joshua Partlow, "Taliban Kills 10 Medical Aid Workers in Northern Afghanistan," *The Washington Post* August 8, 2010.
71 M. Hashim Qayam, "Mūqasir' Pūlī Siā Kīst," *Hasht-i Subh* Saur 11, 1392 *Solār Hijra* Calendar (May 1, 2013).
72 For example, Mahmoud Saikal, former Deputy Minister of Foreign Affairs (2005–2006) and a political analyst, posted the term in his Facebook page on May 1, 2001.
73 Alexander Polikoff, *The Path Still Open* (Indianapolis: Dog Ear Publishing, 2009), 132.
74 BBC, "Karzai Confirms Report of Cash Payments from Iran," October 25, 2010.
75 Dexter Filkins, "Iran Is Said to Give Top Karzai Aide Cash by the Bagful," *The New York Times*, October 23, 2010.
76 Mathew Rosenberg, "With Bags of Cash, C.I.A. Seeks Influence in Afghanistan," *The New York Times* April 28, 2013.

77 Aimal Faizi (Sposksperson of President), "Afghanistan Political Show: Durrand Line," Interview by Jawid Jurat through TV 1 Amaj Programme, Kabul, May 6, 2013.
78 Matthew Rosenberg, "Karzai Says He Was Assured C.I.A. Would Continue Delivering Bags of Cash," *The New York Times* May 4, 2013.
79 ODI (Oversees Development Institue), "Briefing Paper: Promoting Mutual Accountability in Aid Relationships," (London: ODI, April 2006), 1.

6 Interactions between the state and society

Introduction

This chapter explores the fiscal aspect of state–society relations in Afghanistan. In particular, it examines the effects of aid on the formation of independent groups. The chapter examines the dynamics of budget support and off-budget aid and their implications for societal actors – especially CSOs – and state institutions and explores how they affected state–society interactions.

Aid not only had profound effects on state-building processes but also influenced state–society relations, especially as major donors funded and engaged with societal actors. The government budget and donors' direct spending through projects were two important mechanisms for donors' fiscal intervention. The on-budget aid mechanism assisted in financing the government operating budget and development projects. By contrast, off-budget aid sustained the so-called civil society activities, funded the delivery of services by NGOs, empowered individual powerbrokers to either deliver security services to international security forces or to fight the Taliban and Al-Qaeda, and financed projects outside of government systems. The paradox of group formation was that groups remained dependent on aid and accountable to donors for funding.

The chapter argues that the two aid mechanisms had different effects on state building and state–society interactions. On-budget aid assisted in increasing the capacity of the state; by contrast, off-budget aid, in the absence of a greater state capacity and flexibility, fostered service delivery and project implementation, created a "dual public sector" and empowered individual powerbrokers. This aid, however, shifted resources away from building the state permanent institutions and induced parallel mechanisms that further undermined state building. The gap between the state and society was thus reinforced.

Reinforcing the state–society inherited gap

Aid outside government systems and control increased the influence of non-state actors. Existing societal actors, which also formed the nexus of political elites, were empowered and the emergence of new actors was facilitated. The result of this dynamic was mixed. Civil society actors, like NGOs employees and members, became active and powerful on pressing the government for account-ability and demanding for delivery in certain areas including human rights and quality services. Powerful individuals who accessed foreign military aid and delivered security services independent of government became potential com-petitors and challengers for state consolidation. The *mujahidin* commanders and militia groups, among others, comprised powerful individuals. Tribal leaders and community elders, who could be referred as traditional actors here, were also empowered. Especially, they were provided support to undermine the extremism of the Taliban legitimacy and to resist them. These actors and approaches aimed to foster stability and state building. However, especially due to prior state weak-ness and societal fragmentation, they became further complicated, undermining the intended objectives.

Off-budget aid helped to establish a direct fiscal relationship between donor and recipients. Individuals and organizations had to bargain directly with the donors for funding. Neither the Afghan government nor the legislature had discre-tion to discontinue or appropriate off-budget aid. Off-budget aid recipients were accountable to donors.

The availability of such types of aid and demand for particular services in Afghanistan encouraged the societal actors to refocus their activities in response to post-2001 socio-political dynamics. A notable example was the NGOs. Those who formed NGOs invested in building skills in project proposal writing and reporting and, some of them specialized in a particular sector that could yield high returns through aid. While local NGOs were in the process of formation to meet the standards and requirements, NGOs and companies were in a more privileged position to implement projects and use the local NGOs and companies as sub-contractors. They knew how the international system worked, especially having familiarity with the procurement system of donors. In the immediate fall of the Taliban some of the government functions such as public financial management and procurement were outsourced to international consulting companies.[1]

Post-2001 state-building agenda and aid conditionality encouraged the for-mation of NGOs and Civil Society Organisations (CSOs) in Dari referred to as *sāzmān ha-yi jāmah-yi madan-ī*.[2] NGOs and CSOs required registering at the Ministry of Economy and Ministry of Justice respectively. However, it is difficult to distinguish their activities. Thus, here we use the terms NGOs and CSOs inter-changeably for assessing the process of independent group formation. Reliable information does not exist about the total number of NGOs. About 2000 national and international NGOs operated by 2004 in Afghanistan, of which about 83 per cent included the national NGOs.[3] The database of the Foundation for Culture and Civil Society identified 2,918 CSOs in 34 provinces, including Kabul, in 2007. These organizations focused on culture and social activities (41 per cent), services delivery (19 per cent), capacity building (18 per cent), information and advice (14 per cent) a small number on advocacy and representation (8 per cent).[4]

This process strengthened those who had managerial, organizational and mili-tary skills or acquired them to implement aid programmes. Those with military expertise benefited the most in the short-run because the military aid was flexible and easily accessible. The US, particularly, as the major donor for Afghanistan and as a major actor in the war on terror, provided above half of its aid in the form of military assistance (Chapter 3).

The societal actors in post-2001 included urban intelligentsia, Afghan expatriates, *mujahidin* commanders and tribal leaders. They largely supported post-2001 political order or did not oppose it publicly. The societal actors were the generational inheritance of the previous failed state-building projects of the Musahiban family, the People's Democratic Party of Afghanistan (PDPA), the *mujahidin* government and the Taliban emirates, especially, since the 1970s (see Chapter 2). The mentioned regimes had distinct priorities and political orientation; their state-building strategies after the fall of the Daud Khan's government in 1978 resulted to discontinuity in state-existing capacity. There these actors remained politically polarized and fragmented and thus difficult to form a durable coalition among themselves and with other groups. In post-2001 a professional class of youth also emerged, comprising the nexus of the intelligentsia. The following section discusses the role of the societal actors in relation to society, state and donors.

Commanders

The *mujahidin* commanders, who aligned with the US to overthrow the Taliban regime, were given key positions in the provinces by the new government. These commanders operated through their loose networks and had the political backing of *mujahidin tanzīms*, while their accommodation within state institutions expanded their influence among the local populations. They mostly relied on patronage and to a lesser extent on coercion to expand their power. They largely offered government positions, access to contracts and land to their supporters. Their expertise in warfare in Afghanistan put them in a privileged position to provide security services independent of the state and thus access military aid especially from the US.

The *mujahidin* commanders, who lost their influence after the fall of the *mujahidin* government in 1995, re-emerged as influential players in Afghan politics. The acquired wealth and government positions were instrumental in boosting their leverage. Their local power bases included *qawm* (kin, village, tribe or ethnic group) and *mantiqa* (shared locality). Some, like Marshal Qasim Fahim (Defence Minister and First Vice President, 2002–2004), Ismail Khan (governor of Herat [2002–2004] and then Minister of Water and Energy)[5] and General Rashid Dostum (founder of *Jūnbish-i Millī Islamī Afghanistan* [National Islamic Movement of Afghanistan]), upheld their support bases among their *qawm* and *mantiqa* in the north.[6] Meanwhile, a new brand of strongmen also emerged or empowered. They were empowered through an alliance with the US to fight against the Taliban and Al-Qaeda. While they had little independent influence, their power grew through American patronage.[7] Gul Agha Shirzai in Kandahar and in the east, Hazrat Ali, Haji Zaman formally known as Mohammad Zaman Ghamsharik and Haji Zahir were part of this group.[8] The power of Ali, Zaman and Zahir increased when the fighting against Al-Qaeda escalated in the aftermath of the fall of the Taliban regime in the eastern city of Jalalabad. They set up checkpoints to charge the US Special Forces soldiers US$50 each to go through.[9]

In addition, the US and other NATO military contingents, which operated in the south and east of Afghanistan, relied on commanders to provide security for their forward operations and protect their convoys.[10] This was arranged through bilateral contractual agreements in the absence of central government. This arrangement in some cases allied the Afghan expatriates who had, mainly, returned from the US and the militia commanders to form logistic and security companies. The expatriates dealt with donors in regard to funding and contractual management and the commanders and their militias were delivering services. However, the security companies and the commanders, particularly, were safeguarding the convoys by offering a predetermined amount under the name of protection fees to the Taliban and other strong militias who were able to ambush the trucks. The cost per truck depended on the value of goods, ranging between US$800 to US$1,500.

The two Afghan-Americans who earned major contracts were: Hamed Wardak (son of Rahim Wardak, the Afghan Defence Minister, 2005–2012) and Ahmad Ratib Popal, President Karzai's cousin. They ran the NCL Holdings and Watan Risk Management security companies respectively.[11] The parallel security arrangements to that of the state had long-term consequences for state building. It created an imbalance in Afghan politics as, in comparison to other societal actors, it increased the wealth and elevated the autonomy of commanders from the society and government who were neither accountable to their local communities nor the state.

Traditional actors

Traditional actors such as tribal leaders and community elders, who lost their influence after the fall of the Musahiban family in 1978, attempted to preserve their influence in national polity. It was soon prevailed that their rule was limited in post-2001 Afghanistan. Most significant in this respect was when the US approached the former King, Muhammad Zahir, who was expected to have the support of the traditional segments of the society including the Pashtun tribes in the south and southeast, to call on Afghans to rise against the Taliban, complementing the United Islamic Front for Salvation of Afghanistan uprising in 2001. The limits of power of traditional actors were shown when after the former King's call on Afghans to rise there was little evidence to support its intended effects.[12] This was because Afghanistan was economically and socially transformed and military commanders replaced the traditional actors in local communities during war from 1978 to 1992, making it difficult for the traditional actors to dominate power. They were also fragmented around ethnic, tribal and sub-tribal structures. The urban intelligentsia and the *mujahidin* leaders and the commanders also opposed their emergence as dominant players in the national polity. The *mujahidin* leaders and commanders, for instance, strongly resisted the return of the former king to power as the head of Afghan state during the emergency *Loya Jirga* of 2002.[13]

Nonetheless, post-Taliban order had paradoxical effects on the rule of the traditional actors. It offered them opportunities to regain some of their influence but also limited their role because the state-building project focused largely on modernization of the exiting state institutions and building of modern institutions. The latter was the antithesis of tribal governance and their autonomy. The notion that the Taliban's Islamist extremism could be defeated through traditionalism offered traditional actors a reason to demand for more power. Karzai particularly remained an advocate of this doctrine.[14]

Building on its experience of arming the tribal militias in Iraq in 2006 to fight Al-Qaeda,[15] the US lobbied and adopted a similar initiative in Afghanistan. The US funded local tribal militias (*arbakīs*), something which already existed in some parts of the country and was expanded in the Pashtun tribal areas and beyond. The local militias aimed to defend their communities against the Taliban in the areas prone to their attacks, especially in the southern provinces. This approach suffered from lack of consensus among political elites in Kabul and resulted to unintended consequences. Some political elites argued that over-dependence on traditions under the Musahiban rule constrained the emergence of modern institutions and caused many socio-economic problems.[16] Under Zahir Shah's rule which ended in 1972, for example, the senior appointments were largely driven by patron-client arrangement, corruption was widespread and there was apathy towards reforms.[17] Traditional actors constrained building of a modern and effective state. In addition, though the local militias, which were greatly under the influence of *mujahidin* commanders, helped to enhance stability in some areas, their relations with local communities were contentious as they increasingly undermined the rule of law and were involved in criminal activities. The Afghanistan Independent Human Rights Commission found that some of the militias either committed crimes or had a criminal background. Cases of tax extortion by the militias were also reported.[18]

Urban intelligentsia

The role of the urban intelligentsia became important after the fall of the Taliban because they were largely educated and skilled, in comparison to other local actors, and therefore well positioned to run the administration and manage the implementation process of government policies and programmes. Urban intelligentsia had distinct and changing roles in Afghanistan modern history. Their influence in national politics had waned after the fall of the reformist regime of Amanullah Khan (1919–1929). The Musahiban family systematically suppressed the urban intelligentsia at the beginning of their rule. According to G. Muhammad Ghubar, a prominent Afghan historian, the Musahiban family policy was to marginalize the urban intelligentsia whom they saw as a threat to their rule because they largely supported King Amanullah Khan's reforms and his return to power.[19]

While aid-driven development fostered the emergence of a new urbanized educated class after the mid-twentieth century, the rule of *mujahidin* and the Taliban regimes in the late twentieth century reversed their participation in national politics. Post-2001 political order increased the urban intelligentsia participation in state building. An emerging professional class of youth (including high school graduates), members of civil society organizations, private media, women's groups, and some political parties made up this category of societal actors. Donors funded civil society organizations (CSOs) and NGOs advocated for a greater role for them in development and state building.

Donor policy in this regard is well documented in comments which they made on the first draft of the Afghanistan National Development Strategy (ANDS). Accordingly, in 2008, they jointly advised the Afghan government to increase the participation of the CSOs in state building and development processes.[20] Similarly, the "process conditionality" which donors imposed on the Afghan government for the development of the ANDS document prompted the government to consult with different societal actors, including the urban intelligentsia.[21] The government consulted with 13,000 people in 34 provinces, including members of the civil society, NGOs, private sector representatives, government departments, religious leaders, elders and donors.[22]

The intelligentsia comprised the nexus of the state implementers as they mostly worked with the government and NGOs. They therefore remained dependent on the state for their salaries or donor funding through NGOs for their activities. They had skills to understand the complexity of the bureaucracy and relationship with the international system. However, they lacked the power similar to that of the traditional actors and the strongmen in rural Afghanistan because they were not well connected to communities and were incapable of offering patronage in traditional ways as the strongmen did. The contribution by urban intelligentsia to state building was undermined by the weakness of the state and widespread corruption which together seriously damaged their ability to pursue reforms through the state institutions.

Reshaping the state–society relations

State–society relations were essentially dominated by the state capacity to deliver services to the public, protect the citizens and distribute resources. Patronage through allocation of public positions and other privileges to powerful societal actors also impacted the state ties with local communities. Consequently, the state–society relationship was shaped not so much around taxes, but on its distributive capacity, shaped by the level of aid and its delivery mode in particular and as well as the ability of the government to protect the citizens. Additionally, the relationship between the societal actors and local communities for their part depended on the character of the societal actors and how they mobilized communities. In such a relationship, public services, patronage and coercion played a marked role.

Between 2002 and 2004, there was close interaction between Karzai and members of local communities who met with him in Kabul on an *ad hoc* basis. Most of the meetings were focused, among other issues, on demands for distribution of resources to local communities to address their pressing needs. These meetings would generally result in presidential decrees asking the Ministry of Finance to fund projects proposed by communities outside of the budget process. But since the ministry did not have discretionary funding and donors were unwilling to fund such projects, it had to report to the president its inability to finance such projects.[23] However, there was little or no discussion, for instance, about how people could contribute to funding these projects.

As shown in Figure 6.1 below, the government and societal actors were preoccupied with donors to access on-budget and off-budget funding. This further weakened state–society relations and led to the massive number of scattered and uncoordinated projects, mostly funded off-budget. Between 2002 and 2009 there were about 4,851 off-budget and 1,209 on-budget projects, funded by 119 small funding agencies, international organizations and donors, as well as through Afghanistan domestic revenue. Besides the lengthy process of lobbying for donor funding, off-budget projects required quarterly reports in different formats to multiple oversight agencies to meet the various donor requirements. In addition, hundreds of missions monitored and evaluated some of these projects annually, while each mission expected to meet at least with a minister or a deputy minister to obtain their feedback.[24] This process required and encouraged both the government and the off-budget project implementers, be they NGOs or societal actors, to bargain and work with donors.

In addition, the "war on terror" in general and militarization of foreign aid in particular contradicted the state-building agenda and contributed to eroding state–society relations. Between 2002 and 2009, as shown in Figure 6.2, more than half of total aid was disbursed to the security sector and the rest largely followed foreign military priorities, in particular where donors had a military presence.[25] A mismatch thus existed between development needs and aid allocation.

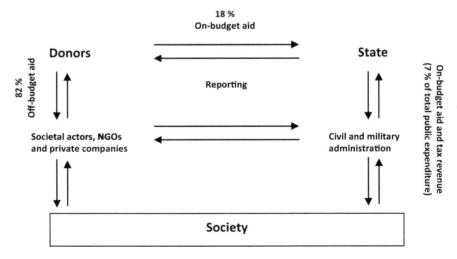

Figure 6.1 Foreign aid and state–society relations, 2002–2009

Source: Author's analysis

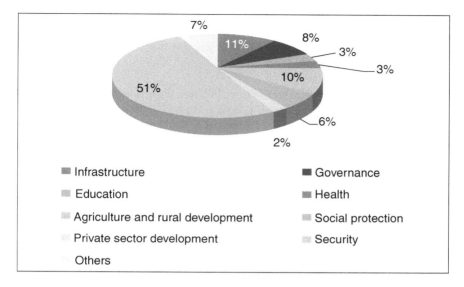

Figure 6.2 Foreign aid by sectors (in US$ million), 2002–2011
Source: Ministry of Finance, 2011

In 2010, the mismatch between the level of provincial poverty and aid distribution was highlighted by a joint study of the World Bank and the Ministry of Economy of Afghanistan. The study estimated the national poverty rate around at 36 per cent (with many more vulnerable people facing poverty). The study divided 34 provinces into five categories based on household per capita consumption (including food and non-food items), ranging from low-poverty provinces with less than 20 per cent poor (living on less than a dollar per day), to high-poverty provinces with poverty rates greater than 57 per cent.[26] Although the study found that between 2002 and 2010 among the top ten recipients of aid (Kabul, Helmand, Kandahar, Ningarhar, Herat, Kunar, Ghazni, Paktika, Paktya and Balkh), only Balkh and Paktika suffered high poverty. Other provinces with high poverty rates (Wardak, Patkya, Badakhshan, Kuna, Laghman, and Logar) received relatively less assistance.[27] The militarization of aid discouraged people in the more stable regions whose efforts contributed to improved local security, but as a result they missed out on this type of donor assistance. Many of the fieldwork interviewees argued that the militarization of aid created a poor incentive for local communities in stable areas. For their projects to be funded it was perceived to be imperative to create an "atmosphere of ambient insecurity."[28]

For quick delivery of results on the ground, militarized aid bypassed state institutions. The bulk of finance for the 26 Provincial Reconstruction Teams (PRTs) was mainly concentrated in insecure areas, aiming to win the "hearts and minds" of local communities.[29] PRTs consulted with the communities to identify and finance their needs, independent of the local state institutions (or the provincial and central government). Projects were then implemented under the auspicious of PRTs.[30] This type of intervention undermined the local state institutions and their ties with the communities. Karl W. Eikenberry, the former US ambassador to Afghanistan, who closely worked with PRTs and the Afghan government argued that

> when people go for their needs to a PRT this undermines the legitimacy of the [Afghan] state. However, if people go to a PRT through government this does not erode the legitimacy of the state. The question is where you go if you want assistance.[31]

In fact, the mechanism was such that instead of going to the government (local state institutions) people needed to go directly to PRTs for assistance. According to Habiba Sorabi, the governor of Bamyan, people in the provinces were going directly to PRTs in order to address their needs. She claimed that the PRTs power grew to an extent that even their translators were able to influence the granting of contracts.[32]

The role of PRTs therefore "substitute[d] the government functions and form[ed] unintentional competition for legitimacy."[33] Karzai and some of his cabinet members publicly criticized PRTs as parallel structures, hindering state building.[34] However, as the state had neither a decentralized resource allocation mechanism nor the capacity to match the expertise of PRTs,[35] this gave the PRTs an unrestricted role in dealing with local communities.

Building and undermining the state

Although the Bonn Agreement of 2001 integrated the international community interest and that of the local ruling elites, it essentially envisaged state institutions as a means of accommodating different political interest groups. While this might have helped to assure short-term stability, in the long run it undermined institution building and stability and how the public interacted with the government in addressing their problems. The public interaction with the government leadership is well observed by Ahmad Zia Masoud, the former Vice President of Afghanistan (2005–2009). He noted that during his term he found that most of his visitors, and those visiting the president and the second Vice President, Karim Khalili, were ethnically biased. Put simply – the Pashtun visitors would prefer to meet Karzai, the Tajiks would choose to meet Masoud and Hazaras would meet with Khalili.[36] However, political affiliation and earlier connections were also important factors. The style of the political leadership at the apex of the state eventually largely became a model for most state bureaucrats to deal with their clients. For example, the timely availability of some government services largely depended on personal connection, ethnic affiliation and the ability to pay bribes. This made the public sceptical of solving their problems through the state as a guardian of the national interest. A senior policy maker, who has advised Karzai since 2001, noted that "a patron-client system is created, so if someone gets a problem where does he/she go, he/she will go to his/her ethnic affiliated support networks, religious support networks and so on [instead of the government departments]."[37] This situation was not the sole result of donors' intervention after 2001, as a patron-client system existed under the previous regimes. However, deficit of government leadership and the aid regime and donors' chaotic approach sustained such a system.

In this context, not only was there a lack of a power balance at the Cabinet, but the power also shifted occasionally with the changing composition of the governing elites at that level. Between 2001 and 2004, Afghan expatriates, especially those who had returned from the US, had a strong influence in shaping public policies through the Cabinet.[38] Many of these expatriate ministers were marginalized in the government and some left the Cabinet of 2005. For example, Ghani, Minister of Finance, did not join the new Cabinet, Ali Ahmad Jalali, Minister of Interior, resigned in 2005 and Rangin Dadfar Spanta, Minister of Foreign Affairs (2005–2010), was given a vote of no-confidence by the Parliament in 2007.[39] However, after 2005 the *mujahidin* leaders and commanders dominated the elected Parliament,[40] with influence in the provinces and capacity to make state bureaucrats work to their will.

As noted earlier, over time Karzai, by his policy of accommodating other powerbrokers, further weakened state institutions. To have the support of strongmen, Karzai appointed them as governors, ministers and senior advisors especially (if he could and had the will) to areas other than their own *mantiqa* (except for Balkh). This policy exacerbated the weakness of the state institutions. For example, Karzai appointed Ismail Khan, the powerful governor of Herat and a former *mujahidin* commander, as the Minister of Energy and Water at a time when the ministry needed to be led by an expert to overcome the energy crises that Afghanistan faced and capitalize on the opportunities made available through aid and the private sector. He in fact constrained the development of the energy sector by failing to reform the ministry and recruit skilled staff.[41]

In 2012, it was revealed that Karzai had 110 advisors, including experts in the Office of Administrative Affairs. He had 30 advisors on ethnic affairs, almost three times more than the total number of major ethnic groups in Afghanistan. The monthly salary of the advisors ranged between US$1,000–5,000, although most of them did not meet the President in a year.[42] Most of these positions were allocated based on patronage and political considerations and were not selected through the civil service recruitment mechanism. Instead, they were chosen at Karzai's pleasure – often based on the degree of threat that an individual could pose to his government. In 2009, this process under Karzai's leadership prompted Ghani to accuse Karzai of "auctioning off the government" for political support.[43] While the advisors could have helped to make the administration more inclusive, it mostly ethnicized the administration and led to inefficiency as they had been appointed based on their personal positions and loyalty to the President rather than to the institutions.[44]

Commanders, who were appointed as administrators reasserted their influence over local communities through coercion and patronage, especially if they were leading the provincial security institutions. Moreover, they selectively applied rules and regulations. It was noted, for example, that Gul Agha Shirzai, Ningarhar's governor (since 2004), rejected a number of provincial appointments made by Kabul, undermining the credibility of the central government's leadership.[45] The control over state institutions helped the commanders to utilize their positions to favour their patronage networks and supporters and to legitimize their role. This deepened a patron-client system which had a significant role in building provincial institutions which were beyond the capacity of the central government to control. However, the institutions were shaped differently in various provinces, depending on the character and aims of governors.

For example, the Balkh and Ningarhar governors, Mohammad Atta Noor (since 2004) and Gul Agha Shirzai, both former *mujahidin* commanders, had different impacts on the development of provincial administrations. Shirzai encouraged the emergence of a more informal governmental system along tribal lines. Noor, on the other hand, while keeping his own informal network, also invested in building the formal institutions of the state.[46] Both largely stabilized their provinces and facilitated implementation of development projects. In case of Shirzai, he "has effectively incorporated American efforts into his own tribal politics of patronage. Like a tribal *khan*, Shirzai spen[t] much of his time holding court in his personal palace."[47]

Noor and Shirzai's success, however, was associated with their informal networks, a number of which benefited from this situation by receiving land and contracts. However, in contrast, the provinces where rivalry among the Pashtun tribes was a problem (such as in Helmand and Uruzgan), the accommodation of strongmen and commanders deepened the grievances among the local communities.

While Karzai and his circle in Kabul offered senior positions, impunity and largesse to buy off strong adversaries, at the local level the authorities instead used their positions to disengage the opponents from the political process. Sometimes local rivals would manipulate the donor intervention for their own interest, damaging society relations with donor and government. In August 2008, for example, the US air forces attack on Aziz Abad, a village of Herat, caused the death of around 100 civilians. Kai Eide, the former United Nations Special Representative to Afghanistan (2008–2010), later wrote in his memoirs that the information which led to the attack was provided by Afghans involved in local disputes.[48] However, Eide's claim is not yet confirmed by an independent source.

The weakness of state institutions undermined the role of Afghan expatriates and urban intelligentsia who focused on pursuing social change through the medium of state institutions and policies. Although most of them had rural backgrounds, their connection with the countryside was weak. This was especially the case with some of the ministers who had lived in the West for a long period, and were not well equipped to relate to the remote countryside.[49] Insecurity exacerbated this kind of disconnect because it was life-threatening for the ministers and other senior government officials to travel to villages as there were chances of Taliban attacks on them, especially in the south and southeast of the country. Likewise, the rural population had little understanding of the processes instituted in Kabul. To borrow from Antonio Giustozzi, there was a "cultural and communication gap" between the rural population and policy makers in Kabul.[50]

The commanders, urban intelligentsia and the traditional actors formally supported the post-2001 state building. Amongst the commanders and the traditional actors were some who, despite the fact that they opposed the oppressive rule of the Taliban and their return, remained suspicious of the emergence of a strong and accountable state, finding it equally threatening to their interests. However, the Taliban, Haqqani network and the Hizb-i Islāmy of Hikmatyar posed a serious threat to the state-building process by waging war against the state and the US and NATO in Afghanistan.[51] They largely reorganized themselves after 2005 due to receiving ongoing support from Pakistan and the failure of the Karzai government and its international supporters to stabilize the country and improve governance. By using coercion, the Taliban in particular expanded their income base through extortion of the local population and taxing of poppy cultivation (Chapter 4), and targeting key politicians and those who worked for the government and international community. The Taliban established a shadow system of governance and justice (according to their own brand of *sharia* law) and a taxation system (see Chapter 4), in a number of areas with an attempt to systematically weaken the state.

While Western donors deliberately channelled foreign aid to elevate the status of some societal actors, they (especially the US) also inadvertently bolstered the Taliban revenue because their military contractors paid taxes to the Taliban (see Chapter 4). The Taliban taxed the passage of the military convoys and charged a fee on construction projects. This process contradicted the Western donors' objective to defeat Al-Qaeda and its Taliban allies and increased the Taliban's revenue. The Taliban threatened the lives of those who did not comply with their demands and policies. In this way, they aimed to prove to the population that the government was not able to protect them.[52] In particular, they had intelligence about the locals, making it easy to take measures to punish evaders.[53] The Taliban skilfully exploited local grievances against the government and against local authorities in the south and southeast in particular.[54] This ultimately altered the behaviour of the population in these areas and prevented them from actively participating in politics and reconstruction.

Although a notable investment by donors took place through the National Solidarity Programme (NSP) to improve state relations with rural communities, the programme was undermined by fragmentation in the donors approach to financing patchy projects of different ministries to improve their relations with the communities.

The NSP was led by the Afghan government and financed by a consortium of donors led by the World Bank through the Afghanistan Reconstruction Trust Fund (ARTF). The NSP offered the rural population an opportunity to participate and decide on their development priorities at the local level, through elected Community Development Councils (CDCs) established in villages across the country. The government gave block grants of US$200 per family and up to a maximum of US$60,000 for each village "to help them build and restore rural infrastructure that communities [chose] through an inclusive decision-making process."[55]

To build ownership, the communities had to make contributions of about 10 per cent of the cost of projects through a voluntary contribution of cash, labour or construction materials. The 2005 evaluation of the NSP demonstrated significant evidence of improved community and state–society relations.[56]

However, the NSP not only remained entirely dependent on aid and donors, but governmental institutional rivalry and inconsistent donor approaches led to duplicated efforts such as the establishment of parallel councils to CDCs. This undermined the CDCs' role, preventing them from emerging as the main forum between the state and local communities. Soon, different ministries and departments such as Ministry of Education and the Independent Directorate of Local Governance (IDLG) established their own *shurās*. However, neither the government and nor foreign donors could provide a reliable data about the number of so-called parallel councils established. In assessing the situation, Ehsan Zia, the former Minister of Rural Rehabilitation and Development (2006–2009), observed that:

> People legitimise the state and their confidence in the state is crucial. The NSP elected *shurās* [CDCs] therefore reflect the trust of people in the Afghan state. Now different ministers are establishing different unelected *shurās* to gain more power. A good example of that is IDLG and education *shurās*. However, instead, these ministries could use the similar *shurās* established under NSP.[57]

Parallel councils confused local communities and consequently undermined the primary aim of improving state–society relations. The councils were funded off-budget and reinforced institutional rivalry, preventing the NSP becoming a vehicle for improving the relationship between the state and local communities.

Conclusion

Post-2001, the state–society relationship formed around a fragmented society that was dominated by its historical context and conflicts on the one hand and by a broken aid system and uncoordinated international community on the other hand. Donors forged their relationships with the Afghan state and society using on- and off-budget mechanisms. This situation facilitated a fiscal divergence in state–society relations by encouraging and requiring the state and societal actors to be preoccupied with donors. The donors boosted the Afghan state capacity by financing its operational and development expenditures through the on-budget mechanism. However, by depriving the government and legislature of the right to allocate and oversee off-budget projects, they pressed and encouraged societal actors to prioritize their relations with donors instead of the state.

In this context, aid largely followed military priorities, and the four-fifths bypassed the state. While off-budget aid was largely justified because of the low government capacity and corruption, this aid – along with competing aims of development and military aid – limited the development of state institutions and reinforced the fragmentation of societal actors, thus maintaining the gap between the state and society.

Notes

1 Seema Ghani and Nematullah Bizhan, "Contracting out Core Government Functions and Services in Afghanistan".
2 Elizabeth Winter, "Civil Society Development in Afghanistan," (NGPA, London School of Economics, London, 2010), 24.
3 IRIN, "Afghanistan: Concern at Ministerial Proposal to Dissolve 2,000 NGOs," 14 December, 2004.
4 Winter, "Civil Society Development in Afghanistan," 24.
5 Qasim Fahim and Ismail Khan fought against the Soviet troops and the Taliban.
6 See Tim Bird and Alex Marshall, *Afghanistan: How the West Lost Its Way* (New Haven: Yale University Press, 2011), 88.
7 Ibid.
8 Ibid., 88–9.
9 Ibid.
10 Gareth Porter, "Afghanistan: U.S., NATO Forces Rely on Warlords for Security," *IPS*, October 29, 2009.
11 Aram Roston, "How the US Funds the Taliban," *The Nation*, November 11, 2009.
12 See for example Mark Baker, "It's Not as Easy as It Looks, US Finds," *The Age* October 27, 2001.
13 Thomas Ruttig, "Flash to the Past: Power Play before the 2002 Emergency *Loya Jirga*," (Afghanistan Analyst Network, April 4, 2012).
14 For more information see Nick Mills, Karzai: The Failing American Intervention and the Struggle for Afghanistan (Hoboken: John Wiley, 2007).
15 Mark Wilbanks and Efraim Karsh, "How the 'Sons of Iraq' Stabilized Iraq," *The Middle East Quarterly* 17, no. 4 (Fall 2010), 57–70.
16 An Afghan Government Official, Interview by Author, Kabul, June 11, 2011.
17 For more information on the fall of Muhammad Zahir see Hasan Kakar, "The Fall of the Afghan Monarchy in 1973," *International Journal of Middle East Studies* 9, no. 2 (1978), 195–214.
18 For more information, see Afghanistan Independent Human Right Commission (AIHRC), "I'Lāmyah-I Matbūātī Dar Maurad-I Guzārish-I 'Az Arbakī Tā Policeh Mahalī' (Press Release about the Report on 'from Arbakī to Local Police')," (Kabul, Sawr 30, 1390 [May 20, 2012]).
19 Mir Ghulām M. Ghubār, *Afghanistan Dar Masyr-I Tārykh (Afghanistan in the Course of History)* (Peshawar: Dārulsalām Kitābkhānah, 1388 *Solār Hijri* Calendar [2009]), 1013.
20 UNDP, "Outcomes from the Donor Dialogue on the First Draft of the Afghanistan National Development Strategy and Consolidated Donor Comments," (Kabul: UNDP, March 10, 2008).
21 Jeremy Gould, *The New Conditionality: The Politics of Poverty Reduction Strategies* (London: Zed Books, 2005). For discussion on aid conditionality see Peter Burnell and Lise Rakner, eds., *Governance and Aid Conditionality in a Globalizing World*, Politics in the Developing World (Oxford: Oxford University Press, 2011).
22 See Islamic Republic of Afghanistan, "Afghanistan National Development Strategy (ANDS), 1387–1391 (2008–2013)," (Kabul: ANDS Secretariat, n.d.), 17–25; and IMF, "Progress Report of ANDS/PRSP Prepared for IMF/World Bank Board of Directors (2006/2007)," (December 2007), 16.
23 Seema Ghani, Executive Director of Joint Committee for Anti Corruption Secretariat, Interview by Author, June 2, 2011. In 2004, the budget department at the Ministry of

Finance established a computerized system to track presidential decrees with financial implications. However, in 2011 the author found that this system no longer existed.

24 An Afghan Deputy Minister-B, Interview by Author, Kabul, May 14, 2011.

25 UNHCR, "Human Rights Dimension of Poverty in Afghanistan," (Kabul: UNHCR, 2010), 11.

26 See Ministry of Economy of Afghanistan and the World Bank, "Poverty Status in Afghanistan: A Profile Based on National Risk and Vulnurability Assesment (NRVA) 2007/2008," (Kabul: Ministry of Economy 2010); A Government Official, May 30, 2012. The poverty status in Afghanistan was assessed based on a per capita household consumption approach, which included food and non-food consumption items. A minimum standard for this approach was selected Afs1,275 per capita per month (around less than a dollar per day per person). Ibid.

27 See Ministry of Economy of Afghanistan and the World Bank, "Poverty Status in Afghanistan: A Profile Based on National Risk and Vulnurability Assesment (NRVA) 2007/2008," 83; and Islamic Republic of Afghanistan, "External Assistance to Afghanistan at a Glance (2002–2010)," (Kabul: Ministry of Finance, n.d.), 8.

28 William Maley, "Reconstruction: A Critical Assesment," in *The Afghanistan Conflict and Australia's Role*, ed. Amin Saikal (Carlton: Melbourne University Press, 2011), 91.

29 Paul Fishstein and Andrew Wilder, "Winning Hearts and Minds? Examining the Relationship between Aid and Security in Afghanistan," (Boston: Feinstein International Center, 2012).

30 See Islamic Republic of Afghanistan and Baawar Consulting Group, "Joint Evaluation of the Paris Declaration Phase 2," (Kabul: Ministry of Finance and Baawar Consulting Group, 2010), 30–3.

31 Eikenberry, Karl, Former US Ambassador to Afghanistan, Interview by Author, Canberra, October 25, 2011.

32 Sorabi, Habiba, Governor of Bamyan, Interview by Author, Kabul, July 17, 2011.

33 Fishstein and Wilder, "Winning Hearts and Minds? Examining the Relationship between Aid and Security in Afghanistan," 23.

34 Ibid.

35 Nematullah Bizhan, Emil Ferhat and Haroon Nayebkhil, "Bringing the State Closer to the People: Deconcentrating Planning and Budgeting in Afghanistan," (Kabul: AREU and GIZ, 2016).

36 1TV, "Mūnazayrah' Kabul: Manāfī Mīlley (Kabul Debate: National Interest)," (July 3, 2013).

37 An Advisor to President Karzai, Interview by Author, Kabul, Canberra, November 28, 2012.

38 See Rangin Dadfar Spanta, "Afghanistan: Nation-Building in the Shadow of the Warlords and the 'War on Terror'," in *Nation-Building: A Key Concept for Peaceful Conflict Transformation?*, ed. Jochen Hippler (London: Pluto, 2005), 70–80.

39 President Karzai challenged the Parliament decision for vote of no-confidence in the Foreign Minister and thus received the Supreme Court's confirmation that the vote did not conform to the provision of law. Therefore, Spanta served in the Cabinet until January of 2010. See Fabrizio Foschini, "Parliament Sacks Key Ministers: Two Birds with One Stone?," (Afghanistan Analyst Network, August 6, 2012).

40 Andrew Wilder, "A House Divided? Analysing the 2005 Afghan Elections," (Kabul: AREU, 2005), 7.

41 However, Ismail Khan was the only regional strongman that Karzai brought to Kabul after getting the assurance of American backing and of Ismail Khan's local rivals. Asrti Surhke, *When More Is Less: The International Project in Afghanistan* (London: Hurst and Company, 2011), 129.

42 The Daily Afghanistan, "110 Tan Ba Hais' Mūshawirin' Riasat' Jamhūrī Kar Mikunand (110 People Are Working as President's Advisers)," (Hamal 14, 1991 *Solār Hijra* Calendar [April 2, 2012]).

43 Dexter Filkins, "Afghan Leader Outmaneuvers Election Rivals," *The New York Times* June 24, 2009.

44 Fieldwork Interviews by Author.

45 Ibid.

46 For discussion on the case of Balkh and Ningarhar, see Dipali Mukhopadhyay, "Warlords as Bureaucrats: The Afghan Experience," (Carnegie Endowment for International Peace, August 2009).

47 Ibid., 18.

48 Kai Eide, Power Struggle over Afghanistan: An Inside Look at What Went Wrong – and What We Can Do to Repair the Damage (New York: Skyhorse Publishing, 2012), 59–65. However, Eide's claim is to be confirmed.

49 See also Barnet Rubin, Amin Saikal and Julian Lindley-French, "The Way Forward in Afghanistan: Three Views," *Survival* 51, no. 1 (2009), 83–96.

50 Antonio Giustozzi, Koran, Kalashnikov and Laptop: The Neo-Taliban Insurgency in Afghanistan (London: Hurst, 2007), 230.

51 Pakistan provided them with critical support including shelter, logistics and fighters through the Pakistani *madrasas*.

52 See Henry Litman, "The Circular Dilemma of State Building in Afghanistan," *Penn State Journal of International Affairs* 1, no. 2 (Spring 2012): 102.

53 Giustozzi et al. notes "the Taliban judiciary had taken the shape of mobile courts, lean structures, and little record keeping. A major consequence of the new organisation was that the appeal system became largely dysfunctional, even if it continued to exist in theory." Antonio Giustozzi, Claudio Franco and Adam Baczk, "Shadow Justice: How the Taliban Run Their Judiciary?," (Kabul: IWA [Integrity Watch Afghanistan], 2012), 5.

54 Giustozzi, Koran, Kalashnikov and Laptop, 234.

55 IDA, "Afghanistan: Expanding Access to Quality Education," http://web.worldbank.org/WBSITE/EXTERNAL/EXTABOUTUS/IDA/0,,contentMDK:21289161~menuPK:3266877~pagePK:51236175~piPK:437394~theSitePK:73154,00.html.

56 Sultan Barakat, "Mid-Term Evaluation Report of the National Solidarity Programme (NSP), Afghanistan," (Kabul: The York University and Ministry of Rural Rehabilitation and Development of Afghanistan, 2006), 5.

57 Zia, Ehsan, Former Minister of Rural Rehabilitation and Development, Interview by Author, Kabul, August 16, 2011.

Conclusion
Findings and implications

This book has examined the effects of foreign aid on state building in Afghanistan between 2001 and 2009 against the backdrop of Afghanistan's history since 1747. It has explored theories of state building and revenue as well as Afghanistan's post-9/11 developments, including the rebuilding of an aid-based rentier state, the development of the taxation system, budget spending and transparency, and state–society relations.

Three key findings have emerged from the preceding discussions. First, Afghanistan historically suffered from a poor economy with inadequate domestic income to pay for state expenditures, weak institutions, conflicts and invasion by powerful states. The reliance of the Afghan state on tributes, subsidies and foreign aid in this complex environment has been crucial to the creation and reshaping of state institutions. Since 1747, except for a brief period in the 1920s, external revenue has constituted a substantial portion of state income. The degree of state dependence on such income has varied over time, but reliance on external support has been a virtually constant feature of the Afghan state, shaping its structures and its practices.

Second, post-2001 state building followed a path of dependency in which foreign aid reinforced the building of a fragmented aid-based rentier state. In the process, aid has had a mixed – and, at times, contradictory – effect on state building. On the one hand, aid greatly contributed to economic growth, the expansion of public services and road building. On the other hand, heavy aid dependence and overreliance on off-budget spending had negative consequences for accountability and state building. High aid dependence has made the government increasingly accountable to donors rather than to Afghan citizens, and the flow of the bulk of aid (82 per cent) outside the government budget and national mechanisms have created a parallel public sector. These processes, along with a divergence between Afghanistan needs and donors' interests, thus created a form of aid dependency that has actually hindered effective state building.

Third, we noted in Chapter I that oil-based rentier states use fiscal measures such as lowering tax rates or not taxing the population at all, increasing government spending (especially on patronage to buy off adversaries), and preventing the formation of independent social groups. These mechanisms relieve social pressure for greater accountability, and the effects can be severe when institutions are weak. However, given the conditionality and unreliability of aid as well as recipients' lack of control over aid, its effects differ from those of natural resources and seem better in some ways, especially when donors seek to strengthen state institutions and make them more democratic, which could be the case for budget support aid in particular. Thus, both schools of thought about aid effects – that "aid is oil" and "aid is not oil" – underestimate the complexities of and differences and similarities between aid and oil revenue and their impacts. The paradoxical effect of this type of aid is that it makes the government increasingly accountable to donors rather than to citizens. But when donors abandon the goal of facilitating the recipient government reforms by spending the bulk of their aid outside the recipient government budget and the national systems, such actions may undermine the central objectives of state building and democratic decision making by diverting political attention and financial resources from state institutions and depriving the recipient country's parliament of the right to oversee outside budgetary spending. Although government accountability to donors in the former case largely seems inevitable, such problems should be recognized and limited in the latter case.

Drawing on lessons from Afghanistan and the literature on state building, this book demonstrates that aid is less desirable than tax revenue for state building. However, when a country has a poor economy and is devastated by war or is failing to deliver services and protect citizens, domestic revenue may not sustain state building. Foreign aid may thus be necessary until domestic institutions and the economy thrive. This stage of state development may have lasting implications. Aid may reinforce or hinder state building, depending on the alignment of donors' interests with recipients' needs, the recipient's type of state, the state's capacity and whether interactions between aid and domestic institutions ensure continuity and support or undermine state capacity. The relationship between aid and state building is thus highly complex, and the question of how aid affects state building cannot be answered unconditionally. These findings are discussed in more detail in the following section, in addition to the lessons that can be applied to future externally aided state building.

Path dependency: Afghan state reliance on external revenue

Historically, Afghanistan had a subsistence-based economy and a weak tax system, and external revenue was important in sustaining and reshaping the state-building process. The interplay of social and political dynamics and geopolitical factors as well as the availability and types of revenue were all crucial to this process. Although the country has shown resilience in maintaining its independence from outside occupations, it has failed to pay for government expenditures from its domestic income, except for a brief period under the reign of Amanullah Khan (1919–1929). Hence, Afghan rulers have always made it a top priority to find external revenue sources to overcome this financial handicap.

The relationship between external revenue and state building was significant in three periods of Afghanistan's modern history. The Durrani Empire (1747–1809) at its peak derived more than three-quarters of its revenue in the form of a tribute.

Following the collapse of the Empire due to internal decay and the expansion of regional powers such as the Sikhs and the British, access to British subsidies partially replaced the tribute, but it was not adequate to make Afghanistan a rentier state. However, since the mid-twentieth century, foreign aid has played a marked role in the state-building process.

In particular, aid became vital for the sustainability of the state after the Soviet Union invasion of Afghanistan in 1978. The loss of aid from the Soviet Union, which paid for increasing proportions of Afghan state expenditures, contributed to the collapse of the PDPA regime (1978–1992). Subsequently, the *mujahidin* government (1992–1996) not only suffered from internal armed conflict but also lacked a viable source of revenue especially as the central revenue collection mechanism disintegrated. Additionally, the government did not have strong patron to replace those who had provided substantial amounts of aid to Afghan governments in the past. With such fiscal weakness, aid and military support from Pakistan helped the Taliban movement (1996–2001) to overthrow the *mujahidin* government and establish its theocratic regime in most parts of Afghanistan.

The conditions upon which external revenue was available and the strings attached to it had consequences for state building in Afghanistan. The Durrani Empire was required to maintain its military domination over conquests to secure the flow of tributes. After the Empire disintegrated, it became a situation of external states providing aid to secure Afghanistan's allegiance for their own rival geopolitical reasons. For example, the British granted Abdur Rahman Khan subsidies and weapons to build a modern buffer state to prevent the advancement of Russian influence over Afghanistan, which the British perceived as a threat to their interests in the region. In this situation, the subsidies and foreign aid were given to only a small segment of society and were allocated for building the coercive capacity of the state, such as the army to maintain internal order and defend Afghanistan especially against external threats by rivals of the patron states.

From the mid-twentieth century, external revenue provided rulers with capital and coercive power and shaped state institutions and state–society relations by increasing the capacity of the state and bypassing a domestic path through taxation. However, because the external revenue was not sufficiently generous to make the state fully autonomous from society, the rulers occasionally needed to compromise with strong actors, such as powerful tribal chieftains and religious leaders, and offer concessions to assure their loyalties.

Between 1747 and 2000, except for the aid that the *mujahidin* groups received during the Soviet Union invasion of Afghanistan, the state was the main recipient of external revenue. Although this delivery method helped build the capacity of the state and maintain the power of its rulers, this approach did not result in rulers being accountable to the people. Abdul Rahman Khan, the *Musahiban* family, and the PDPA regime were the main recipients of the subsidies and foreign aid. In addition, Western donors and Saudi Arabia gave aid to different *mujahidin* groups through fragmented channels that reinforced and institutionalized the differences among them.

We found, however, that the absence of external revenue and heavy reliance on taxation does not improve accountability. Abdur Rahman Khan heavily taxed the population and declared taxation an Islamic duty, depriving taxpayers of the right to have a voice in state affairs. Similarly, under the *mujahidin* government, the absence of significant aid did not prompt improved governance. Hence, the absence of external revenue and dependence on taxation, although important for state formation, do not necessarily guarantee that the government will be accountable to its people.

Building and undermining the state: Afghanistan after 9/11

Following the Taliban regime's fall in late 2001, the new government, with support from the international community, made efforts to rebuild the existing weak unitary state with a strong executive. In these efforts, aid dependency had paradoxical affects. On the one hand, aid financed democratic efforts such as the elections and building of the legislature, promoted economic growth and expanded public services. On the other hand, the type of aid dependency that Afghanistan endured made the government overly accountable to foreign donors and overly focused on short-term gains, thus undermining a cohesive process of state building. The government became preoccupied with lobbying for the flow of aid and complying with donors' conditions; aid largely bypassed government departments and ministries, resulting in the creation of a parallel public sector. Major donors strongly concentrated on short-term gains mainly as a result of the war on terror. The formation of groups independent of the state remained donor dependent and fragmented. Hence, the deficit of government accountability, the creation of a parallel public sector and paradoxical efforts to improve the budget process and the taxation system along unfavourable social, economic and political preconditions hindered the process of building an effective and sustainable state.

Upward accountability to donors

The type of aid dependency that Afghanistan endured caused the government to be preoccupied with and increasingly accountable to donors. While this process helped the government to ensure the flow of aid and to comply with aid conditions, it adversely affected government legitimacy in the eyes of ordinary Afghans and in the ways that the government handled domestic problems. The government concentrated its political and administrative efforts on adhering to the conditions attached to the aid and on lobbying to ensure the flow of aid. This process unintentionally diverted the political and administrative focus of the government from pursuing a balanced strategy for building institutions and effectively investing in long-term development.

Although the government's upward accountability to donors might have substituted for the reduced demand from Afghan citizens, especially in the absence of an elected legislature until 2005, it compromised the government's accountability to Afghan citizens in the long term and hindered state–society interactions.

Donors were less likely to provide significant budget support without detailed conditions, or discretionary funds, to the Afghan government. At least the US Congress would not tolerate such expenditure. While this aid conditionality distinguishes the aid which Afghanistan received from states that are dependent on oil revenue, the aid conditionality lacked coherence, consistency and a long-term orientation. This situation was exacerbated by the fact that pre-9/11 Afghanistan did not have a democratically accountable government or strong state capacity. Because of the increasing activities of the Taliban insurgency and groups such as Al-Qaeda, the time pressure to "win the hearts and minds" of people did not facilitate a political process in which the government and societal actors could effectively address collective problems.

While aid from Western donors was largely conditional on advancing the democratization process and implementing specific reforms, such as reforms in the area of budget and taxation, the aid modality was full of inherited contradictions. Given the government preoccupation with donors to negotiate on major national policies and the divergence between donors' short-term agenda to defeat the Taliban and Al-Qaeda in Afghanistan and the long-term domestic imperative of building the state and the economy, the flow of aid was largely rendered ineffective for achieving the expected outcomes. In this regard, while the government preoccupation with and accountability to foreign donors was inevitable in the situation of high aid dependence, how aid was spent had adverse implications for state building, which could have been managed more effectively.

Creating a parallel public sector

The flow of more than four-fifths of aid outside the Afghan government budget created a parallel public sector. This type of aid aimed to improve project implementation and overcome the problem of corruption in the public sector. With regard to the rentier effects of aid, this type of aid was designed to constrain the Afghan government from spending aid on patronage. Donors' concerns were valid to some extent because the government suffered from a low budget implementation capacity and widespread corruption. However, reliance on off-budget mechanisms was not a sound strategy for supporting state building, which had the unintentional effect of prolonging the weakness of the state.

Thus, off-budget aid became counterproductive, undermining institution building and democratic decision making. It neither effectively helped to build the state capacity nor prevented corruption. To manage off-budget aid, donors established parallel structures and mechanisms outside the state system, referred to as a parallel public sector. This approach diverted political and financial resources from state institutions, weakened potential pressure to reform the state, and deprived the government of budgetary control over the bulk of public expenditures. Off-budget aid even constrained the government in conducting need-based strategic planning, as the availability of aid would determine what programmes could be implemented. President Karzai's lack of a pragmatic vision for Afghanistan's future and his personalized politics along with the poor quality of institutions reduced the effectiveness of state-building efforts.

Off-budget spending further fragmented the fiscal management and budget. The budget was divided into on- and off-budgets, which undermined fiscal management and transparency. Although the government budget process and transparency gradually improved, the situation with off-budget aid spending did not improve. Donors paid less attention to improving the availability of their direct spending and informing the Afghan public and even the government in some cases. Some off-budget transactions also remained hidden from public view while being fully spent on patronage. Some politicians, such as those in Karzai's office and strongmen, received hidden funds from the US and Iran. The funds were given to individuals using off-budget channels rather than institutions, and details remained secret. Although budget transparency improved over time, the credibility of the state-building process suffered much damage.

Paradoxical tax outcomes

We noted in Chapter 2 that aid can generally have positive and negative implications for tax revenue collection in different countries. However, an in-depth analysis from Afghanistan shows that aid can have mixed effects on taxation even within a single country. Efforts to partially reform the taxation system to sustain state building were ineffective. The recentralization of revenue collection, the adoption of new laws and regulations, and the upgrading of revenue infrastructure such as customs buildings helped to increase domestic revenue, especially as the country had started from a very low baseline. However, tax revenue as percentage of GDP remained low and efforts to build the taxation system suffered from a number of shortcomings and contradictions. Widespread extortion and corrupt practices on the top of the formal taxes placed a heavy burden on Afghan citizens. The government failed to overcome these problems. The Taliban and local militias extorted illegal taxes from businesses, local communities and poppy cultivation, although they did not provide any services to the public. Any revenue that the Taliban and other groups earned perpetuated their activities, posing major threats to stability and undermining state building. Despite the taxpayers' desire to promote a social contract surrounding taxation, tax reforms failed to achieve this objective.

In addition, tax exemption and evasion remained a challenge. Powerful taxpayers with political connections often evaded taxation, and even those who wanted to pay their taxes could face delays. Those with limited knowledge of the system, including many small business owners, accumulated enormous fines for late payment from the Ministry of Finance. Moreover, tax exemption for donor-funded contractors not only reduced the possible tax income but also created a sense of injustice among taxpayers. The government failed to stop extortion and implement its anti-corruption measures; hence, with the government and donors preoccupied with tax reforms as a technical process, they neglected the politics of taxation and the role that taxation could play in state–society relations by increasing their interactions.

Divergence in state–society fiscal relations

The effects of aid in Afghanistan on the formation of independent groups not only were paradoxical but also reinforced fragmentation. In the former, the sustainability of CSOs, whose activities were important for strengthening civil society, remained dependent on donor funding. In the latter, many competing individual actors and groups emerged and were reinforced. Perhaps Afghanistan's inherited societal fragmentation and multiplicity of donors with diverse interests facilitated this situation. The government's dependence on aid and the dependence of societal actors such as CSOs and strongmen on off-budget aid led to a fiscal divergence between the state and society. The government no longer needed to increase its interactions with societal actors to negotiate on tax policies, and societal actors did not need the government to approve their funding. The government and societal actors were thus preoccupied with donors to receive funding.

Thus, donors participated in state-building efforts while also directly intervening to promote social change or achieve specific objectives through societal actors using off-budget aid. In the process, some strongmen and private entities unintentionally competed with the state in implementing projects. This was particularly the case with the Provincial Reconstruction Teams (PRTs) that directly funded local projects while largely neglecting the role of state institutions. The availability of funding for the government and societal actors enabled them to bypass the lengthy bureaucratic process and to overcome the problem of scarcity of resources, but as a permanent mechanism, the preoccupation of both the government and societal actors with donors undermined state–society interactions, which are important for the state-building process.

The future

Although multifaceted factors have made state building without aid dependency difficult in Afghanistan, the broader question that arises is whether such a path will exist in the future. Incomes from natural resources and transit for connecting neighbouring countries could be alternatives to substitute for aid in the long term. Afghanistan is categorized as a prospective resource-rich country with the potential to become a land bridge between Central and South Asia. According to an estimate by the US, Afghanistan has nearly US$ 1 trillion untapped mineral deposits.[1] However, resource extraction is costly, and to date, little investment has been made in this area in Afghanistan; furthermore, the implementation of regional transit projects through Afghanistan takes a long period of time and requires stability. In this situation, the state-building pattern thus not only indicates the imperative of aid for the foreseeable future but also shows the risk that, even if natural resources are utilized, they may reinforce a rentier dynamic with severe adverse effects on government accountability. Unless the conditions and socio-political relations that prolong the institutional weakness and poor checks and balances are addressed at the institutional level, the flow of resource and transit revenue may not be a guarantee for building an accountable and effective state.

Afghanistan's post-2001 state building represents success stories in some areas and failures in others. On the one hand, public services were successfully expanded, but on the other hand, Afghanistan lagged behind in building effective state institutions and in effectively promoting government accountability. Although the unfavourable social, economic and political preconditions that Afghanistan inherited constrained effective state building, the way that aid was spent and the over-concentration on the war on terror's short-term gains compromised the long-term agenda of building state institutions and promoting accountability. In this regard, domestic revenue seems unlikely to fully finance the state operation and development budget in the foreseeable future because of Afghanistan's poor economy and high public expenditure. The country will thus need a sizable amount of aid in the foreseeable future. Effective state building requires fundamental governance reforms, elite cohesion and a balanced approach in building the state and the economy. Aid and aid modalities may work as a catalyst that can either support or hinder state building and societal cohesion.

Implications for externally aided state building

This book argues that because of the conditionality and unreliability of aid and the recipients' lack of control, aid produces distinctive rentier outcomes through the mechanisms of taxation, government spending and independent group formation. These outcomes differ from oil-revenue rentier effects. Unlike in oil-rich states with a weak taxation function and low revenue collection, the impact of aid on revenue collection is mixed in this case. Aid is often conditional on increases in revenue collection, and the recipient government may also have the incentive to strengthen the taxation system because the flow of aid is not permanent. The problem of aid conditionality is that it could force the government's upward accountability to donors. If a greater portion of aid flows outside the recipient budget while constraining the recipient government from spending aid on patronage, a parallel public sector may arise and undermine the state.

Moreover, unlike oil revenue, aid tends to promote the formation of groups independent of the recipient government, especially CSOs. However, while such groups are independent of the recipient state, they are dependent on foreign donors for funding, making these groups largely accountable to donors rather than *vice versa*. If the recipient suffers from legacies of social fragmentation, off-budget aid may further reinforce this fragmentation. Aid impacts are paradoxical and dependent on donors' intention and strategy as well as the recipient's state capacity and polity.

In addition, state building requires coherent and continued efforts on the part of domestic and external actors. Although aid-dependent countries tend to inherit weak states, state weakness is not the norm. In the aftermath of World War II, for example, South Korea and Taiwan inherited strong cohesive states. It is important to consider how post-war state building addresses state weakness. The pattern in which the state is bypassed either by foreign donors (for example, when donors use a large portion of their aid outside the recipient state) or by the recipient leadership (for example, when the recipient leaders rely on informal networks) does not render state building effective. Such an approach instead exacerbates the state weakness and relieves the state of the necessary pressure and resources to pursue necessary reforms and building public institutions – which we observed in the case of Afghanistan. In addition, over-concentration of the recipient government and donors on short-term objectives to deliver quick results, although important for gaining public support for the state-building project, may undermine prospects for long-term development and effective state building. A balance between short-and long-term objectives is imperative.

The characteristics and capacity of the existing state institutions are important for the subsequent state-building project. The interaction of internal factors such as state institutions and the polity with external factors such as donors' interests has major implications for state building. Whether such interactions reinforce or transform the existing characteristics of a state is crucial. A state may be neo-patrimonial or Weberian. When internal instability and insecurity pose a major challenge in the recipient country, foreign donors tend to focus on short-term objectives. Donors may dispense aid to buy off adversaries and undermine the rule of law in exchange for short-term stability. This type of intervention may foster short-term stability, but in the long term, it may undermine both stability and effective state building.

The fragmentation of elites and of state or non-state institutions makes it difficult for the state to effectively address problems that pose a threat to the wellbeing and security of citizens and to effectively negotiate with donors. While this is a dilemma for the recipient state, aid can help to either reduce or reinforce such fragmentation. How donors spend their aid can affect both institutions and elite cohesion. We can also argue the opposite – that the characteristics of elites and institutions determine the types of aid that a country receives. As we noted in the case of Afghanistan, donor interests and strategic preferences considerably explain how and where donors might spend their aid. In this regard, on-budget aid – budget support or aid that flows through the recipient systems – seems to be relatively more effective for state building.

The effects of aid on group formation are important for state–society interactions and for long-term state building. The paradox in the current aid system is that it finances CSOs to improve democratization of the recipient state, but such efforts tend to be fiscally less sustainable when CSOs are largely dependent on foreign donors. Like the recipient state, these organizations may suffer from upward accountability to donors, largely compromising the ability to provide downward accountability to citizens. In conflict-ridden situations in particular, even individuals can have access to aid to deliver (security) services, but if the society is fragmented and institutions are weak, such behaviour tends to undermine accountability and state building because individuals can participate in unlawful activities.

It is less likely that donors provide budget support without detailed conditionality. For instance, in the case of US, the Congress may not tolerate such kind of expenditure. But increasing aid conditionality may undermine democratic state building because it gives donors greater leverage to shape the recipient government's policy. However, the view that aid conditionality substitutes for the weakness of citizens in the recipient country in holding their government accountable has limitations. Although this could be true when the aim is the implementation of technical reform, such as the modernization of the recipient budget process, the interests of donors and the recipient country's citizens are unlikely to be fully aligned, as foreign aid largely follows donors' interests. While government accountability to external actors may be better than the absence of accountability, which is typically the case in undemocratic oil-based rentier states, it can undermine democratic state building and deprive the recipient parliament of the right to hold the executive accountable.

In summary, aid is less desirable than tax revenue for state building. However, when a country has a poor economy and is devastated by war or is failing to deliver services and protect citizens, domestic revenue may not sustain state-building efforts. Foreign aid may thus be necessary until domestic institutions and economy thrive. This stage of state development may have lasting implications. Aid can reinforce or hinder state building, depending on the alignment of donors' interests with recipients' needs, the recipient's type of state, the state's capacity, and whether the interactions between aid and domestic institutions ensures continuity and supports or undermines the state capacity. The relationship between aid and state building is thus highly complex, and the question of how aid affects state building cannot be answered unconditionally.

Note

1 James Risen, "U.S. Identifies Vast Mineral Riches in Afghanistan," *The New York Times*, June 13, 2010.

Bibliography

1TV. "Mūnazayrah' Kabul: Manāfī Mīlley (Kabul Debate: National Interest)." July 3, 2013.

Abdur Rahman Khan. *Tāj ul-Tawārikh (Amir Abdur Rahman Khan's Autobiography)*. 2 vols. Kabul: Maiwand, 1387 Solār *Hijri* Calendar (2008).

Abu Bakr. *Taqwim Din*. 2nd ed. Kabul: Government Press, 1306 A.H.

ACSFO (Afghan Civil Society Forum Organisation). "About ACSFO: Background." www. acsf.af/english/index.php?option=com_content&view=article&id=1:background& catid=29&Itemid=3.

Afghanistan Chamber of Commerce and Industries (ACCI). "About ACCI: Background." www.acci.org.af/about-us/about-acci.html.

———. "About ACCI: Background." ACCI, www.acci.org.af/about-us/about-acci.html.

Afghanistan Independent Human Right Commission (AIHRC). "I'lāmyah-i Matbūātī Dar Maurad-i Guzārish-i 'Az Arbakī Tā Policeh Mahalī' (Press Release about the Report on 'From Arbakī to Local Police')." Kabul, Sawr 30, 1390. (May 20, 2012).

Afghanistan Reconstruction and Development Services (ARDS). "Who We Are?" ARDS, www.ards.gov.af/index.php.

Ahmed, Faisal Z. "The Perils of Unearned Foreign Income: Aid, Remittances, and Government Survival." *American Political Science Review* 106, no. 1 (2012): 146–65.

Altincekic, Ceren and David H. Bearce. "Why There Should Be No Political Foreign Aid Curse." *World Development* 64 (2014): 18–32.

ANDS and JCMB Secretariat. "Joint Coordination and Monitoring Board (JCMB) Reports." 2006–2008.

ANDS Secretariat. "The London Conference on Afghanistan: The Afghanistan Compact." London, 2006.

The Asia Foundation. *Afghanistan in 2009: A Survey of Afghan People*. Kabul: The Asia Foundation, 2009.

Ayubi, Nazih. "Arab Bureaucracies: Expanding Size, Changing Roles." In *The Arab State*, edited by Giacomo Luciani, 129–49. Berkeley: University of California Press, 1990.

Baker, Mark. "It's Not as Easy as It Looks, US Finds." *The Age*, October 27, 2001.

Bandstein, Sara. "What Determines the Choice of Aid Modalities? A Framework for Assessing Incentive Structures." Karlstad: SADEV, 2007.

Barakat, Sultan. "Mid-Term Evaluation Report of the National Solidarity Programme (NSP), Afghanistan." Kabul: The York University and Ministry of Rural Rehabilitation and Development of Afghanistan, 2006.

Barfield, Thomas. *Afghanistan: A Cultural and Political History*. Princeton: Princeton University Press, 2010.

Bazdresch, Carlos and Santiago Levy. "Populism and Economic Policy in Mexico, 1970–1982." In *The Macroeconomics of Populism in Latin America*, edited by Rudiger Dornbush and Sebastian Edwards, 223–62. Chicago: University of Chicago Press, 1991.

BBC. "Karzai Confirms Report of Cash Payments From Iran." October 25, 2010.

BBC Persian. "Hafta' Hasābdihay Dawlat' Afghanistan (Accountability Week of the Afghan State)." November 26, 2005.

———. "Matn-i Qānūn-i Shurā'ha-i Vulāyaty-i Afghanistan (Afghanistan's Provincial Councils Law Text)." August 29, 2005.

BBC Persian-Afghanistan. "Fālīat Hā-i Nehād Hai' Kūmak Dihindah Dar Afghanistan Shīfaf Nīst (Donor Activities Are Not Transparent in Afghanistan)." November 21, 2011.

Beblawi, Hazem. "The Rentier State in the Arab World." In *The Rentier State*, edited by Hazem Beblawi and Giacomo Luciani. London: Croom Helm, 1987.

Beblawi, Hazem and Giacomo Luciani. *The Rentier State*, 49-62 London: Croom Helm, 1987.

Belasco, Amy. "The Cost of Iraq, Afghanistan, and Other Global War on Terror Operations since 9/11." Washington: Congressional Research Service, March 29, 2011.

Bennett, Dashiel. "Report: Pakistan Is Supporting the Taliban in Afghanistan." *The Atlantic Wire*, February 1, 2012.

Bird, Tim and Alex Marshall. *Afghanistan: How the West Lost Its Way*. New Haven: Yale University Press, 2011.

Bizhan, Nematullah. "Beyond Armed Stabilization in Afghanistan: Poverty and Unemployment." In *Petrsberg Papers on Afghanistan and the Region*, edited by Wolfgang Danspeckgruber, 124–8. Princeton: Princeton University Press, 2009.

———. "Budget Transparency in Afghanistan: A Pathway to Building Public Trust in the State." Washington: International Budget Partnership, 2013.

———. "Continuity, Aid and Revival: State Building in South Korea, Taiwan, Iraq and Afghanistan." Working Paper 2015/109, the Global Economic Governance Programme, Oxford: University of Oxford, 2015.

———. "The Limits of U.S. Aid in Afghanistan." *Foreign Policy*, 2014.

———. "Re-Engaging in a Fragmented Context: Development Approaches and Aid Modalities in Afghanistan, 2001–2004." In *Failed, Fragile and Pariah States: Development in Difficult Socio-Political Contexts*, edited by Anthony Ware. London: Palgrave, 2014.

Bizhan, Nematullah, Emil Ferhat, and Haroon Nayebkhil. "Bringing the State Closer to the People: Deconcentrating Planning and Budgeting in Afghanistan." Kabul: AREU and GIZ, 2016.

Blodgett, Bermeo Sarah. "Aid Is Not Oil: Donor Utility, Heterogeneous Aid, and the Aid-Democratization Relationship." *International Organization*, 70, no. 1 (Winter 2016): 1–32.

Boone, Jon. "Hamid Karzai: Too Nice, Too Weak: How West's Own Man Fell out of Favour." *The Guardian*, March 23, 2009.

Bowley, Graham and Matthew Rosenberg. "Mining Contract Details Disclosed in Afghanistan." *The New York Times*, October 15, 2012.

Brautigam, Deborah. *Aid Dependence and Governance*. Stockholm: Almqvist and Wiksell International, 2000.

———. "Building Leviathan: Revenue, State Capacity, and Governance." *IDS Bulletin* 33, no. 3 (2002): 1–17.

———. "Introduction: Taxation and State-Building in Developing Countries." In *Taxation and State-Building in Developing Countries: Capacity and Consent*, edited by Deborah Brautigam, Odd-Helge Fjeldstad and Mick Moore, 1–33. Cambridge: Cambridge University Press, 2008.

Brautigam, Deborah, Odd-Helge Fjeldstad and Mick Moore. *Taxation and State-Building in Developing Countries: Capacity and Consent.* Cambridge: Cambridge University Press, 2008.

Browne, Stephen. *Foreign Aid in Practice.* London: Pinter Reference, 1990.

Burg, David F. *A World History of Tax Rebellions: An Encyclopedia of Tax Rebels, Revolts, and Riots from Antiquity to the Present.* New York: Routledge, 2004.

Burnell, Peter and Lise Rakner, eds. *Governance and Aid Conditionality in a Globalizing World.* Edited by Peter Burnell, Vicky Randall and Lise Rakner, Politics in the Developing World. Oxford: Oxford University Press, 2011.

Byrd, William. "Changing Financial Flows during Afghanistan's Transition: The Political Economy Fallout." Washington: United States Institute of Peace, 2013.

Carnahan, Michael. "Options for Revenue Generation in Post-Conflict Environments." Working Paper 137, Center for International Cooperation and Political Economy Research Institute and Center on International Cooperation, New York, New York University, 2007.

Carnahan, Michael, Nick Manning, Richard Bontjer and Stephane Guimbert. *Reforming Fiscal and Economic Management in Afghanistan.* Washington: World Bank, 2004.

Centeno, Miguel A. "Blood and Debt: War and Taxation in Nineteenth-Century Latin America." *American Journal of Sociology* 102, no. 6 (1997): 1565–605.

Chaudhry, Kiren Aziz. "Economic Liberalization and the Lineages of the Rentier State." *Comparative Politics* 27, no. 1 (1994): 1–25.

Chayes, Sarah. Thieves of State: Why Corruption Threatens Global Security. New York: W. W. Norton & Company, 2015.

Collier, Paul. "Aid Dependency: A Critique." *Journal of African Economies* 8, no. 4 (1999): 528–45.

———. "Is Aid Oil? An Analysis of Whether Africa Can Absorb More Aid." *World Development* 34, no. 9 (2006): 1482–97.

Commisiun Mu'zaf Ba Artibat' Juz' (14) Mādah Aval' Farmān Shūmārah (45) Mu'rikh 1391/05/05 Mūqam' Riāsat' Jamhūrī Aislāmī Afghanistan. "Gūzarish Commisiun (the Commission Report)." Kabul, n.d.

Crown Agents. "Where We Work: Afghanistan." Crown Agents, www.crownagents.com/Afghanistan.aspx.

The Daily Afghanistan. "110 Tan Ba Hais' Mūshawirin' Riasat' Jamhūrī Kar Mikunand (110 People Are Working as Presidential Advisers)." Hamal 14, 1991 *Solār Hijra* Calendar (April 2, 2012).

The Daily Beast. "A Harvest of Treachery." www.thedailybeast.com/newsweek/2006/01/08/a-harvest-of-treachery.html.

Dalrymple, William. *Return of a King: The Battle for Afghanistan.* London: Bloomsbury, 2013.

Dauderstadt, Michael and Arne Schildberg. *Dead Ends of Transition: Rentier Economies and Protectorates.* Frankfurt: Campus Verlag, 2006.

De Renzio, Paolo and Harika Masud. "Measuring and Promoting Budget Transparency: The Open Budget Index as a Research and Advocacy Tool." *Governance* 24, no. 3 (2011): 607–16.

Dietrich, Simone. "Donor Political Economies and the Pursuit of Aid Effectiveness." *International Organization* 70, no. 1 (2014): 1–38.

Doner, Richard F., Bryan K. Ritchie and Dan Slater. "Systemic Vulnerability and the Origins of Developmental States: Northeast and Southeast Asia in Comparative Perspective." *International Organization* 59, no. 2 (April 2005): 327–61.

Dupree, Louis. *Afghanistan* [in English]. Karachi: Oxford University Press, 1973.

Eichengreen, Barry, Marc Uzan, Nicholas Crafts and Martin Hellwig. "The Marshall Plan: Economic Effects and Implications for Eastern Europe and the Former USSR." *Economic Policy* 7, no. 14 (1992): 13–75.

Eide, Kai. *Power Struggle over Afghanistan: An Inside Look at What Went Wrong – and What We Can Do to Repair the Damage.* New York: Skyhorse Publishing, 2012.

Entelis, John P., ed. *Oil Wealth and the Prospects for Democratization in the Arabian Peninsula: The Case of Saudi Arabia.* Edited by Naiem A. Sherbiny and Mark A. Tessler, Arab Oil: Impact on the Arab Countries and Global Implications. New York: Praeger, 1976.

Evans, Anne, Nick Manning, Yasin Osmani, Anne Tully and Andrew Wilder. *A Guide to Government in Afghanistan.* Washington: World Bank and the Afghanistan Research and Evaluation Unit, 2004.

Fahimi, Subhan. "LTO Strategy for Year 1390." Director of Large Taxpayers Office (LTO) of Afghanistan's Ministry of Finance, April 2, 2010.

Faizi, Aimal (Spokesperson of President Karzai). "Afghanistan Political Show: Durrand Line." Interview by Jawid Jurat through TV 1 Amaj Programme, Kabul, May 6, 2013.

Faramarz, Abdul Waheb. "Afghanistan More Open about Finances." Institute for War and Peace Reporting, February 10, 2011.

Farhang, Mir M. Seddiq. *Afghanistan Dar Panj Qarn-i Akhyr* [in Dari]. Vol. 1. Sadir Qum: Ismāaylian, 1371 Solār *Hijri* Calendar (1992).

Filkins, Dexter. "Afghan Leader Outmaneuvers Election Rivals." *The New York Times,* June 24, 2009.

———. "Iran Is Said to Give Top Karzai Aide Cash by the Bagful." *The New York Times,* October 23, 2010.

First, Ruth. "Libya: Class and State in an Oil Economy." In *Oil and Class Struggle,* edited by Petter Nore and Terisa Turner, 119–42. London: Zed Press, 1980.

Fishstein, Paul, and Andrew Wilder. "Winning Hearts and Minds? Examining the Relationship between Aid and Security in Afghanistan." Boston: Feinstein International Center, 2012.

Foschini, Fabrizio. "Parliament Sacks Key Ministers: Two Birds with One Stone?" Afghanistan Analyst Network, Kabul, August 6, 2012.

Fry, Maxwell J. *The Afghan Economy: Money, Finance, and the Critical Constraints to Economic Development.* Leiden: Brill, 1974.

Fukuyama, Francis. *The Origins of Political Order: From Prehuman Times to the French Revolution.* New York: Farrar, Straus and Giroux, 2011.

———. "What Is Governance?" *Governance* 26, no. 3 (2013): 347–68.

Gankovski, Yuri. "The Durrani Empire: Taxes and Tax System, State Incomes and Expenditures." In *Afghanistan Past and Present,* edited by Social Sciences Editorial Board, 76–98. Moscow: USSR Academy of Sciences, 1981.

Ashraf Ghani, "Afghanistan xi Administration," in Encyclopedia Iranica, Online Edition, 1982, available at www.iranicaonline.org/articles/afghanistan-xi-admin

———. "Islam and State-Building in a Tribal Society, Afghanistan: 1880–1901." *Modern Asian Studies* 12, no. 2 (1978): 269–84.

———. "Production and Domination: Afghanistan, 1747–1901." PhD Dissertation, Columbia University, New York, 1982.

———. "A Ten-Year Framework for Afghanistan: Executing the Obama Plan and Beyond." Washington: The Atlantic Council of the United States, 2009.

Ghani, Ashraf and Clare Lockhart. *Fixing Failed States: A Framework for Rebuilding a Fractured World.* New York: Oxford University Press, 2008.

Ghani, Asrhaf, Clare Lockhart, Nargis Nehan and Baqer Massoud. "The Budget as the Linchpin of the State." In *Peace and the Public Purse: Economic Policies for Postwar*

Statebuilding, edited by James K. Boyce and Madalene O'Donnell, 153–84. London: Lynne Rienner, 2007.

Ghani, Seema and Nematullah Bizhan. "Contracting out Core Government Functions and Services in Afghanistan." In *Contracting out Government Functions and Services: Emerging Lessons from Post-Conflict and Fragile Situations*, edited by OECD, 97–113. Paris: OECD, 2009.

Ghanizada. "Afghanistan Reduce Penalties for Failure to Pay Taxes." *Khāmah Press*, January 2, 2012.

Ghubār, Mir Ghulām M. *Afghanistan Dar Masyr-i Tārykh (Afghanistan in the Course of History)* [in Dari]. Peshawar: Dārulsalām Kitābkhānah, 1388 *Solār Hijri* Calendar (2009).

Giustozzi, Antonio. Koran, Kalashnikov and Laptop: The Neo-Taliban Insurgency in Afghanistan. London: Hurst, 2007.

Giustozzi, Antonio, Claudio Franco and Adam Baczk. "Shadow Justice: How the Taliban Run Their Judiciary?" Kabul: IWA (Integrity Watch Afghanistan), 2012.

Gould, Jeremy. The New Conditionality: The Politics of Poverty Reduction Strategies. London: Zed Books, 2005.

Government of Afghanistan. "List of Working Overlaps among State Institutions." n.d.

———. *Resala Mawaza* (Book of Preaching). Kabul: Government Press, 1311 *Solār Hijri* Calendar (1932).

Government of Islamic Republic of Afghanistan. "Public Finance Framework, Annex 2, Kabul Process: Building Afghanistan from Within." Kabul: Government of Islamic Republic of Afghanistan 2011.

Gray, Matthew. "A Theory of 'Late Rentierism' in the Arab States of the Gulf." Qatar: Georgetown University School of Foreign Service in Qatar, 2011.

Gregorian, Vartan. *The Emergence of Modern Afghanistan*. Stanford: Stanford University Press, 1969.

Gupta, Sanjeev, Robert Powell and Yongzheng Yang. The Macroeconomic Challenges of Scaling up Aid to Africa: A Checklist for Practitioners. Washington, DC: IMF, 2006.

Habib, Asma. "Awalīn Rūzi 'Hafta' Hasābdihay' Dawlat' Afghanistan (the First Day of 'Accountability Week' of the Afghan State)." *BBC Persian*, November 20, 2005.

Hanifi, Shah. Connecting Histories in Afghanistan: Market Relations and State Formation on a Colonial Frontier. Stanford: Stanford University Press, 2011.

Haqjo, Kabir. "Chief Executive Officer (CEO), Afghanistan Chamber of Commerce and Industries (ACCI)." 2011.

Harakat. "Current Activities: Featured Project, Small Taxpayers Office Reform Project (November 2010–November 2013)." www.harakat.af/index.php?page=en_Our+Activities.

Hashimi, Said S. *The First Book on Constitutional Movement in Afghanistan, during the First Quarter of the Twentieth Century*. 2nd ed., Vol. 1. Kabul: Afghanistan Cultural Association, 2008.

Herbst, Jeffrey. *States and Power in Africa: Comparative Lessons in Authority and Control*. Princeton: Princeton University Press, 2000.

Hua, Shiping, ed. *Islam and Democratization in Asia*. New York: Cambria Press, 2009.

Ibn Khaldun. *The Muqaddimah: An Introduction to History*, Translated by Franz Rosenthal. Princeton: Princeton University Press, 1967.

IBP. "Open Budget Index 2010: Afghanistan." Washington: OBI, 2010.

———. "Open Budget Survey 2012." Washington: IBP 2012.

———. "Open Budgets Transform Lives: The Open Budget Survey of 2008." 2008.

IDA. "Afghanistan: Expanding Access to Quality Education." http://web.worldbank.org/WBSITE/EXTERNAL/EXTABOUTUS/IDA/0,,contentMDK:21289161~menuPK:3266877~pagePK:51236175~piPK:437394~theSitePK:73154,00.html.

IMF. "Islamic Republic of Afghanistan: First Review under the Extended Credit Facility Arrangement, Request for Waiver of Nonobservance of a Performance Criterion, Modification of Performance Criteria, and Rephasing of Disbursements." Washington: IMF 2012.

———. "Islamic State of Afghanistan: Letter of Intent, Memorandum of Economic and Financial Policies, and Technical Memorandum of Understanding." September 6, 2004.

———. "Islamic State of Afghanistan: Selected Issues and Statistical Appendix (IMF Country Report No. 05/34)." Washington: IMF, 2005.

———. "Progress Report of ANDS/PRSP Prepared for IMF/World Bank Board of Directors (2006/2007)." December 2007.

Interim Administration of Afghanistan. "National Development Framework (Draft for Consultation)." Kabul: Afghanistan Assistance Coordination Authority (AACA), April 2002.

International Budget Partnership (IBP). "Open Budget Index 2008: Afghanistan." 2008.

———. "Open Budget Questionnaire: Afghanistan." Washington: IBP 2007.

International Crises Group. "Aid and Conflict in Afghanistan: Asia Report No 210–4 August 2011." New York: International Crises Group, 2011.

IRIN. "Afghanistan: Concern at Ministerial Proposal to Dissolve 2,000 NGOs." December 14, 2004.

Ishihara, Yoichiro. Afghanistan - Public expenditure trends and fiscal sustainability. Public expenditure review (PER). Washington: World Bank 2010.

Ishihara, Yoichiro, Paul Sisk, Deepal Fernando and Peter Jensen. "Afghanistan: Public Financial Management Performance Assessment, Executive Summary." May 2008.

Islamic Republic of Afghanistan. "1387–90 National Budget (s)." Kabul: Ministry of Finance, 1387–90 [2008–2011].

———. "1387 (2008/09) National Budget." Kabul: Ministry of Finance.

———. "Afghanistan National Development Strategy (ANDS), 1387–1391 (2008–2013)." Kabul: ANDS Secretariat, n.d.

———. "Afghanistan National Development Strategy: An Interim Strategy for Security, Governance, Economic Growth and Poverty Reduction." n.d.

———. "Afghanistan National Development Strategy: An Interim Strategy for Security, Governance, Economic Growth and Poverty Reduction, Summary Report." Kabul: Afghanistan National Development Strategy (ANDS) Secretariat, n.d.

———. "Afghanistan National Development Strategy Progress Report 2006/07." Kabul: ANDS Secretariat, 2007.

———. *Afghanistan Statistical Yearbook (2007/8)*. Kabul: Central Statistics Organization (CSO), 2008.

———. "The Constitution of Afghanistan." 2004.

———. "Da Afghanistan Kalanay." 1388 *Solār Hijra* Calendar (2009).

———. "Development Cooperation Report." Kabul: Ministry of Finance, 2010.

———. "Donor Financial Review: Report 1388." Kabul: Ministry of Finance, 2009.

———. "External Assistance to Afghanistan at a Glance (2002–2010)." Kabul: Ministry of Finance, n.d.

———. "Fact Sheet: Taxpayer Selection Criteria." Kabul: Ministry of Finance, 2010.

———. "HRMD Annual Achievements Report 1390." Kabul: Human Resource Directorate, Ministry of Finance, 1390 (2012).

———. "The Income Tax Law." *Official Gazette*. Kabul: Ministry of Justice, 2009.

———. "The Income Tax Law." *Official Gazette*. Kabul: Ministry of Justice 2005.

———. "An Internal Memo on the Client Assistance Option." Kabul: Afghanistan Revenue Department, 2008.

————. "Ministerial Circular: Tax Exemption Policy for Donor Countries, International Financial Institutions, Non-Governmental Organizations, and Their Contractors Operating within Afghanistan." Kabul: Ministry of Finance, n.d.

————. "Ministry of Finance Releases New Circular Regarding the Taxation of NGOs and Donor-Funded Projects." Kabul: Ministry of Finance Archive, n.d.

————. "National Budget 1387–8 Mid Year Review(s)." Kabul: Ministry of Finance, 1387–8 (2008–2009).

————. "Official Gazette (Extraordinary Issue): Public Finance Management and Expenditure Law." Kabul: Ministry of Justice, June 27, 2005.

————. "Pakistan's Participation in the Construction of Afghanistan: Progress Report." Kabul: Ministry of Finance, n.d.

————. "Policy Directions and Strategies for Sustainable Sources of Revenue for Afghanistan: Official Tax Policy Framework and Revenue System Strategy." Kabul: Ministry of Finance, 2007.

————. "Revenues Forgone as a Result of Tax Exemptions in Afghanistan." Kabul: Ministry of Finance, 2006.

————. "Technical Assistance Summary Report." Office of the Deputy Minister for Administration Reform Implementation and Management Unit, August 2009.

Islamic Republic of Afghanistan and Baawar Consulting Group. "Joint Evaluation of the Paris Declaration Phase 2." Kabul: Ministry of Finance and Baawar Consulting Group, 2010.

Islamic Republic of Afghanistan and European Commission. "Summary of the National Risk and Vulnerability Assessment 2007/8: Profile of Afghanistan." n.d.

IWA (Afghanistan Integrity Watch). "About IWA." www.iwaweb.org/about_iwa.html.

Jackson, Robert H. Quasi-States: *Sovereignty, International Relations, and the Third World.* Cambridge: Cambridge University Press, 1990.

Jahangir, Said Ismail. "Bastah-i Paīshnihādī Musawīdah-i Qānūnī Haq'ī Dastrasī Ba 'Atlāt ba Wuzāratī Adliah Sipūrdah Shūd (the Draft of Access to Information Law Was Sent to the Justice Ministry)." *Jumhūr News*, August 29, 2012.

James, Simon, ed. *Taxation: Critical Perspectives on the World Economy.* Vol. 3. London: Routledge, 2002.

JCMB Secretariat. "Joint Coordination and Monitoring Board, Annual Report, March 2007–March 2008." Kabul: JCMB Secretariat, n.d.

John, Jonathan Di. "The Political Economy of Taxation and Tax Reform in Developing Countries." Tokyo: World Institute for Economic Development Research, 2006.

Journeyman Pictures. A Decaying State, Afghanistan (a Documentary Film). Journeyman Pictures.

Jumhūr News. "Pasūkh' Majlīs' Ba Wūzārat' Māliah: Būdīja-i Bīdun' Taghīr (the Legislature Response to the Ministry of Finance: Budget without Change)." June 27, 2012.

Kahler, Miles. "Aid and State Building." In *Annual Meeting of the American Political Science Association*, Chicago, August 30–September 2, 2007.

Kakar, Hasan. "The Fall of the Afghan Monarchy in 1973." *International Journal of Middle East Studies* 9, no. 2 (1978): 195–214.

————. *Government and Society in Afghanistan: The Reign of Amir 'Abd al-Rahman Khan.* Austin: University of Texas Press, 1979.

————. *A Political and Diplomatic History of Afghanistan, 1863–1901.* Leiden: Brill, 2006.

Karsh, Efraim and Mark Wilbanks. "How the 'Sons of Iraq' Stabilized Iraq." *The Middle East Quarterly* 17, no. 4 (Fall 2010), 57–70.

Karzai, Hamid. "A Vision for Afghanistan: Statement of the Chairman of the Interim Administration of Afghanistan in Tokyo Conference." Tokyo, January 2002.

Katzman, Kenneth. "Afghanistan: Politics, Elections, and Government Performance." Congressional Research Service, April 18, 2013.

Khan, Mushtaq Husain and Hazel Gray. "State Weakness in Developing Countries and Strategies of Institutional Reform: Operational Implications for Anti-Corruption Policy and a Case Study of Tanzania." Working Paper, London School of Economics and Political Science, London, May 2003.

Kilcullen, David. *Counterinsurgency.* New York: Oxford University Press, 2010.

Knack, Stephen. "Aid Dependence and the Quality of Governance: Cross-Country Empirical Tests." *Southern Economic Journal* 68, no. 2 (2001): 310–29.

Knack, Stephen, and Aminur Rahman. "Donor Fragmentation and Bureaucratic Quality in Aid Recipients." Policy Research Working Paper 3186, World Bank, 2004. Available at doi:10.1596/1813-9450-3186. doi:10.1596/1813-9450-3186.

Kohli, Atul. *State-Directed Development: Political Power and Industrialization in the Global Periphery.* Cambridge, UK; New York: Cambridge University Press, 2004.

Kopits, George and Jon D. Craig. *Transparency in Government Operations.* Occasional paper. Washington: IMF, 1998.

Kotkin, Stephen and Andras Sajo. *Political Corruption in Transition: A Skeptic's Handbook.* Budapest: Central European University Press, 2002.

Krelove, Russell and Graham Harrison. "Building a Strong Foundation for Domestic Taxation." Washington: IMF, June 2004.

Kwon, Huck-ju. "Transforming the Developmental Welfare State in East Asia." *Development and Change* 36, no. 3 (2005): 477–97.

Levi, Margaret. *Of Rule and Revenue.* Berkeley: University of California Press, 1988.

Lister, Sarah and Hamish Nixon. "Provincial Governance Structures in Afghanistan: From Confusion to Vision?" Kabul: AREU, May 2006.

Litman, Henry. "The Circular Dilemma of State Building in Afghanistan." *Penn State Journal of International Affairs* 1, no. 2 (Spring 2012): 93–109.

Lockhart, Clare. "The Aid Relationship in Afghanistan: Struggling for Government Leadership." Global Economic Governance Programme, Managing Aid Dependency Project, GEG Working Paper, University of Oxford, Oxford 2007.

Londono, Ernesto. "Afghanistan Officials Agree to Dissolve Kabul Bank under Pressure from US and IMF." *The Washington Post*, March 27, 2011.

Luciani, Giacomo. "Allocation vs. Production States." In *The Rentier State*, edited by Hazem Beblawi and Giacomo Luciani, 63–82. London: Croom Helm, 1987.

———. "Introduction." *In The Arab State*, edited by Hazem Beblawi and Giacomo Luciani, xvii–xxxii. Berkeley: University of California Press, 1990.

Luoga, Florens. "Taxpayers' Right in the Context of Democratic Governance: Tanzania." *IDS Bulletin* 33, no. 3 (July 2002): 1–14.

Macrory, Patrick. Retreat from Kabul: The Catastrophic British Defeat in Afghanistan, 1842. Guilford, CT: Lyons, 2002. (1966).

Mahdavy, Hossein. "The Patterns and Problems of Economic Development in Rentier States: The Case of Iran." In *Studies in the Economic History of the Middle East*, edited by M. A. Cook, 428–67. London: Oxford University Press, 1970.

Maley, William. *The Afghanistan Wars.* Basingstoke: Palgrave MacMillan, 2009.

———. "Reconstruction: A Critical Assesment." In *The Afghanistan Conflict and Australia's Role*, edited by Amin Saikal, 77–98. Carlton: Melbourne University Press, 2011.

Mann, Michael. "The Crises of the Latin American Nation-State." In *Conference on the Political Crises and Internal Conflict in Colombia.* Bogota: University of the Andes, April 10–13, 2003.

————. *The Sources of Social Power: The Rise of Classes and Nation-States, 1760–1914, Vol. II.* Cambridge: Cambridge University Press, 1993.

————. *States, War and Capitalism: Studies in Political Sociology.* Oxford: Basil Blackwell, 1988.

Mesquita, Bruce Bueno de and Alastair Smith. "Leader Survival, Revolutions, and the Nature of Government Finance." *American Journal of Political Science* 54, no. 4 (2010): 936–50.

Miakhel, Shahmahmood. "The Afghanistan Stabilisation Program (ASP): A National Programme to Improve Security and Governance." Middle East Institute, June 19, 2012. Available at www.mei.edu/content/afghanistan-stabilisation-program-asp-national-program-improve-security-and-governance

Mills, Nick. *Karzai: The Failing American Intervention and the Struggle for Afghanistan.* Hoboken: John Wiley, 2007.

Milner, Helen V., and Dustin Tingley, eds. *Introduction.* Edited by Helen V. Milner and Dustin Tingley, Geopolitics of Foreign Aid. Cheltenham: Edward Elgar, 2013.

Ministry of Economy of Afghanistan and the World Bank. "Poverty Status in Afghanistan: A Profile Based on National Risk and Vulnerability Assessment (NRVA) 2007/2008." Kabul: Ministry of Economy and World Bank, 2010.

Ministry of Finance. "Corrective Actions for Revenue Collection." Kabul: Revenue Department, n.d.

————. "Proposal for Clarification of Tax and Duties of the USAID under Technical Cooperation Agreement of 1951." Kabul: Director General of LTO (Large Taxpayers Office), 2005.

Ministry of Finance of Afghanistan. "Ministerial Circular: Tax Exemption Policy for Donor Countries, International Financial Institutions, Non-Governmental Organizations, and Their Contractors Operating within Afghanistan." Kabul: Revenue Department, n.d.

————. "Press Release (Clarification of the Special Inspector General for Afghanistan Reconstruction [SIGAR] Report)." Kabul: Media Department, July 26, 2011.

————. "Tackling Airline's Unpaid Taxes and Fees." Kabul: Revenue Department, n.d.

Ministry of Foreign Affairs of Denmark. "Partners: Civil Society Organisations." http://um.dk/en/danida-en/partners/civil-society-organisations/.

Ministry of Justice of Afghanistan. "Qānoni Asāsī Afghanistan." http://moj.gov.af/fa/page/1684.

Montagnat-Rentier, Gilles and William E. LeDrew. "Islamic State of Afghanistan: Strategy and Priorities for Customs Administration Modernization." Washington: IMF, 2004.

Moore, Mick. "Between Coercion and Contract." In *Taxation and State-Building in Developing Countries: Capacity and Consent*, edited by Deborah Brautigam, Odd-Helge Fjeldstad and Mick Moore, 34–63. Cambridge: Cambridge University Press, 2008.

————. "Political Underdevelopment: What Causes Bad Governance." *Public Management Review* 3, no. 3 (2001): 385–418.

————. "Revenues, State Formation, and the Quality of Governance in Developing Countries." *International Political Science Review* 25, no. 3 (2004): 297–319.

Morrison, Kevin M. *Nontaxation and Representation.* Cambridge: Cambridge University Press, 2014.

————. "Oil, Nontax Revenue, and the Redistributional Foundations of Regime Stability." *International Organization* 63, no. 1 (2009): 107–38.

Moss, Todd, Gunilla Pettersson and Nicolas Van de Walle. "An Aid-Institutions Paradox? A Review Essay on Aid Dependency and State Building in Sub-Saharan Africa." 1–28. Working Paper, Center for Global Development, Washington, January 2006.

Moyo, Dambisa. Dead Aid: Why Aid Is Not Working and How There Is a Better Way for Africa. New York: Farrar, Straus and Giroux, 2009.

Mūjʻtamiʻayʻ Jāmiʻayʻ Madanīʻ Afghanistan (Afghanistan Civil Society Forum). Khatʻ Mashī Nukhūstīn Nāmzadān-i Riāsatʻ Jamhūr-i Afghanistan (Afghanistan First Presidential Candidates Manifestos). Kabul, 1384 Solār *Hijri* Calendar (2005).

Mukhopadhyay, Dipali. "Warlords as Bureaucrats: The Afghan Experience." Working Paper, Carnegie Endowment for International Peace, Washington, August 2009.

Mūsharikat Millī Weekly. "Kharjʻ Jibʻ Qumandānān Kam Mīshawad." June 1, 2003.

Muzhda, Wahid. *Afghanistan Wa Panj Sal Salta-i Taliban*. Kabul: Maiwand, 1381 *Solār Hijri* Calendar (2002).

Myers, Robert. "Tax Collectors, Appendix C." Ministry of Finance of Afghanistan Archive, August 14, 2005.

Najmabadi, Afsaneh. "Depoliticisation of a Rentier State: the Case of Iran Pahlavi" In *The Rentier State*, edited by Hazem Beblawi and Giacomo Luciani, 211–27. London, Croom Helm, 1987.

Noelle, Christine. State and Tribe in Nineteenth-Century Afghanistan: The Reign of Amir Dost Muhammad Khan (1826–1863). London: Routledge Curzon, 1997.

Nojumi, Neamatollah, Dyan Mazurana and Elizabeth Stites. *After the Taliban: Life and Security in Rural Afghanistan*. Lanham: Rowman and Littlefield, 2009.

Noori, Khalil. "Kashmakashi Afghanistan Wa Sifaratkhana Ha Bar Sari Maliati Karmandan." *BBC Persian*, May 23, 2011.

Noorzoy, M. Siddieq. "Long-Term Economic Relations between Afghanistan and the Soviet Union: An Interpretive Study." *International Journal of Middle East Studies* 17, no. 2 (1985): 151–73.

ODI (Oversees Development Institute). "Briefing Paper: Promoting Mutual Accountability in Aid Relationships." London: ODI, April 2006.

OECD. "Aid for CSOs." 2013.

———. Do No Harm: International Support for State Building. Paris: OECD, 2009.

———. "States of Fragility 2015: Meeting Post-2015 Ambitions." Paris: OECD Publishing, 2015.

———. "Total Flows by Donors." April 9, 2016.

Omran, Ahmed A. L. and Summer Said. "Saudi Arabia Cuts Spending, Raises Domestic Fuel Prices." *The Wall Street Journal*, December 28, 2015. www.wsj.com/articles/saudi-arabia-announces-2016-budget-1451312691.

O'Neil, Tam. "Neopatrimonialism and Public Sector Performance and Reform." September 2007.

One India News. "India Completes Zaranj-Delaram Highway in Afghanistan." August 4, 2008.

Owusu, Francis Y. "Post-9/11 U.S. Foreign Aid, the Millennium Challenge Account and Africa: How Many Birds Can One Stone Kill?" Ames: Iowa State University, 2004.

Partlow, Joshua. "Taliban Kills 10 Medical Aid Workers in Northern Afghanistan." *The Washington Post*, August 8, 2010.

Pattanayak, Sailendra. "Sustainability in PFM Capacity-Building in Post-Conflict Countries-Afghanistan's Experience." Public Financial Management Blog, IMF, http://blog-pfm.imf.org/pfmblog/2009/08/sustainability-in-pfm-capacitybuilding-in-postconflict-countries-afghanistans-experience.html#comment-captcha.

Pierson, Christopher. *The Modern State*. London: Routledge, 1996.

Polikoff, Alexander. *The Path Still Open*. Indianapolis: Dog Ear Publishing, 2009.

Poole, Lydia. "Afghanistan: Tracking Major Resource Flows, 2002–2010." Global Humanitarian Assistance: A Development Initiative, January 2011.

Porter, Gareth. "Afghanistan: U.S., NATO Forces Rely on Warlords for Security." *IPS*, October 29, 2009.

Poston, Toby. "The Battle to Rebuild Afghanistan." *BBC News*, February 26, 2006.

Poullada, Leon B. Reform and Rebellion in Afghanistan, 1919–1929: King Amanullah's Failure to Modernize a Tribal Society. Ithaca: Cornell University Press, 1973.

Qassem, Ahmad Shayeq. Afghanistan's Political Stability: A Dream Unrealised. Farnham: Ashgate, 2009.

Qayam, Mohamad Hashim. "Mūqasir' Pūlī Siā Kīst." *Hasht-i Subh*, Saur 11, 1392 *Solār Hijra* Calendar (May 1, 2013).

Rāhī Nijāt Daily. "Wolūsī Jirga Dar Tala'sh Bāraī Kāhish' Akhāzī Ha Az Tājiran: Mūshkil Aqtisād' Afghanistan Bay Qānoni 'Ast (the Lower House Seeks to Address Illegal Extortion: The Economic Problem of Afghanistan is Absence of the Rule of Law)." *Rahe Nejat Daily*, Hamal 31, 1388 *Solār Hijra* Calendar (April 20, 2009).

Ramkumar, Vivek and Paolo de Renzio. "Improving Budget Transparency and Account-ability in Aid Dependent Countries: How Can Donors Help?" Washington: International Budget Partnership 2009.

Rasanayagam, Angelo. *Afghanistan: A Modern History*. London: I.B. Tauris, 2005.

Rashid, Ahmad. *Taliban: Islam, Oil and the New Great Game in Central Asia*. London: I.B. Tauris, 2002.

Rasuly, Jafar. "Tāsir-i Siāsati Khārijy Bar Tawseah Nayāftagy-i Afghanistan (The Impact of Foreign Policy on Afghanistan's Underdevelopment)." Kabul: Maiwand, 1384 *Solār Hijra* Calendar (2005).

Renzio, Paolo de and Diego Angemi. "Comrades or Culprits? Donor Engagement and Bud-get Transparency in Aid Dependent Countries." Institut Barcelona D'Estudid Internation-als (IBEI), 2011.

Republic of Afghanistan. "Graduated Land Tax Law." The World Law Guide, n.d.

Revenue Watch Institute. "The 2013 Resource Governance Index: A Measure of Transpar-ency and Accountability in the Oil, Gas and Mining Sector." New York: Revenue Watch Institute 2013.

Riā'sat-i 'Aumumī Aidārah-i Aumūr Va Dār al-ainshā-yi Shorā-yi Vazirān (Office of Administrative Affairs and Cabinet Secretariat). "Dast Āward'hā-yi Ūmda-yi Hukūmat Dar Haft Sāli Guzashta Wa Barnāmah'hā-yi Panj Sāli Āinda (the Last Seven Years Government Achievements and the Next Five Years Programmes)." Kabul: Aidārah-'i Aumūr Va Arziābay, 1388 *Solār Hijra* Calendar (2009).

Riddell, Roger C. *Does Foreign Aid Really Work?* Oxford: Oxford University Press, 2007.

Riechmann, Deb and Richard Lardner. "Taliban, Criminals Get $360 Million from US Taxes." Associated Press, www.nbcnews.com/id/44171605/ns/politics/t/taliban-criminals-get-million-us-taxes/#.Ub5K4Zw1d8F.

Risen, James. "U.S. Identifies Vast Mineral Riches in Afghanistan." *The New York Times*, June 13, 2010.

Rockmore, Tom, Joseph Margolis and Armen Marsoobian. *The Philosophical Challenge of September 11*. Metaphilosophy Series in Philosophy. Oxford: Blackwell, 2005.

Rosenberg, Mathew. "With Bags of Cash, C.I.A. Seeks Influence in Afghanistan." *The New York Times*, April 28, 2013.

———. "Karzai Says He Was Assured C.I.A. Would Continue Delivering Bags of Cash." *The New York Times*, May 4, 2013.

Ross, Michael L. "Does Oil Hinder Democracy?" *World politics* 53, no. 03 (2001): 325–61.

———. *The Oil Curse: How Petroleum Wealth Shapes the Development of Nations*. Princeton: Princeton University Press, 2012.

Roston, Aram. "How the US Funds the Taliban." *The Nation*, November 11, 2009.

RT (Russia Today). "Karzai Blames the US for Afghan Corruption." December 7, 2012, http://rt.com/usa/news/karzai-us-afghan-president-546/.

Rubin, Alissa J. and James Risen. "Losses at Afghan Bank Could Be $900 Million." *The New York Times*, January 30, 2011.

Rubin, Barnett R. *The Fragmentation of Afghanistan: State Formation and Collapse in the International System*. London: Yale University Press, 1995.

———. *The Fragmentation of Afghanistan: State Formation and Collapse in the International System*. 2nd ed. New Haven: Yale University Press, 2002.

———. "Lineages of the State in Afghanistan." *Asian Survey* 28, no. 11 (1988): 1188–209.

———. *The Search for Peace in Afghanistan: From Buffer State to Failed State*. Karachi: Oxford University Press, 1995.

Rubin, Barnett R., Amin Saikal and Julian Lindley-French. "The Way Forward in Afghanistan: Three Views." *Survival* 51, no. 1 (2009): 83–96.

Ruttig, Thomas. "Flash to the Past: Power Play before the 2002 Emergency Loya Jirga." Kabul: Afghanistan Analyst Network, April 4, 2012.

Sachdeva, Gulshan. "Rethinking Reconstruction." Geopolitics 1, no. xii (April 2011): 58–60.

Sadiq, Malyar. "Ra'zi Taqarur-i Vāli Ha: Gūzarish Vīzha (the Secret of Governors Appointments: Special Report)." Kabul: The Killid Group, December 9, 2010.

Saikal, Amin. "Afghanistan's Weak State and Strong Society." In *Making States Work: State Failure and the Crisis of Governance*, edited by Simon Chesterman, Michael Ignatieff and Ramesh Chandra Thakur, 193–210. Tokyo: United Nations University Press, 2005.

———. Modern Afghanistan: A History of Struggle and Survival. London: I.B. Tauris, 2004.

———. Modern Afghanistan: A History of Struggle and Survival. London: I.B. Tauris, 2012.

Schumpeter, Joseph A. "The Crises of the Tax State." In *The Economics and Sociology of Capitalism*, edited by Richard Swedberg. 99–140. Princeton: Princeton University Press, 1991.

Scott, Zoe. "Literature Review on State-Building." Governance and Social Development Resource Center, University of Birmingham, Birmingham 2007.

Shahrani, M. Nazif, ed. "State Building and Social Fragmentation in Afghanistan: A Historical Perspective." In T*he State, Religion, and Ethnic Politics: Afghanistan, Iran, and Pakistan*. Edited by Ali Banuazizi and Myron Weiner, 23-74. Syracuse: Syracuse University Press, 1986.

SIGAR. "Quarterly Report to the United States Congress." Arlington, July 30, 2014.

Skocpol, Theda, ed. *Bringing the State Back In: Strategies of Analysis in Current Research*. Edited by Peter B. Evans, Dietrich Rueschemeyer and Theda Skocpol, Bringing the State Back In. Cambridge: Cambridge University Press, 1985.

Snyder, Richard and Ravi Bhavnani. "Diamonds, Blood, and Taxes: A Revenue Centered Framework for Explaining Political Order." *Journal of Conflict Resolution* 49, no. 4 (2005): 563–97.

Sorel, Eliot and Pier Carlo Pdoan, eds. *The Marshall Plan: Lessons Learned for the 21st Century*. Paris: OECD, 2008.

Spanta, Rangin Dadfar. "Afghanistan: Nation-Building in the Shadow of the Warlords and the 'War on Terror'." In *Nation-Building: A Key Concept for Peaceful Conflict Transformation?* edited by Jochen Hippler, 70–80. London: Pluto, 2005.

Starr, S. Frederick. Lost Enlightenment: Central Asia's Golden Age from the Arab Conquest to Tamerlane. Princeton: Princeton University Press, 2013.

Stephens, Moore. "Afghanistan First EITI Reconciliation Report: 1387 and 1388." Afghanistan Extractive Industries Transparency Initiative (AEITI), 2012.

Stewart, Frances and Graham Brown. "Fragile States." Centre for Research on Inequality, Human Security and Ethnicity, 2010.

Story, Thomas, Frank Bosch and Darryn Jenkins. "Afghanistan: Reforming Tax and Customs Administration." Washington: IMF, 2009.

Suhrke, Astri, ed. *The Dangers of a Tight Embrace: Externally Assisted Statebuilding in Afghanistan.* Edited by Ronald Paris and Timothy D. Sisk, The Dilemmas of Statebuilding: Confronting the Contradictions of Postwar Peace Operations. London: Taylor and Francis, 2009.

Sunley, Emil M., and Borja Gracia. "Afghanistan: Tax Reform: The Next Steps." Washington: IMF, Fiscal Affairs Department, November 2010.

Sunley, Emil M., John Isaac, and Thomas Story. "Afghanistan: Tax Reform-Selected Issues." Washington: IMF, 2006.

Surhke, Asrti. When More Is Less: The International Project in Afghanistan. London: Hurst and Company, 2011.

Sykes, Percy Molesworth. *History of Persia.* 2nd ed. London: Routledge, 2004.

Symansky, Steven, Abdelrahmi Bessaha, Edouard Martin, Abhisek Banerjee and Theo Thomas. "Selected Issues and Statistical Appendix: IMF Country Report No. 06/114." Washington: IMF, 2006.

Tandberg, Eivind, Priyaranjan Desai, Peter Fairman and Janne Stene. "Afghanistan: Consolidating Budget Management Systems." Washington: IMF, December 2003.

Tarzi, Amin H. "A Tax Reform of the Afghan Amir, 'Abd Al-Rahman Khan'." *Journal of Asian History* 27, no. 1 (1993), 30-50.

Therkildsen, Ole. "Keeping the State Accountable: Is Aid No Better Than Oil?" *IDS Bulletin* 33, no. 3 (2002): 1–17.

Tilly, Charles, ed. *The Formation of National States in Western Europe.* Princeton: Princeton University Press, 1975.

———. "War Making and State Making as Organized Crime." In *Bringing the State Back In,* edited by Peter B. Evans, Dietrich Rueschemeyer and Theda Skocpol, 169–91. Cambridge: Cambridge University Press, 1985.

Timmons, Jeffrey F. "The Fiscal Contract: States, Taxes, and Public Services." *World Politics* 57, no. 4 (2005): 530–67.

Tolo News. "Kankāsh: Approval of 1391 (2012/13) Budget (a Roundtable Discussion with Shukraia Barakzai and Sediq Ahmad Osmani Members of Lower House, and Hamidullah Farooqi Professor of Kabul University)." Kabul: Tolonews, April 22, 2012.

———. "Taliban Destroy 7 Communication Antennas in Helmand." March 29, 2011.

Transitional Government of Afghanistan. "Financial Report, 4th Quarter 1380–2nd Quarter 1383 (21 January 2001–20 September 2004)." Kabul: Ministry of Finance, October 2004.

———. "Securing Afghanistan's Future: Accomplishments and the Strategic Path Forward." March 2004.

UNDP. Human Development Report 2001, *Making New Technologies Work for Human Development.* New York: Oxford University Press, 2011.

———. "Outcomes from the Donor Dialogue on the First Draft of the Afghanistan National Development Strategy and Consolidated Donor Comments." Kabul: UNDP, March 10, 2008.

———. "Project in Spotlight: Making Budgets and Aid Work Project." Kabul: UNDP, October 2012.

UNHCR. "Human Rights Dimension of Poverty in Afghanistan." Kabul: UNHCR, 2010.

UNITAR. "Implementation of the Afghanistan Civil Service New Pay and Grade Reform: Case Study." n.d.

United Nations Security Council. "Agreement on Provisional Arrangements in Afghanistan Pending the Re-Establishment of Permanent Government Institutions." December 5, 2011.

UNODC. "Corruption in Afghanistan: Bribery as Reported by the Victims." 2010.

UNSC. "Report of the Security Council Mission to Afghanistan, 11 to 16 November 2006 (S/2006/935)." New York: UNSC December 4, 2006.

USAID. "Afghanistan: Education." www.usaid.gov/afghanistan/education.

USAID Afghanistan. "Report on the Assessment of the Capability of the Ministry of Finance (MoF), Da Afghanistan Bank (DAB) and the Control and Audit Office (CAO) in Regard to Managing Direct Donor Assistance." July 27, 2009.

The Fund for Peace. "The Failed States Index," 2017.

The US Embassy. "Afghan Parliament Flexes Its Muscles: [Foreign Minister] Spanta Loses No-Confidence Vote, Supreme Court to Review Decision (07KABUL1605)." Kabul: Wikileaks, May 14, 2007.

US Embassy Kabul. "Duelling Afghan Chamber of Commerce." Wikileaks, http://wikileaks. org/cable/2005/12/05KABUL5118.html.

Vandewalle, Dirk J. *Libya since Independence: Oil and State-Building*. Ithaca: Cornell University Press, 1998.

Walder, Andrew George. *The Waning of the Communist State: Economic Origins of Political Decline in China and Hungary*. Berkeley: University of California Press, 1995.

Waldman, Matt. "Falling Short: Aid Effectiveness in Afghanistan." Agency Coordinating Body for Afghan Relief (ACBAR), Kabul: March 2008.

Waterbury, John. "Democracy without Democrats? The Potential for Political Liberalization in the Middle East." In *Democracy without Democrats*, edited by Ghassan Salame, 23–47. London: I.B. Tauris 1994.

Weber, Max, ed. *Economy and Society: An Outline of Interpretive Sociology*. Vol. 2. Edited by Guenther Roth and Claus Wittich. Berkeley: University of California Press, 1978.

Werker, Eric and Faisal Z. Ahmed. "What Do Nongovernmental Organizations Do?" *The Journal of Economic Perspectives* 22, no. 2 (2008): 73–92.

Wilder, Andrew. "A House Divided? Analysing the 2005 Afghan Elections." Kabul: AREU, 2005.

Wily, Liz Alden. Land Rights in Crises: Restoring Tenure Security in Afghanistan. Kabul: AREU, 2003.

Winter, Elizabeth. "Civil Society Development in Afghanistan." NGPA, London School of Economics, London, 2010.

World Bank. "Afghanistan: Building an Effective State, Priorities for Public Administration Reform." Kabul: AINA Media and Culture Center, 2007.

———. "Afghanistan: Managing Public Finances for Development, Main Report." Washington: World Bank, 2005.

———. "Afghanistan: Modernizing Customs Control." 2009.

———. "Afghanistan-State Building, Sustaining Growth, and Reducing Poverty." Washington: World Bank 2005.

———. "Afghanistan in Transition: Looking beyond 2014." 2012.

———. "ARTF Incentive Program and SY1388 (2009/10) Benchmarks: Memorandum of Understanding." Washington: ARTF, 2009.

———. Context and Prospects for Reform. n.d.

———. "Global Development Finance." http://data.worldbank.org/data-catalog/global-financial-development.

———. "Governance: Governance in Afghanistan." http://go.worldbank.org/N41DIJDKG0.

———. "Implementation Completion and Results Report (IDA-H2970)." 2012.

————. "Issues and Challenges for Economic Growth and Sustainability in Afghanistan after 2014." Kabul: World Bank, July 16, 2011.

————. "Poverty Reduction Strategy Papers." http://web.worldbank.org/WBSITE/EXTERNAL/PROJECTS/0,,contentMDK:20120705~menuPK:51557~pagePK:41367~piPK:51533~theSitePK:40941,00.html.

————. "Review of Technical Assistance and Capacity Building in Afghanistan: Discussion Paper for the Afghanistan Development Forum." April 26, 2007.

————. "Two Decades of Conflict Cost US$240 Billion: Now Afghanistan will Need US$27.5 Billion to Recover." http://web.worldbank.org/WBSITE/EXTERNAL/NEWS/0,,contentMDK:20186600~menuPK:34463~pagePK:34370~piPK:34424~theSitePK:4607,00.html.

————. "World Data Bank: World Development Indicators." http://data.worldbank.org/indicator/GC.TAX.TOTL.GD.ZS/countries?display=default.

————. "World Development Indicators." 2014.

The World Factbook. "Afghanistan: People and Society." CIA, www.cia.gov/library/publications/the-world-factbook/geos/af.html.

Index

Page numbers in italics indicate tables.

For Product Safety Concerns and Information please contact our EU
representative GPSR@taylorandfrancis.com
Taylor & Francis Verlag GmbH, Kaufingerstraße 24, 80331 München, Germany